Managerial Accounting

Managerial Accounting

Edited by
Christopher Keegan

Willford Press
www.willfordpress.com

Published by Willford Press,
118-35 Queens Blvd., Suite 400,
Forest Hills, NY 11375, USA

ISBN: 978-1-68285-466-2

Cataloging-in-Publication Data

Managerial accounting / edited by Christopher Keegan.
p. cm.
Includes bibliographical references and index.
ISBN 978-1-68285-466-2
1. Managerial accounting. 2. Accounting. I. Keegan, Christopher.
HF5657.4 .M36 2018
658.151 1--dc23

For information on all Willford Press publications
visit our website at www.willfordpress.com

Willford Press

Printed in China.

Contents

Preface VII

Chapter 1 **Managerial Accounting and Business Organizations** 1

i. Management Accounting 1
ii. Business Model 1
iii. Money 11
iv. Double Entry 24
v. Single Entry 25
vi. Forms of Business Organization 26
vii. Partnership 31
viii. Company / Corporation 43
ix. Co-operative Society 65
x. Stakeholder 66

Chapter 2 **Accounting: Recording Finanacial Transactions and Standards** 70

i. General Journal 70
ii. Journal 70
iii. Ledger 75
iv. Mercantilism 79
v. System of Accounting 91
vi. Share Capital 93
vii. Debenture 105
viii. Accounting Principles 111
ix. Accounting Standards 113
x. Generally Accepted Accounting Principles 113
xi. IASs 133
xii. GAAP 134

Chapter 3 **Basics of Financial Statement** 136

i. Financial Statement 136
ii. Balance Sheet 141
iii. Liabilities 149
iv. Income Statement 156
v. Entity Concept 164

vi. Basis of Accounting 165
vii. Earnings Before Interest and Taxes 167

Chapter 4 **Financial Statement Analysis and Related Concepts** 171
i. Financial Statement Analysis 171
ii. Common-size Statements 173
iii. Balance Sheet Horizontal Format 185
iv. Ratio 186
v. Financial Ratio 187
vi. Liquidity Ratio 197
vii. Capital Structure/Leverage Ratios 203
viii. Activity Ratios 205
ix. Depreciation 214
x. Goodwill (Accounting) 226
xi. Inventory 229
xii. Window Dressing 242

Permissions

Index

Preface

Managerial accounting in business is one of the most important functions of economics. It refers to the use of accounting principles in order to make managerial decisions and improve performance control functions. The main aspects of this subject are performance management, strategic management and risk management. The theories used in it are transfer pricing, throughput accounting, etc. This book is a valuable compilation of topics, ranging from the basic to the most complex theories and principles in the field of managerial accounting. Different approaches, evaluations and methodologies on managerial accounting have been included in it. The textbook is appropriate for those seeking detailed information in this area.

A foreword of all Chapters of the book is provided below:

Chapter 1 - Managerial accounting is the use of accounting information of a company to be better informed, which helps in future decision-making and enhancing the management and performance of the company concerned. The chapter also discusses the concepts of business model, money, and other aspects related to business. This chapter on basics of accounting offers an insightful focus, keeping in mind the complex subject matter; **Chapter 2 -** All transactions are recorded in a journal to find the accounts which have been affected. A journal forms the basis of recording financial transactions. A few distinct forms of journals are special journal and sales journal. After the transactions are recorded, they are sorted through preparation of accounts called a ledger. In order to completely understand financial transactions and accounting standards, it is necessary to understand the processes related to it. The following section elucidates the varied processes and mechanisms associated with this area of study; **Chapter 3 -** A financial statement is the formal record of the financial activities of a company or a person. Its purposes include balance sheet, statement of change in equity, income statement, profit and loss account and cash flow statement. The profit and loss account calculates the profit or loss incurred by a company or a person. Income can be defined as benefits made in terms of inflows, increase in asset or decrease in liability. The major components of financial statements and profit and loss account are discussed in this chapter; **Chapter 4 -** The recorded transactions are treated as raw data. To retrieve useful information from the data, they are analysed, organized and processed. This process can be divided into horizontal and vertical analysis. The latter part follows preparation of common-size statements. This chapter discusses the methods of managerial accounting in a critical manner providing key analysis to the subject matter.

I would like to thank the entire editorial team who made sincere efforts for this book and my family who supported me in my efforts of working on this book. I take this opportunity to thank all those who have been a guiding force throughout my life.

Editor

1

Managerial Accounting and Business Organizations

Managerial accounting is the use of accounting information of a company to be better informed, which helps in future decision-making and enhancing the management and performance of the company concerned. The chapter also discusses the concepts of business model, money, and other aspects related to business. This chapter on basics of accounting offers an insightful focus, keeping in mind the complex subject matter.

Management Accounting

- Any form of accounting which enables a business to be conducted more efficiently can be regarded as Management Accounting. (Institute of Chartered Accountants of India-ICAI).
- Management Accounting is the application of professional knowledge and skill in the preparation of accounting information in such a way as to assist management in the formation of policies and in the planning and control of operations of undertaking. (International Capital Market Association, London- ICMA).

Financial Management

- Financial Accounting, Managerial Accounting and Financial Management: Relationship.
- Financial Management deals with raising and utilization of funds.
- Raising of funds may include Cost of Capital, Capital Structure decisions, Capital Markets, IPOs and so on.
- Financial Management deals with raising and utilization of funds.
- Utilization of funds may include Capital Budgeting, Portfolio Management, Working Capital Management and so on.

Business Model

A business model is an "abstract representation of an organization, be it conceptual, textual, and/or graphical, of all core interrelated architectural, co-operational, and financial arrangements designed and developed by an organization presently and in the future, as well as all core products and/or services the organization offers, or will offer, based on these arrangements that are needed to achieve its strategic goals and objectives." This definition by Al-Debei, El-Haddadeh and Avison (2008) indicates that value proposition, value architecture (the organizational infrastructure and technological architecture that allows the movement of products, services, and information), value finance (modeling information related to total cost of ownership, pricing methods, and revenue structure), and value network articulate the primary constructs or dimensions of business models.

A business model describes the rationale of how an organization creates, delivers, and captures value, in economic, social, cultural or other contexts. The process of business model construction is part of business strategy.

In theory and practice, the term *business model* is used for a broad range of informal and formal descriptions to represent core aspects of a business, including purpose, business process, target customers, offerings, strategies, infrastructure, organizational structures, sourcing, trading practices, and operational processes and policies including culture. The literature has provided very diverse interpretations and definitions of a business model. A systematic review and analysis of manager responses to a survey defines business models as the design of organizational structures to enact a commercial opportunity. Further extensions to this design logic emphasize the use of narrative or coherence in business model descriptions as mechanisms by which entrepreneurs create extraordinarily successful growth firms.

Business models are used to describe and classify businesses, especially in an entrepreneurial setting, but they are also used by managers inside companies to explore possibilities for future development. Well-known business models can operate as "recipes" for creative managers. Business models are also referred to in some instances within the context of accounting for purposes of public reporting.

History

Over the years, business models have become much more sophisticated. The *bait and hook* business model (also referred to as the "razor and blades business model" or the "tied products business model") was introduced in the early 20th century. This involves offering a basic product at a very low cost, often at a loss (the "bait"), then charging compensatory recurring amounts for refills or associated products or services (the "hook"). Examples include: razor (bait) and blades (hook); cell phones (bait) and air time (hook); computer printers (bait) and ink cartridge refills (hook); and cameras (bait) and prints (hook). A variant of this model is Adobe, a software developer that gives away its document reader free of charge but charges several hundred dollars for its document writer.

In the 1950s, new business models came from McDonald's Restaurants and Toyota. In the 1960s, the innovators were Wal-Mart and Hypermarkets. The 1970s saw new business models from FedEx and Toys R Us; the 1980s from Blockbuster, Home Depot, Intel, and Dell Computer; the 1990s from Southwest Airlines, Netflix, eBay, Amazon.com, and Starbucks.

Today, the type of business models might depend on how technology is used. For example, entrepreneurs on the internet have also created entirely new models that depend entirely on existing or emergent technology. Using technology, businesses can reach a large number of customers with minimal costs. In addition, the rise of outsourcing and globalization has meant that business models must also account for strategic sourcing, complex supply chains and moves to collaborative, relational contracting structures.

Theoretical and Empirical Insights

Design Logic and Narrative Coherence

Design logic views the business model as an outcome of creating new organizational structures or changing existing structures to pursue a new opportunity. Gerry George and Adam Bock (2011) conducted a comprehensive literature review and surveyed managers to understand how they perceived the components of a business model. In that analysis these authors show that there is a design logic behind how entrepreneurs and managers perceive and explain their business model. In further extensions to the design logic, George and Bock (2012) use case studies and the IBM survey data on business models in large companies, to describe how CEOs and entrepreneurs create narratives or stories in a coherent manner to move the business from one opportunity to another. They also show that when the narrative is incoherent or the components of the story are misaligned, that these businesses tend to fail. They recommend ways in which the entrepreneur or CEO can create strong narratives for change.

Complementarities of Between Partnering Firms

Studying collaborative research and the accessing of external sources of technology, Hummel et al. (2010) found that in deciding on business partners, it is important to make sure that both parties' business models are complementary. For example, they found that it was important to identify the value drivers of potential partners by analyzing their business models, and that it is beneficial to find partner firms that understand key aspects of our own firm's business model.

The University of Tennessee conducted research into highly collaborative business relationships. Researchers codified their research into a sourcing business model known as Vested (also referred to as Vested Outsourcing). Vested is a hybrid sourcing business model in which buyers and suppliers in an outsourcing or business relationship focus on shared values and goals to create an arrangement that is highly collaborative and mutually beneficial to each.

Categorization

From about 2012, some research and experimentation has theorized about a so-called "liquid business model".

V4 BM Framework

Al-Debei and Avison (2010) V[4] BM Framework - four main dimensions encapsulating sixteen elements: Value Proposition, Value Architecture, Value Network, and Value Finance

- Value Proposition: This dimension implies that a BM should include a description of the products/services a digital organization offers, or will offer, along with their related information. Furthermore, the BM needs also to describe the value elements incorporated within the offering, as well as the nature of targeted market segment(s) along with their preferences.

- Value Architecture: portrays the concept as a holistic structural design of an organization, including its technological architecture, organizational infrastructure, and their configurations.
- Value Network: depicts the cross-company or inter-organization perspective towards the concept and has gained much attention in the BM literature.
- Value Finance: depicts information related to costing, pricing methods, and revenue structure

Shift from Pipes to Platforms

Sangeet Paul Choudary (2013) distinguishes between two broad families of business models in an article in *Wired* magazine. Choudary contrasts pipes (linear business models) with platforms (networked business models). In the case of pipes, firms create goods and services, push them out and sell them to customers. Value is produced upstream and consumed downstream. There is a linear flow, much like water flowing through a pipe. Unlike pipes, platforms do not just create and push stuff out. They allow users to create and consume value.

In an op-ed on MarketWatch, Choudary, Van Alstyne and Parker further explain how business models are moving from pipes to platforms, leading to disruption of entire industries.

Platform

There are three elements to a successful platform business model. The *Toolbox* creates connection by making it easy for others to plug into the platform. This infrastructure enables interactions between participants. The *Magnet* creates pull that attracts participants to the platform. For transaction platforms, both producers and consumers must be present to achieve critical mass. The *Matchmaker* fosters the flow of value by making connections between producers and consumers. Data is at the heart of successful matchmaking, and distinguishes platforms from other business models.

Chen (2009) stated that the business model has to take into account the capabilities of Web 2.0, such as collective intelligence, network effects, user-generated content, and the possibility of self-improving systems. He suggested that the service industry such as the airline, traffic, transportation, hotel, restaurant, information and communications technology and online gaming industries will be able to benefit in adopting business models that take into account the characteristics of Web 2.0. He also emphasized that Business Model 2.0 has to take into account not just the technology effect of Web 2.0 but also the networking effect. He gave the example of the success story of Amazon in making huge revenues each year by developing an open platform that supports a community of companies that re-use Amazon's on-demand commerce services.

Applications

Malone et al. found that some business models, as defined by them, indeed performed better than others in a dataset consisting of the largest U.S. firms, in the period 1998 through 2002, while they did not prove whether the existence of a business model mattered.

In the context of the Software-Cluster, which is funded by the German Federal Ministry of

Education and Research, a business model wizard for software companies has been developed. It supports the design and analysis of software business models. The tool's underlying concept and data were published in various scientific publications.

The concept of a business model has been incorporated into certain accounting standards. For example, the International Accounting Standards Board (IASB) utilizes an "entity's business model for managing the financial assets" as a criterion for determining whether such assets should be measured at amortized cost or at fair value in its financial instruments accounting standard, IFRS 9. In their 2013 proposal for accounting for financial instruments, the Financial Accounting Standards Board also proposed a similar use of business model for classifying financial instruments. The concept of business model has also been introduced into the accounting of deferred taxes under International Financial Reporting Standards with 2010 amendments to IAS 12 addressing deferred taxes related to investment property.

Both IASB and FASB have proposed using the concept of business model in the context of reporting a lessor's lease income and lease expense within their joint project on accounting for leases. In its 2016 lease accounting model, IFRS 16, the IASB chose not to include a criterion of "stand alone utility" in its lease definition because "entities might reach different conclusions for contracts that contain the same rights of use, depending on differences between customers' resources or suppliers' business models." The concept has also been proposed as an approach for determining the measurement and classification when accounting for insurance contracts. As a result of the increasing prominence the concept of business model has received in the context of financial reporting, the European Financial Reporting Advisory Group (EFRAG), which advises the European Union on endorsement of financial reporting standards, commenced a project on the "Role of the Business Model in Financial Reporting" in 2011.

Design

Business model design generally refers to the activity of designing a company's business model. It is part of the business development and business strategy process and involves design methods. Massa and Tucci (2014) highlighted the difference between crafting a new business models when none is in place, as it is often the case with academic spinoffs and high technology entrepreneurship, and changing an existing business model, such as when the tooling company Hilti shifted from selling its tools to a leasing model. They suggested that the differences are so profound (for example, lack of resource in the former case and inertia and conflicts with existing configurations and organisational structures in the latter) that it could be worthwhile to adopt different terms for the two. They suggest business model design to refer to the process of crafting a business model when none is in place and business model reconfiguration for process of changing an existing business model, also highlighting that the two process are not mutually exclusive, meaning reconfiguration may involve steps which parallel those of designing a business model.

Definitions

Al-Debei and Avison (2010) define a business model as an abstract representation of an organization. This may be conceptual, textual, and/or graphical, of all core interrelated architectural, co-operational, and financial arrangements designed and developed by an organization presently and in the future, as well all core products and/or services the organization offers, or will offer, based on these arrangements that are needed to achieve its strategic goals and objectives. This definition indicates that value proposition, value architecture, value finance, and value network articulate the primary constructs or dimensions of business models.

Economic Consideration

Al-Debei and Avison (2010) consider value finance as one of the main dimensions of BM which depicts information related to costing, pricing methods, and revenue structure. Stewart and Zhao (2000) defined the business model as *a statement of how a firm will make money and sustain its profit stream over time.*

Component Consideration

Osterwalder et al. (2005) consider the Business Model as the blueprint of how a company does business. Slywotzky (1996) regards the business model as *the totality of how a company selects its customers, defines and differentiates it offerings, defines the tasks it will perform itself and those it will outsource, configures its resources, goes to market, creates utility for customers and captures profits.*

Strategic Outcome

Mayo and Brown (1999) considered the business model as *the design of key interdependent systems that create and sustain a competitive business.* Casadesus-Masanell and Ricart (2011) explain a business model as a set of *choices (policy, assets and governance)* and *consequences (flexible and rigid)* and underline the importance of considering *how it interacts with models of other players in the industry* instead of thinking of it in isolation.

Definitions of Design or Development

Zott and Amit (2009) consider business model design from the perspectives of design themes and design content. Design themes refer to the system's dominant value creation drivers and design content examines in greater detail the activities to be performed, the linking and sequencing of the activities and who will perform the activities.

Design Themes Emphasis

Environment-Strategy-Structure-Operations (ESSO) Business Model Development

Developing a Framework for Business Model Development with an emphasis on Design Themes, Lim (2010) proposed the Environment-Strategy-Structure-Operations (ESSO) Business Model Development which takes into consideration the alignment of the organization's strategy with the organization's structure, operations, and the environmental factors in achieving competitive advantage in varying combination of cost, quality, time, flexibility, innovation and affective.

Design Content Emphasis

Business model design includes the modeling and description of a company's:

- value propositions

- target customer segments
- distribution channels
- customer relationships
- value configurations
- core capabilities
- commercial network
- partner network
- cost structure
- revenue model

Business model design is distinct from business modeling. The former refers to defining the business logic of a company at the strategic level, whereas the latter refers to business process design at the operational level.

A business model design template can facilitate the process of designing and describing a company's business model.

Daas et al. (2012) developed a decision support system (DSS) for business model design. In their study a decision support system (DSS) is developed to help SaaS in this process, based on a design approach consisting of a design process that is guided by various design methods.

Examples

In the early history of business models it was very typical to define business model types such as bricks-and-mortar or e-broker. However, these types usually describe only one aspect of the business (most often the revenue model). Therefore, more recent literature on business models concentrate on describing a business model as a whole, instead of only the most visible aspects.

The following examples provide an overview for various business model types that have been in discussion since the invention of term *business model*:

- Bricks and clicks business model

  Business model by which a company integrates both offline (*bricks*) and online (*clicks*) presences. One example of the bricks-and-clicks model is when a chain of stores allows the user to order products online, but lets them pick up their order at a local store.

- Collective business models

  Business system, organization or association typically composed of relatively large numbers of businesses, tradespersons or professionals in the same or related fields of endeavor, which pools resources, shares information or provides other benefits for their members. For example, a science park or high-tech campus provides shared resources (e.g. cleanrooms and other lab facilities) to the firms located on its premises, and in addition seeks to create an innovation community among these firms and their employees.

- Cutting out the middleman model

  The removal of intermediaries in a supply chain: "cutting out the middleman". Instead of going through traditional distribution channels, which had some type of intermediate (such as a distributor, wholesaler, broker, or agent), companies may now deal with every customer directly, for example via the Internet.

- Direct sales model

  Direct selling is marketing and selling products to consumers directly, away from a fixed retail location. Sales are typically made through party plan, one-to-one demonstrations, and other personal contact arrangements. A text book definition is: "The direct personal presentation, demonstration, and sale of products and services to consumers, usually in their homes or at their jobs."

- Distribution business models, various

- Fee in, free out

  Business model which works by charging the first client a fee for a service, while offering that service free of charge to subsequent clients.

- Franchise

  Franchising is the practice of using another firm's successful business model. For the franchisor, the franchise is an alternative to building 'chain stores' to *distribute* goods and avoid investment and liability over a chain. The franchisor's success is the success of the franchisees. The franchisee is said to have a greater incentive than a direct employee because he or she has a direct stake in the business.

- Sourcing business model

  A sourcing business model is a type of business model that is applied specifically to business relationships where more than one party needs to work with another party to be successful. It is the combination of two concepts: the contractual relationship framework a company uses with its supplier (transactional, relational, investment based), and the economic model used (transactional, output or outcome-based).

- Freemium business model

  Business model that works by offering basic Web services, or a basic downloadable digital product, for free, while charging a premium for advanced or special features.

- Pay what you can (PWYC)

  A non-profit or for-profit business model which does not depend on set prices for its goods, but instead asks customers to pay what they feel the product or service is worth to them. It is often used as a promotional tactic, but can also be the regular method of doing business. It is a variation on the gift economy and cross-subsidization, in that it depends on reciprocity and trust to succeed.

  "Pay what you want" (PWYW) is sometimes used synonymously, but "pay what you can" is often more oriented to charity or socially oriented uses, based more on *ability* to pay, while "pay what you want" is often more broadly oriented to perceived value in combination with willingness and ability to pay.

- Value-added reseller model

Value Added Reseller is a model where a business makes something which is resold by other businesses but with modifications which add value to the original product or service. These modifications or additions are mostly industry specific in nature and are essential for the distribution. Businesses going for a VAR model have to develop a VAR network. It is one of the latest collaborative business models which can help in faster development cycles and is adopted by many Technology companies especially software.

Other examples of business models are:

- Auction business model
- All-in-one business model
- Chemical leasing
- Low-cost carrier business model
- Loyalty business models
- Monopolistic business model
- Multi-level marketing business model
- Network effects business model
- Online auction business model
- Online content business model
- Online media cooperative
- Premium business model
- Professional open-source model
- Pyramid scheme business model
- Razor and blades business model
- Servitization of products business model
- Subscription business model

Frameworks

Technology centric communities have defined "frameworks" for business modeling. These frameworks attempt to define a rigorous approach to defining business value streams. It is not clear, however, to what extent such frameworks are actually important for business planning. Business model frameworks represent the core aspect of any company; they involve "the totality of how a company selects its customers defines and differentiates its offerings, defines the tasks it will perform itself and those it will outsource, configures its resource, goes to market, creates utility for customers, and captures profits". A business framework involves internal factors (market analysis; products/services promotion; development of trust; social influence and knowledge sharing) and external factors (competitors and technological aspects).

A review on business model frameworks can be found in Krumeich et al. (2012). In the following some frameworks are introduced.

- Business reference model

  Business reference model is a reference model, concentrating on the architectural aspects of the core business of an enterprise, service organization or government agency.

- Component business model

  Technique developed by IBM to model and analyze an enterprise. It is a logical representation or map of business components or "building blocks" and can be depicted on a single page. It can be used to analyze the alignment of enterprise strategy with the organization's capabilities and investments, identify redundant or overlapping business capabilities, etc.

Although Webvan failed in its goal of disintermediating the North American supermarket industry, several supermarket chains (like Safeway Inc.) have launched their own delivery services to target the niche market to which Webvan catered.

- Industrialization of services business model

  Business model used in strategic management and services marketing that treats service provision as an industrial process, subject to industrial optimization procedures

- Business Model Canvas

  Developed by A. Osterwalder, Yves Pigneur, Alan Smith, and 470 practitioners from 45 countries, the business model canvas is one of the most used frameworks for describing the elements of business models.

- OGSM

  The OGSM is developed by Marc van Eck and Ellen van Zanten of Business Openers into the 'Business plan on 1 page'. Translated in several languages all over the world. #1 Management book in The Netherlands in 2015. The foundation of Business plan on 1 page is the OGSM. Objectives, Goals, Strageties and Measures (dashboard and actions).

Related Concepts

The process of business model design is part of business strategy. Business model design and innovation refer to the way a firm (or a network of firms) defines its business logic at the strategic level.

In contrast, firms implement their business model at the operational level, through their business operations. This refers to their process-level activities, capabilities, functions and infrastructure (for example, their business processes and business process modeling), their organisational structures (e.g. organigrams, workflows, human resources) and systems (e.g. information technology architecture, production lines).

Consequently, an operationally viable and feasible business model requires lateral alignment with the underlining business operations.

The brand is a consequence of the business model and has a symbiotic relationship with it, because the business model determines the brand promise, and the brand equity becomes a feature of the model. Managing this is a task of integrated marketing.

The standard terminology and examples of business models do not apply to most nonprofit organizations, since their sources of income are generally not the same as the beneficiaries. The term 'funding model' is generally used instead.

The model is defined by the organization's vision, mission, and values, as well as sets of boundaries for the organization—what products or services it will deliver, what customers or markets it will target, and what supply and delivery channels it will use. While the business model includes high-level strategies and tactical direction for how the organization will implement the model, it also includes the annual goals that set the specific steps the organization intends to undertake in the next year and the measures for their expected accomplishment. Each of these is likely to be part of internal documentation that is available to the internal auditor.

Money

A sample picture of a fictional ATM card.

Money is any item or verifiable record that is generally accepted as payment for goods and services and repayment of debts in a particular country or socio-economic context, or is easily converted to such a form. The main functions of money are distinguished as: a medium of exchange; a unit of account; a store of value; and, sometimes, a standard of deferred payment. Any item or verifiable record that fulfills these functions can be considered as money.

Money is historically an emergent market phenomenon establishing a commodity money, but nearly all contemporary money systems are based on fiat money. Fiat money, like any check or note of debt, is without use value as a physical commodity. It derives its value by being declared by a government to be legal tender; that is, it must be accepted as a form of payment within the boundaries of the country, for "all debts, public and private".

The money supply of a country consists of currency (banknotes and coins) and, depending on the particular definition used, one or more types of bank money (the balances held in checking accounts, savings accounts, and other types of bank accounts). Bank money, which consists only of records (mostly computerized in modern banking), forms by far the largest part of broad money in developed countries.

Etymology

The word "money" is believed to originate from a temple of Juno, on Capitoline, one of Rome's seven hills. In the ancient world Juno was often associated with money. The temple of Juno Moneta at Rome was the place where the mint of Ancient Rome was located. The name "Juno" may derive from the Etruscan goddess Uni (which means "the one", "unique", "unit", "union", "united") and "Moneta" either from the Latin word "monere" (remind, warn, or instruct) or the Greek word "moneres" (alone, unique).

In the Western world, a prevalent term for coin-money has been *specie*, stemming from Latin *in specie*, meaning 'in kind'.

History

A 640 BC one-third stater electrum coin from Lydia

The use of barter-like methods may date back to at least 100,000 years ago, though there is no evidence of a society or economy that relied primarily on barter. Instead, non-monetary societies operated largely along the principles of gift economy and debt. When barter did in fact occur, it was usually between either complete strangers or potential enemies.

Many cultures around the world eventually developed the use of commodity money. The Mesopotamian shekel was a unit of weight, and relied on the mass of something like 160 grains of barley. The first usage of the term came from Mesopotamia circa 3000 BC. Societies in the Americas, Asia, Africa and Australia used shell money – often, the shells of the cowry (*Cypraea moneta L.* or *C. annulus L.*). According to Herodotus, the Lydians were the first people to introduce the use of gold and silver coins. It is thought by modern scholars that these first stamped coins were minted around 650–600 BC.

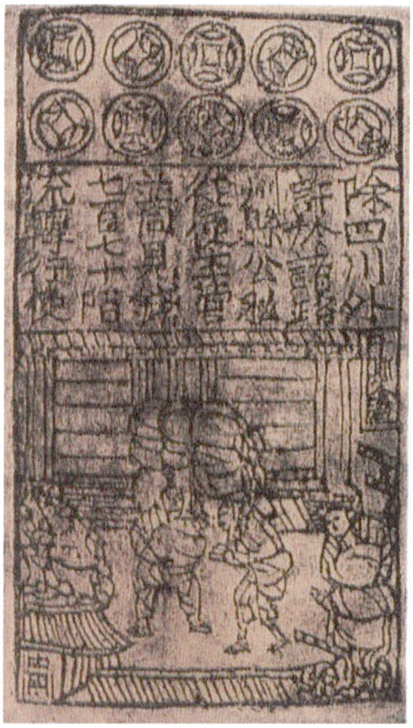

Song Dynasty *Jiaozi,* the world's earliest paper money

The system of commodity money eventually evolved into a system of representative money. This occurred because gold and silver merchants or banks would issue receipts to their depositors – redeemable for the commodity money deposited. Eventually, these receipts became generally accepted as a means of payment and were used as money. Paper money or banknotes were first used in China during the Song Dynasty. These banknotes, known as "jiaozi", evolved from promissory notes that had been used since the 7th century. However, they did not displace commodity money, and were used alongside coins. In the 13th century, paper money became known in Europe through the accounts of travelers, such as Marco Polo and William of Rubruck. Marco Polo's account of paper money during the Yuan Dynasty is the subject of a chapter of his book, *The Travels of Marco Polo*, titled "How the Great Kaan Causeth the Bark of Trees, Made Into Something Like Paper, to Pass for Money All Over his Country." Banknotes were first issued in Europe by Stockholms Banco in 1661, and were again also used alongside coins. The gold standard, a monetary system where the medium of exchange are paper notes that are convertible into pre-set, fixed quantities of gold, replaced the use of gold coins as currency in the 17th-19th centuries in Europe. These gold standard notes were made legal tender, and redemption into gold coins was discouraged. By the beginning of the 20th century almost all countries had adopted the gold standard, backing their legal tender notes with fixed amounts of gold.

After World War II and the Bretton Woods Conference, most countries adopted fiat currencies that were fixed to the U.S. dollar. The U.S. dollar was in turn fixed to gold. In 1971 the U.S. government suspended the convertibility of the U.S. dollar to gold. After this many countries de-pegged their currencies from the U.S. dollar, and most of the world's currencies became unbacked by anything except the governments' fiat of legal tender and the ability to convert the money into goods via payment. According to proponents of modern money theory, fiat money is also backed by taxes. By imposing taxes, states create demand for the currency they issue.

Functions

In *Money and the Mechanism of Exchange (1875)*, William Stanley Jevons famously analyzed money in terms of four functions: a *medium of exchange*, a *common measure of value* (or unit of account), a *standard of value* (or standard of deferred payment), and a *store of value*. By 1919, Jevons's four functions of money were summarized in the couplet:

Money's a matter of functions four,

A Medium, a Measure, a Standard, a Store.

This couplet would later become widely popular in macroeconomics textbooks. Most modern textbooks now list only three functions, that of medium of exchange, unit of account, and store of value, not considering a standard of deferred payment as it is a distinguished function, but rather subsuming it in the others.

There have been many historical disputes regarding the combination of money's functions, some arguing that they need more separation and that a single unit is insufficient to deal with them all. One of these arguments is that the role of money as a medium of exchange is in conflict with its role as a store of value: its role as a store of value requires holding it without spending, whereas its role as a medium of exchange requires it to circulate. Others argue that storing of value is just deferral of the exchange, but does not diminish the fact that money is a medium of exchange that can be transported both across space and time. The term "financial capital" is a more general and inclusive term for all liquid instruments, whether or not they are a uniformly recognized tender.

Medium of Exchange

When money is used to intermediate the exchange of goods and services, it is performing a function as a *medium of exchange*. It thereby avoids the inefficiencies of a barter system, such as the "coincidence of wants" problem. Money's most important usage is as a method for comparing the values of dissimilar objects.

Measure of Value

A *unit of account* (in economics) is a standard numerical monetary unit of measurement of the market value of goods, services, and other transactions. Also known as a "measure" or "standard" of relative worth and deferred payment, a unit of account is a necessary prerequisite for the formulation of commercial agreements that involve debt.

Money acts as a standard measure and common denomination of trade. It is thus a basis for quoting and bargaining of prices. It is necessary for developing efficient accounting systems.

Standard of Deferred Payment

While *standard of deferred payment* is distinguished by some texts, particularly older ones, other texts subsume this under other functions. A "standard of deferred payment" is an accepted way to settle a debt – a unit in which debts are denominated, and the status of money as legal tender, in those jurisdictions which have this concept, states that it may function for the discharge of debts.

When debts are denominated in money, the real value of debts may change due to inflation and deflation, and for sovereign and international debts via debasement and devaluation.

Store of Value

To act as a *store of value*, a money must be able to be reliably saved, stored, and retrieved – and be predictably usable as a medium of exchange when it is retrieved. The value of the money must also remain stable over time. Some have argued that inflation, by reducing the value of money, diminishes the ability of the money to function as a store of value.

Money Supply

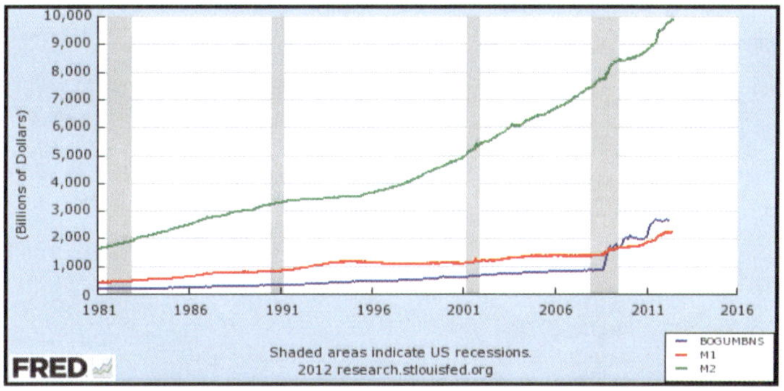

Money Base, M1 and M2 in the U.S. from 1981 to 2012

Printing paper money at a printing press in Perm

In economics, money is a broad term that refers to any financial instrument that can fulfill the functions of money (detailed above). These financial instruments together are collectively referred to as the money supply of an economy. In other words, the money supply is the amount of financial instruments within a specific economy available for purchasing goods or services. Since the money supply consists of various financial instruments (usually currency, demand deposits and various other types of deposits), the amount of money in an economy is measured by adding together these financial instruments creating a *monetary aggregate*.

Modern monetary theory distinguishes among different ways to measure the money supply, reflected in different types of monetary aggregates, using a categorization system that focuses on the liquidity of the financial instrument used as money. The most commonly used monetary aggregates (or types of money) are conventionally designated M1, M2 and M3. These are successively larger aggregate categories: M1 is currency (coins and bills) plus demand deposits (such as checking accounts); M2 is M1 plus savings accounts and time deposits under $100,000; and M3 is M2 plus larger time deposits and similar institutional accounts. M1 includes only the most liquid financial instruments, and M3 relatively illiquid instruments. The precise definition of M1, M2 etc. may be different in different countries.

Another measure of money, M0, is also used; unlike the other measures, it does not represent actual purchasing power by firms and households in the economy. M0 is base money, or the amount of money actually issued by the central bank of a country. It is measured as currency plus deposits of banks and other institutions at the central bank. M0 is also the only money that can satisfy the reserve requirements of commercial banks.

Market Liquidity

"Market liquidity" describes how easily an item can be traded for another item, or into the common currency within an economy. Money is the most liquid asset because it is universally recognised and accepted as the common currency. In this way, money gives consumers the freedom to trade goods and services easily without having to barter.

Liquid financial instruments are easily tradable and have low transaction costs. There should be no (or minimal) spread between the prices to buy and sell the instrument being used as money.

Types

Currently, most modern monetary systems are based on fiat money. However, for most of history, almost all money was commodity money, such as gold and silver coins. As economies developed, commodity money was eventually replaced by representative money, such as the gold standard, as traders found the physical transportation of gold and silver burdensome. Fiat currencies gradually took over in the last hundred years, especially since the breakup of the Bretton Woods system in the early 1970s.

Commodity

A 1914 British gold sovereign

Many items have been used as commodity money such as naturally scarce precious metals, conch shells, barley, beads etc., as well as many other things that are thought of as having value. Commodity money value comes from the commodity out of which it is made. The commodity itself constitutes the money, and the money is the commodity. Examples of commodities that have been used as mediums of exchange include gold, silver, copper, rice, Wampum, salt, peppercorns, large stones, decorated belts, shells, alcohol, cigarettes, cannabis, candy, etc. These items were sometimes used in a metric of perceived value in conjunction to one another, in various commodity valuation or price system economies. Use of commodity money is similar to barter, but a commodity money provides a simple and automatic unit of account for the commodity which is being used as money. Although some gold coins such as the Krugerrand are considered legal tender, there is no record of their face value on either side of the coin. The rationale for this is that emphasis is laid on their direct link to the prevailing value of their fine gold content. American Eagles are imprinted with their gold content and legal tender face value.

Representative

In 1875, the British economist William Stanley Jevons described the money used at the time as "representative money". Representative money is money that consists of token coins, paper money or other physical tokens such as certificates, that can be reliably exchanged for a fixed quantity of a commodity such as gold or silver. The value of representative money stands in direct and fixed relation to the commodity that backs it, while not itself being composed of that commodity.

Fiat

Gold coins are an example of legal tender that are traded for their intrinsic value, rather than their face value.

Fiat money or fiat currency is money whose value is not derived from any intrinsic value or guarantee that it can be converted into a valuable commodity (such as gold). Instead, it has value only by government order (fiat). Usually, the government declares the fiat currency (typically notes and coins from a central bank, such as the Federal Reserve System in the U.S.) to be legal tender, making it unlawful not to accept the fiat currency as a means of repayment for all debts, public and private.

Some bullion coins such as the Australian Gold Nugget and American Eagle are legal tender, however, they trade based on the market price of the metal content as a commodity, rather than their legal tender face value (which is usually only a small fraction of their bullion value).

Fiat money, if physically represented in the form of currency (paper or coins) can be accidentally damaged or destroyed. However, fiat money has an advantage over representative or commodity money, in that the same laws that created the money can also define rules for its replacement in case of damage or destruction. For example, the U.S. government will replace mutilated Federal Reserve Notes (U.S. fiat money) if at least half of the physical note can be reconstructed, or if it can be otherwise proven to have been destroyed. By contrast, commodity money which has been lost or destroyed cannot be recovered.

Coinage

These factors led to the shift of the store of value being the metal itself: at first silver, then both silver and gold, and at one point there was bronze as well. Now we have copper coins and other non-precious metals as coins. Metals were mined, weighed, and stamped into coins. This was to assure the individual taking the coin that he was getting a certain known weight of precious metal. Coins could be counterfeited, but they also created a new unit of account, which helped lead to banking. Archimedes' principle provided the next link: coins could now be easily tested for their fine weight of metal, and thus the value of a coin could be determined, even if it had been shaved, debased or otherwise tampered with.

In most major economies using coinage, copper, silver and gold formed three tiers of coins. Gold coins were used for large purchases, payment of the military and backing of state activities. Silver coins were used for midsized transactions, and as a unit of account for taxes, dues, contracts and fealty, while copper coins represented the coinage of common transaction. This system had been used in ancient India since the time of the Mahajanapadas. In Europe, this system worked through the medieval period because there was virtually no new gold, silver or copper introduced through mining or conquest. Thus the overall ratios of the three coinages remained roughly equivalent.

Paper

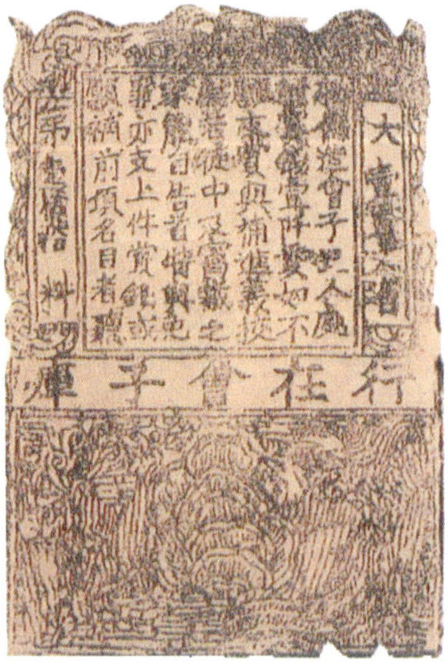

Huizi currency, issued in 1160

In premodern China, the need for credit and for circulating a medium that was less of a burden than exchanging thousands of copper coins led to the introduction of paper money, commonly known today as banknotes. This economic phenomenon was a slow and gradual process that took place from the late Tang Dynasty (618–907) into the Song Dynasty (960–1279). It began as a means for merchants to exchange heavy coinage for receipts of deposit issued as promissory notes from shops of wholesalers, notes that were valid for temporary use in a small regional territory. In the 10th century, the Song Dynasty government began circulating these notes amongst the traders in their monopolized salt industry. The Song government granted several shops the sole right to issue banknotes, and in the early 12th century the government finally took over these shops to produce state-issued currency. Yet the banknotes issued were still regionally valid and temporary; it was not until the mid 13th century that a standard and uniform government issue of paper money was made into an acceptable nationwide currency. The already widespread methods of woodblock printing and then Pi Sheng's movable type printing by the 11th century was the impetus for the massive production of paper money in premodern China.

Paper money from different countries

At around the same time in the medieval Islamic world, a vigorous monetary economy was created during the 7th–12th centuries on the basis of the expanding levels of circulation of a stable high-value currency (the dinar). Innovations introduced by Muslim economists, traders and merchants include the earliest uses of credit, cheques, promissory notes, savings accounts, transactional accounts, loaning, trusts, exchange rates, the transfer of credit and debt, and banking institutions for loans and deposits.

In Europe, paper money was first introduced in Sweden in 1661. Sweden was rich in copper, thus, because of copper's low value, extraordinarily big coins (often weighing several kilograms) had to be made. The advantages of paper currency were numerous: it reduced transport of gold and silver, and thus lowered the risks; it made loaning gold or silver at interest easier, since the specie (gold or silver) never left the possession of the lender until someone else redeemed the note; and it allowed for a division of currency into credit and specie backed forms. It enabled the sale of stock in joint stock companies, and the redemption of those shares in paper.

However, these advantages held within them disadvantages. First, since a note has no intrinsic value, there was nothing to stop issuing authorities from printing more of it than they had specie to back it with. Second, because it increased the money supply, it increased inflationary pressures, a fact observed by David Hume in the 18th century. The result is that paper money would often lead to an inflationary bubble, which could collapse if people began demanding hard money, causing the demand for paper notes to fall to zero. The printing of paper money was also associated with wars, and financing of wars, and therefore regarded as part of maintaining a standing army. For these reasons, paper currency was held in suspicion and hostility in Europe and America. It was also addictive, since the speculative profits of trade and capital creation were quite large. Major nations established mints to print money and mint coins, and branches of their treasury to collect taxes and hold gold and silver stock.

At this time both silver and gold were considered legal tender, and accepted by governments for taxes. However, the instability in thc ratio between the two grew over the course of the 19th century, with the increase both in supply of these metals, particularly silver, and of trade. This is called bimetallism and the attempt to create a bimetallic standard where both gold and silver backed currency remained in circulation occupied the efforts of inflationists. Governments at this point could use currency as an instrument of policy, printing paper currency such as the United States Greenback, to pay for military expenditures. They could also set the terms at which they would redeem notes for specie, by limiting the amount of purchase, or the minimum amount that could be redeemed.

Banknotes with a face value of 5000 of different currencies

By 1900, most of the industrializing nations were on some form of gold standard, with paper notes and silver coins constituting the circulating medium. Private banks and governments across the world followed Gresham's Law: keeping gold and silver paid, but paying out in notes. This did not happen all around the world at the same time, but occurred sporadically, generally in times of war or financial crisis, beginning in the early part of the 20th century and continuing across the world until the late 20th century, when the regime of floating fiat currencies came into force. One of the last countries to break away from the gold standard was the United States in 1971.

No country anywhere in the world today has an enforceable gold standard or silver standard currency system.

Commercial Bank

Commercial bank money or demand deposits are claims against financial institutions that can be used for the purchase of goods and services. A demand deposit account is an account from which funds can be withdrawn at any time by check or cash withdrawal without giving the bank or financial institution any prior notice. Banks have the legal obligation to return funds held in demand deposits immediately upon demand (or 'at call'). Demand deposit withdrawals can be performed in person, via checks or bank drafts, using automatic teller machines (ATMs), or through online banking.

A check, used as a means of converting funds in a demand deposit to cash

Commercial bank money is created through fractional-reserve banking, the banking practice where banks keep only a *fraction* of their deposits in reserve (as cash and other highly liquid assets) and lend out the remainder, while maintaining the simultaneous obligation to redeem all these deposits upon demand. Commercial bank money differs from commodity and fiat money in two ways: firstly it is non-physical, as its existence is only reflected in the account ledgers of banks and other financial institutions, and secondly, there is some element of risk that the claim will not be fulfilled if the financial institution becomes insolvent. The process of fractional-reserve banking has a cumulative effect of money creation by commercial banks, as it expands money supply (cash and demand deposits) beyond what it would otherwise be. Because of the prevalence of fractional reserve banking, the broad money supply of most countries is a multiple larger than the amount of base money created by the country's central bank. That multiple (called the money multiplier) is determined by the reserve requirement or other financial ratio requirements imposed by financial regulators.

The money supply of a country is usually held to be the total amount of currency in circulation plus the total amount of checking and savings deposits in the commercial banks in the country. In modern economies, relatively little of the money supply is in physical currency. For example, in December 2010 in the U.S., of the $8853.4 billion in broad money supply (M2), only $915.7 billion (about 10%) consisted of physical coins and paper money.

Electronic or Digital

Many digital currencies, in particular Flooz and Beenz, had gained momentum before the Dot-com bubble of the early 2000s. Not much innovation occurred until the conception of Bitcoin in 2009, which introduced the concept of a cryptocurrency.

Monetary Policy

US dollar banknotes

When gold and silver are used as money, the money supply can grow only if the supply of these metals is increased by mining. This rate of increase will accelerate during periods of gold rushes and discoveries, such as when Columbus discovered the New World and brought back gold and silver to Spain, or when gold was discovered in California in 1848. This causes inflation, as the value of gold goes down. However, if the rate of gold mining cannot keep up with the growth of the economy, gold becomes relatively more valuable, and prices (denominated in gold) will drop, causing deflation. Deflation was the more typical situation for over a century when gold and paper money backed by gold were used as money in the 18th and 19th centuries.

Modern day monetary systems are based on fiat money and are no longer tied to the value of gold. The control of the amount of money in the economy is known as monetary policy. Monetary policy is the process by which a government, central bank, or monetary authority manages the money supply to achieve specific goals. Usually the goal of monetary policy is to accommodate economic growth in an environment of stable prices. For example, it is clearly stated in the Federal Reserve Act that the Board of Governors and the Federal Open Market Committee should seek "to promote effectively the goals of maximum employment, stable prices, and moderate long-term interest rates."

A failed monetary policy can have significant detrimental effects on an economy and the society that depends on it. These include hyperinflation, stagflation, recession, high unemployment, shortages of imported goods, inability to export goods, and even total monetary collapse and the adoption of a much less efficient barter economy. This happened in Russia, for instance, after the fall of the Soviet Union.

Governments and central banks have taken both regulatory and free market approaches to monetary policy. Some of the tools used to control the money supply include:

- changing the interest rate at which the central bank loans money to (or borrows money from) the commercial banks
- currency purchases or sales
- increasing or lowering government borrowing
- increasing or lowering government spending
- manipulation of exchange rates
- raising or lowering bank reserve requirements
- regulation or prohibition of private currencies
- taxation or tax breaks on imports or exports of capital into a country

In the US, the Federal Reserve is responsible for controlling the money supply, while in the Euro area the respective institution is the European Central Bank. Other central banks with significant impact on global finances are the Bank of Japan, People's Bank of China and the Bank of England.

For many years much of monetary policy was influenced by an economic theory known as monetarism. Monetarism is an economic theory which argues that management of the money supply should be the primary means of regulating economic activity. The stability of the demand for money prior to the 1980s was a key finding of Milton Friedman and Anna Schwartz supported by the work of David Laidler, and many others. The nature of the demand for money changed during the 1980s owing to technical, institutional, and legal factors and the influence of monetarism has since decreased.

Counterfeit

Counterfeit money is imitation currency produced without the legal sanction of the state or government. Producing or using counterfeit money is a form of fraud or forgery. Counterfeiting is almost as old as money itself. Plated copies (known as Fourrées) have been found of Lydian coins which are thought to be among the first western coins. Before the introduction of paper money, the most prevalent method of counterfeiting involved mixing base metals with pure gold or silver. A form of counterfeiting is the production of documents by legitimate printers in response to fraudulent instructions. During World War II, the Nazis forged British pounds and American dollars. Today some of the finest counterfeit banknotes are called *Superdollars* because of their high quality and likeness to the real U.S. dollar. There has been significant counterfeiting of Euro banknotes and coins since the launch of the currency in 2002, but considerably less than for the U.S. dollar.

Laundering

Money laundering is the process in which the proceeds of crime are transformed into ostensibly legitimate money or other assets. However, in a number of legal and regulatory systems the term money laundering has become conflated with other forms of financial crime, and sometimes used more generally to include misuse of the financial system (involving things such as securities, digital currencies, credit cards, and traditional currency), including terrorism financing, tax evasion and evading of international sanctions.

Money Measurement Concept

The money measurement concept underlines the fact that in accounting and economics generally, every recorded event or transaction is measured in terms of money, i.e., the local currency monetary unit of measure. Using this principle, a fact or a happening or event which cannot be expressed in terms of money is not recorded in the accounting books. Thus, it is not acceptable to record such non-quantifiable items as employee skill levels or the quality of customer service.

One of the basic principles in historical cost accounting is "The Measuring Unit principle" (or stable measuring unit assumption): The unit of measure in accounting shall be the base money unit of the most relevant currency.

This principle also assumes the unit of measure is stable; that is, changes in its general purchasing power are not considered sufficiently important to require adjustments to the basic financial statements.The inflation which occurs over the passage of time is not considered."

Money is the medium of exchange and the standard of economic value. Hence money measurement concept requires that only those transactions which are capable of being measured in terms of money are to be recorded in books of accounts.

Transactions that cannot be expressed in terms of money are not recorded in books.

Example 1

Successful meeting with a prospective customer may be very important but can not be recorded in the books of accounts.

Example 2

Employees are the valuable resources of the organisation but their measurement in monetary terms is not possible therefore, not recorded in books.

Double Entry

- Dual aspect concept is the core of double entry book-keeping system.
- According to it, every transaction has two aspects and both aspects are to be recorded in the books of accounts.
- Double entry system of book-keeping means that all transactions are recorded in two aspect one involving the receiving benefit and other giving benefit in the accounts system.

  For instance, buying a machinery for Rs.25,000 would be entered as a decrease in the cash account, and as an increase in the 'machinery' account.
- The advantage of a double entry system is that it is comprehensive.
- It will give you an accurate picture of your true financial position, not just your cash position. As non-cash transactions can be huge, this is extremely important for robust financial management.

- The disadvantage of double entry bookkeeping is that it needs significant details for regular maintenance of books and not always easy to use.
- It generally needs a qualified accountant to run it.
- Every transaction has two aspects:
    i. it increases one asset and decreases other asset.
    ii. it increases an asset and increases other liability.
    iii. it decreases an asset and decreases a liability.
    iv. it decreases one liability and increases other liability.

Single Entry

- It is difficult to define single entry system because, in fact, there exists no system like single entry system. Broadly speaking, it is a defective double entry system. Any system that falls short of complete double entry method is called single entry system. Under this method, sometimes both the aspects of transactions are recorded, sometimes only one aspect is recorded or sometime no aspects of transactions is recorded in the books.
- In short single entry system may be called a mix of double entry, single entry and no entry.
- For instance, buying a Machinery for Rs.25,000 would be entered as a payment in a cashbook.
- It has the advantage of being simple, and spontaneous to use.
- However, it may not account for non-cash (or non-bank) transactions. These are transactions that will have a significant effect on the accounts, but do not immediately cause a change on the cash or bank accounts.
- Example

  Goods sold on one month's credit are not be recorded in the system at the time of sale of goods. This will create a situation where a businessman can not anticipate exact cash position of the particular month and therefore wrong planning.

- Example of a non-cash transaction is ordering a Machinery for Rs.25,000. The machinery might take a month to arrive. During that month, a single entry system would not record the transaction on the formal accounts. This would mean that the accounting system has not shown liability of Rs.25,000 payable to machinery suppliers: a dangerous situation.

Forms of Business Organization

- Sole Proprietorship.
- Hindu Undivided Family.
- Partnership.
- Company.
- Co-operative Society.

Sole Proprietorship

A sole proprietorship, also known as the sole trader or simply a proprietorship, is a type of business entity that is owned and run by one natural person and in which there is no legal distinction between the owner and the business. The owner is in direct control of all elements and is legally accountable for the finances of such business and this may include debts, loans, loss, etc.

The owner receives all profits (subject to taxation specific to the business) and has unlimited responsibility for all losses and debts. Every asset of the business is owned by the proprietor and all debts of the business are the proprietor's. It is a "sole" proprietorship in contrast with partnerships (which have at least two owners).

A sole proprietor may use a trade name or business name other than his, her, or its legal name. They may have to legally trademark their business name if it differs from their own legal name, the process varying depending upon country of residence.

Other Countries

An exact translation of "sole proprietorship" is unusual, because the focus of the concept can change. An example is the Brazilian concept of "sole business" that was split into two main kinds of formal freelancer:

- sole professional: with higher level academic certificate and regulations for formal control of autonomous exercise (ex. sole doctor's office).
- sole entrepreneur: typical "little entrepreneurs", as sole craftsman, autonomous taxi driver, and many others, that can be formal. An informal freelancer, through a simple process, can be formalized as *sole microentrepreneur*

German and Austrian tax law also differentiates between sole professionals and other sole proprietors

Advantages and Disadvantages of Sole Proprietorship

Registration of a business name for a sole proprietor is generally uncomplicated, unless it involves the selection of a name that is fictitious, or "assumed." The business owner is required to register with the appropriate local authorities, who will determine that the name submitted is not duplicated by another business entity. Furthermore, the business owner must complete a form submitted to the governing authority to acquire title as a "DBA" or "doing business as". The authority in some states is the Secretary of State.

The license for a sole proprietary business entitles the owner to hire employees and enlist the services of independent consultants. Although an employee or consultant may be requested by the owner to complete a specific project or participate in the company's decision-making process, their contribution to the project or decision is considered a *recommendation* under the law. Under the legal doctrine *Respondeat superior* (Latin: "let the master answer"), the legal liability for any business decision arising from such a contribution remains upon the owner and cannot be renounced or apportioned.

This is transposed by the unlimited liability attached to a sole proprietary business. The owner carries the financial responsibility for all debts and/or losses suffered by the business, to the extent of using personal or other assets, to discharge any outstanding liabilities. The owner is exclusively liable for all business activities conducted by the sole proprietorship and accordingly, entitled to full control and all earnings associated with it. The general aspect according to general business law is that this type of business ownership does not embody a "legal entity" Furthermore, any attempted and unreliable distinctions of the business do not change the classification under this title.

According to the Small Business Administration (SBA) a sole proprietor and their business are considered as one and the same; therefore, the business is not subjected to separate taxation and regarded as the direct income of the owner. Income, losses and expenses may be listed on a Schedule C Download, which is then transferred to the personal tax return of the owner. It is the responsibility of the owner to ensure all due income taxes and self-employment contributions are paid.

Foundation and Development

Time is an extremely valuable commodity. Recognized tax, business attorney and author, Barbara Weltman, states that a sole proprietor must be prepared to devote their time, utilizing business methods towards establishing a sound and appropriate foundation. This will significantly contribute to increased turnover, profits and minimizing taxes; K. Lasser Small Business Taxes (Wiley 2010) and avoidance of potential adversities. The setting-up process of a sole proprietorship to comply with local laws and regulations, is obtainable from the Small Business Development Center (SBDC), using their locator facility.

A sole proprietor starting a new business involves his or her compiling a business plan related to ambitions for development and determined results to be achieved. Sole owners are engaged in many varieties of industry and commerce and a comprehensive list of the primary categories, is found in the North American Industry Classification System (NAICS). The selection of a business type by a new sole proprietor is in many instances, motivated by appropriate business experience in a particular field, especially those pertaining to enterprises involving the marketing and selling of defined products and services.

A crucial component of a sole proprietorship within a business plan is the provision of an inherent guideline, for actions that require implementing for a business to achieve growth. The business name and products are critical aspects in the founding of a sole proprietorship and once selected, should be protected. In the event of a determined brand name being legalized, information regarding trademark protection is available from the U.S. Patent and Trademark Office.

Finances

For the sole proprietor there are a variety of options in obtaining financial support for their business, including loan facilities available from the U.S. Small Business Administration. The loans are not originated by the SBA, but the administration does guarantee loans made by various independent lending institutions. The primary loan facility for small businesses offered by this agency is the 7(a) loan program, designed for general applications. Sole proprietors are able to finance legitimate operating expenses; for example, working capital, furniture, leasehold improvements and building renovations.

Many and varied private organizations and individuals seek opportunities to invest and fund a business that may not qualify for traditional financing from institutions, such as banks. For the sole proprietor, seeking to take advantage of this facility, there are various factors that must be understood and adhered to regarding the loan application.

The Small Business Administration (SBA), advises there are traditionally two forms of financing; debt and equity. For any small business owner seeking funding, they must consider the debt-to-equity ratio of their enterprise. This means the inter-action between the sum of dollars borrowed and the financial dollars invested in the business. The mathematics are simple; greater the finance invested by sole proprietors in their business; easier the obtaining of finance! The SBA statistics show that the majority of small enterprises favor the use of limited equity financing; for example, friends and relatives.

Loans and Options

According to the Small Business Administration, there are various private organizations prepared to fund sole proprietor business operations that do not qualify for traditional financing from banks. These private investors can provide loans, credit lines, leasing facilities for equipment, or other forms of capital, to sole proprietorship that have exhausted alternative financial resources. It is also possible for these owners to obtain financing by way of business partners or others, with cash to invest. Financial partners are frequently "silent" and although they do not participate in any business related decisions, they generally receive a percentage of the profits, generated by the business.

To assist sole proprietors, there are business grants available from the Federal Government or private organizations, providing certain criteria are met. To qualify for Federal grants, small businesses must comply with determined business size and income standards. For consideration regarding various grant opportunities, sole proprietors may apply for a grant in their capacity as an individual. Local governments and state economic development agencies, frequently make grants available, for businesses that stimulate their local economies.

For any sole proprietor applying for a loan, before starting the loan procedure, it is essential their personal and business credit history is in order and up-to-date. A personal credit report should be obtained from a credit bureau; for example, Trans-Union, Equifax or Experian. This action should be initiated by a business owner well before starting the borrowing process.

The Small Business Administration specifies that all credit reports received from any source should be carefully reviewed to ensure that all relevant personal information is correct. Other content in the report should also be examined particularly that related to the past credit obtained, from sources such as, credit cards, mortgages, student loans, as well as details pertaining to how the credit was repaid.

Rules for Sole Proprietorships in Different Countries

United Kingdom

In Britain, anyone who begins work for themselves is considered by the Government to be a self-employed sole trader, regardless of whether or not they have advised HM Revenue and Customs.

A sole trader can keep all the profits of their business after tax has been paid. They must lodge a self-assessment tax return each year, and pay Income Tax as well as National Insurance. If revenue is expected to be more than £83,000 a year, they must also register for the Value Added Tax.

A sole trader can employ staff, but is personally responsible for any losses the business makes.

United States

A permitted exception to the sole proprietor (single owner) stipulation is made by the Internal Revenue Service (IRS) permitting the spouse of a sole proprietor to work for the business. They are not classified as partners in the enterprise, or an independent contractor, enabling the business to retain its sole proprietorship status and not be required to submit a partnership income tax return.

Hindu Joint Family

Hindu Undivided Family (HUF) business is a form of business organisation found only in India. In this form of business, all the members of a Hindu undivided family own the business jointly. The affairs of business are managed by the head of the family, who is known as the "KARTA" (can be male or female).

HUF business comes into existence as per the Hindu Inheritance Laws of India. The membership is limited up to three successive generations. Thus, an individual, his child(ren), and his grandchild(ren) become the members of a HUF by birth. They are called Co-parceners. A daughter can also be a coparcener.

A joint family or undivided family is an extended family arrangement prevalent throughout the Indian subcontinent, particularly in India, consisting of many generations living in the same household, all bound by the common relationship.

Family Structure

Historically, for generations India had a prevailing tradition of the *joint family system* or *undivided family*. The system is an extended family arrangement prevalent throughout the Indian subcontinent, particularly in India, consisting of many generations living in the same home, all bound by the common relationship. A patrilineal joint family consists of an older man and his wife, his sons and daughters and his grandchildren from his sons and daughters.

The family is headed by a karta, usually the oldest male, who makes decisions on economic and social matters on behalf of the entire family. The patriarch's wife generally exerts control over the household and minor religious practices and often wields considerable influence in domestic matters. Family income flows into a common pool, from which resources are drawn to meet the needs of all members, which are regulated by the heads of the family. However, with urbanisation and economic development, India has witnessed a break up of traditional joint family into more nuclear-like families, and the traditional joint family in India accounted for a small number of Indian households.

A Hindu undivided family or HUF is a legal term related to the Hindu Marriage Act. The female members are also given the right of share to the property in the HUF. The term finds reference in the provisions of the Income Tax Act, but the expression is not defined in the act. There are various aspects of Hindu law relevant for the purpose assessment of income and wealth in the status of HUF, as well as the impact of the provisions of Hindu Succession Act 1956 as amended by Hindu Succession (Amendment) Act 2005 relevant for the purpose of assessment of income and wealth in the status of HUF under the Income Tax Act 1961.

In the case of Surjit lal Chhabra 101 ITR 776 SC, joint family and undivided family are synonymous: "A joint Hindu family consists of persons lineally descended from a common ancestor and includes their wives and unmarried daughters. The daughter, on marriage, ceases to be a member of her father's family and becomes a member of her husband's family."

In 2016, a judgment of the Delhi High Court ruled that the eldest female member of a Hindu Undivided Family can be its "karta" (manager).

Relationships

Different relationships are addressed via different names. The nature of relationship also varies. Relations can be of equivalence, mutual respect or teasing in nature.

In joint families in northern and central India between a bride or sister-in-law and her younger brother-in-law, a joking or teasing relationship is common, and the relationship towards an older brother-in-law is that of respectfulness.

In a traditional joint Hindu family, there is a subservient relationship between the wives of the brothers: the patriarch's wife is addressed as "Badi Bhabhi" (in Hindi), meaning "eldest brother's wife." She is traditionally considered the mistress of the house and is in charge of running the household affairs and overseeing the servants (if any). The subsequent younger brothers' wives typically seek her advice and permission for any matter his/decisions regarding the household and rearing of the children.

Partnership

A partnership is an arrangement where parties, known as partners, agree to cooperate to advance their mutual interests. The partners in a partnership may be individuals, businesses, interest-based organizations, schools, governments or combinations. Organizations may partner together to increase the likelihood of each achieving their mission and to amplify their reach. A partnership may result in issuing and holding equity or may be only governed by a contract. Partnership agreements can be formed in the following areas:

- Business: two or more companies join forces in a joint venture or a consortium to i) work on a project (e.g. industrial or research project) which would be too heavy or too risky for a single entity, ii) join forces to have a stronger position on the market, iii) comply with specific regulation (e.g. in some emerging countries, foreigners can only invest in the form of partnerships with local entrepreneurs). In this case, the alliance may be structured in a process comparable to a Mergers & Acquisitions transaction.
- Politics (or geopolitics): In what is usually called an alliance, governments may partner to achieve their national interests, sometimes against allied governments holding contrary interests, as occurred during World War II and the Cold War.
- Knowledge: In education, accrediting agencies increasingly evaluate schools, or universities, by the level and quality of their partnerships with local or international peers and a variety of other entities across societal sectors.
- Individual: Some partnerships occur at personal levels, such as when two or more individuals agree to domicile together, while other partnerships are not only personal, but private, known only to the involved parties.

Partnerships present the involved parties with complex negotiation and special challenges that must be navigated unto agreement. Overarching goals, levels of give-and-take, areas of responsibility, lines of authority and succession, how success is evaluated and distributed, and often a variety of other factors must all be negotiated. Once agreement is reached, the partnership is typically enforceable by civil law, especially if well documented. Partners who wish to make their agreement affirmatively explicit and enforceable typically draw up Articles of Partnership. Trust and pragmatism are also essential as it cannot be expected that everything can be written in the initial partnership agreement, therefore quality governance and clear communication are critical success factors in the long run. It is common for information about formally partnered entities to be made public, such as through a press release, a newspaper ad, or public records laws.

While industrial partnerships stand to amplify mutual interests and accelerate success, some forms of collaboration may be considered ethically problematic. When a politician, for example, partners with a corporation to advance the latter's interest in exchange for some benefit, a conflict of interest results; consequentially, the public good may suffer. While technically lawful in some jurisdictions, such practice is broadly viewed negatively or as corruption.

Partnerships recognized by a government body may enjoy special benefits from taxation policy. Among developed countries, for example, business partnerships are often favored over corporations in taxation policy, since dividend taxes only occur on profit before they are distributed to the partners. However, depending on the partnership structure and the jurisdiction in which it operates, owners of a partnership may be exposed to greater personal liability than they would as shareholders of a corporation. In such countries, partnerships are often regulated via anti-trust laws, so as to inhibit monopolistic practices and foster free market competition. Enforcement of the laws, however, varies considerably. Domestic partnerships recognized by governments typically enjoy tax benefits, as well.

Common Law

Under common law legal systems, the basic form of partnership is a general partnership, in which all partners manage the business and are personally liable for its debts. Two other forms which have developed in most countries are the limited partnership (LP), in which certain limited partners relinquish their ability to manage the business in exchange for limited liability for the partnership's debts, and the limited liability partnership (LLP), in which all partners have some degree of limited liability.

There are two types of partners. General partners have an obligation of strict liability to third parties injured by the Partnership. General partners may have joint liability or joint and several liability depending upon circumstances. The liability of limited partners is limited to their investment in the partnership.

A *silent partner* is one who still shares in the profits and losses of the business, but who is not involved in its management, and/or whose association with the business is not publicly known; these partners usually provide capital in the expectation of a return on their investment.

Australia

Summarising s. 5 of the *Partnership Act 1958* (Vic) (hereinafter the "Act"), for a partnership in Australia to exist, four main criteria must be satisfied. They are:

- Valid Agreement between the parties;
- To carry on a business – this is defined in s. 3 as "any trade, occupation or profession";
- In Common – meaning there must be some mutuality of rights, interests and obligations;
- View to Profit – thus charitable organizations cannot be partnerships (charities are typically incorporated associations under *Associations Incorporations Act 1981* (Vic))

Partners share profits and losses. A partnership is basically a settlement between two or more groups or firms in which profit and loss are equally divided

Bangladesh

In Bangladesh, the relevant law for regulating partnership is the Partnership Act 1932. A partnership is defined as the relation between persons who have agreed to share the profits of a business carried on by all or any of them acting for all. The law does not require written partnership agreement between the partners to form a partnership. A partnership does not also required to be registered, however an unregistered partnership has a number of limitation regarding enforcing its rights in any court. A partnership is considered as a separate legal identity (i.e. separate from its owners) in Bangladesh only if the partnership is registered. There must be a minimum of 2 partners and maximum of 20 partners.

Canada

Statutory regulation of partnerships in Canada fall under provincial jurisdiction. A partnership is not a separate legal entity and partnership income is taxed at the rate of the partner receiving the income. It can be deemed to exist regardless of the intention of the partners. Common elements considered by courts in determining the existence of a partnership are that two or more legal persons:

- Are carrying on a business
- In common
- With a view to profit.

Hong Kong

A partnership in Hong Kong is a business entity formed by the Hong Kong Partnerships Ordinance, which defines a partnership as "the relation between persons carrying on a business in common with a view of profit" and is not a joint stock company or an incorporated company. If the business entity registers with the Registrar of Companies it takes the form of a limited partnership defined in the Limited Partnerships Ordinance. However, if this business entity fails to register with the Registrar of Companies, then it becomes a general partnership as a default.

India

According to section 4 of the Partnership Act of 1932,"Partnership is defined as the relation between two or more persons who have agreed to share the profits of a business run by all or any one of them acting for all". This definition superseded the previous definition given in section 239 of Indian Contract Act 1872 as – "Partnership is the relation which subsists between persons who have agreed to combine their property, labor, skill in some business, and to share the profits thereof between them". The 1932 definition added the concept of mutual agency. The Indian Partnerships have the following common characteristics:

1) A partnership firm is not a legal entity apart from the partners constituting it. It has limited identity for the purpose of tax law as per section 4 of the Partnership Act of 1932.

2) Partnership is a concurrent subject. Contracts of partnerships are included in the Entry no.7 of List III of The Constitution of India (the list constitutes the subjects on which both the State government and Central (National) Government can legislate i.e. pass laws on).

3) Unlimited Liability. The major disadvantage of partnership is the unlimited liability of partners for the debts and liabilities of the firm. Any partner can bind the firm and the firm is liable for all liabilities incurred by any firm on behalf of the firm. If property of partnership firm is insufficient to meet liabilities, personal property of any partner can be attached to pay the debts of the firm.

4) Partners are Mutual Agents.The business of firm can be carried on by all or any of them for all. Any partner has authority to bind the firm. Act of any one partner is binding on all the partners. Thus, each partner is 'agent' of all the remaining partners. Hence, partners are 'mutual agents'. Section 18 of the Partnership Act, 1932 says "Subject to the provisions of this Act, a partner is the agent of the firm for the purpose of the business of the firm"

5) Oral or Written Agreements. The Partnership Act, 1932 nowhere mentions that the Partnership Agreement is to be in written or oral format. Thus the general rule of the Contract Act applies that the contract can be 'oral' or 'written' as long as it satisfies the basic conditions of being a contract i.e. the agreement between partners is legally enforceable. A written agreement is advisable to establish existence of partnership and to prove rights and liabilities of each partner, as it is difficult to prove an oral agreement.

6) Number of Partners is minimum 2 and maximum 50 in any kind of business activities.Since partnership is 'agreement' there must be minimum two partners. The Partnership Act does not put any restrictions on maximum number of partners. However, section 464 of Companies Act 2013, and Rule 10 of Companies (Miscellaneous) Rules, 2014 prohibits partnership consisting of more than 50 for any businesses, unless it is registered as a company under Companies Act, 2013 or formed in pursuance of some other law. Some other law means companies and corporations formed via some other law passed by Parliament of India.

7) Mutual agency is the real test. The real test of 'partnership firm' is 'mutual agency' set by the Courts of India, i.e. whether a partner can bind the firm by his act, i.e. whether he can act as agent of all other partners.

United Kingdom Limited Partnership

A limited partnership in the United Kingdom consists of:

- One or more people called general partners, who are liable for all debts and obligations of the firm; and
- One or of the firm beyond the amount contributed.

Limited partners may not:

- Draw out or receive back any part of their contributions to the partnership during its lifetime; or
- Take part in the management of the business or have power to bind the firm.

If they do, they become liable for all the debts and obligations of the firm up to the amount drawn out or received back or incurred while taking part in the management, as the case may be.

United States

The federal government of the United States does not have specific statutory law governing the establishment of partnerships. Instead, each of the fifty states as well as the District of Columbia has its own statutes and common law that govern partnerships. These states largely follow general common law principles of partnerships whether a general partnership, a limited partnership or a limited liability partnership. In the absence of applicable federal law, the National Conference of Commissioners on Uniform State Laws has issued non-binding model laws (called uniform act) in which to encourage the adoption of uniformity of partnership law into the states by their respective legislatures. This includes the Uniform Partnership Act and the Uniform Limited Partnership Act. Although the federal government does not have specific statutory law for establishing partnerships, it has an extensive and hyperdetailed statutory scheme for the taxation of partnerships in the Internal Revenue Code. The IRC is Title 26 of the United States Code wherein Subchapter K of Chapter 1 creates tax consequences of such great scale and scope that it effectively serves as a federal statutory scheme for governing partnerships.

History

Partnerships have a long history, they were already in use in Medieval times in Europe and in the Middle East. In Europe, the partnerships contributed to the Commercial Revolution which started in the 13th century. In the 15th, century the cities member of the Hanseatic League, would mutually strengthen each other; a ship from Hamburg to Danzig, would not only carry its own cargo but was also commissioned to transport freight for other members of the league. This practice not only saved time and money; but also constituted a first step toward partnership. This capacity to join forces in reciprocal services became a distinctive feature, and a long lasting success factor, of the Hanseatic team spirit.

A close examination of Medieval trade in Europe shows that numerous significant credit based trades were not bearing interest. Hence, pragmatism and common sense called for a fair compensation for the risk of lending money, and a compensation for the opportunity cost of lending money without using it for other fruitful purposes. In order to circumvent the usury laws edicted by the Church, other forms of reward were created, in particular through the widespread form of partnership called *commenda*, very popular with Italian merchant bankers. Florentine merchant banks were almost sure to make a positive return on their loans, but this would be before taking into account solvency risks.

In the Middle East, the *Qirad* and *Mudarabas* institutions developed when trade with the Levant, namely the Ottoman Empire and the Muslim Near East, flourished and when early trading companies, contracts, bills of exchange and long-distance international trade were established. After the fall of the Roman Empire, the Levant trade revived in the tenth to eleventh centuries in Byzantine Italy. The eastern and western Mediterranean formed part of a single commercial civilization in the Middle Ages, and the two regions were economically interdependent through trade (in varying degrees).

Partner Compensation

In certain partnerships of individuals, particularly law firms and accountancy firms, equity partners are distinguished from salaried partners (or contract or income partners). An equity partner is a part-owner of the business, and is entitled to a proportion of the distributable profits of the partnership, while a salaried partner who is paid a salary but does not have any underlying ownership interest in the business and will not share in the distributions of the partnership (although it is quite common for salaried partners to receive a bonus based on the firm's profitability). Although they are both regarded as partners, in legal and economic terms, equity partners and salaried partners have little in common other than joint and several liability. The degree of control which each type of partner exerts over the partnership depends on the relevant partnership agreement.

In their most basic form, equity partners enjoy a fixed share of the partnership (usually, but not always an equal share with the other partners). However, in more sophisticated partnerships, different models exist for determining either ownership or profit distribution (or both). Two common forms are "lockstep" and "eat what you kill" compensation (sometimes referred to as, less graphically, a "source of origination").

Lockstep involves new partners joining the partnership with a certain number of "points". As time passes, they accrue additional points, until they reach a set maximum sometimes referred to as a plateau. The length of time it takes to reach the maximum is often used to describe the firm (so, for example, one could say that one firm has a "seven-year lockstep" and another has a "ten-year lockstep" depending on the length of time it takes to reach maximum equity).

Eat-what-you-kill is rarely, if ever, seen outside of law firms. The principle is simply that each partner receives a share of the partnership profits up to a certain amount, with any additional profits being distributed to the partner who was responsible for the "origination" of the work that generated the profits.

British law firms tend to use the lockstep principle, whereas American firms are more accustomed to eat-what-you-kill. When British firm Clifford Chance merged with American firm Rogers & Wells, many of the difficulties associated with that merger were blamed on the difficulties of merging a lockstep culture with an eat-what-you-kill culture.

Limited Liability Partnership

A limited liability partnership (LLP) is a partnership in which some or all partners (depending on the jurisdiction) have limited liabilities. It therefore exhibits elements of partnerships and corporations. In an LLP, one partner is not responsible or liable for another partner's misconduct or negligence. This is an important difference from the traditional unlimited partnership under the Partnership Act 1890 (for the UK), in which each partner has joint and several liability. In an LLP, some partners have a form of limited liability similar to that of the shareholders of a corporation. In some countries, an LLP must also have at least one thing called as a "general partner" with unlimited liability. Unlike corporate shareholders, the partners have the right to manage the business directly. In contrast, corporate shareholders have to elect a board of directors under the laws of various state charters. The board organizes itself (also under the laws of the various state charters) and hires corporate officers who then have as "corporate" individuals the legal responsibility to manage the corporation in the corporation's best interest. A LLP also contains a different level of tax liability from that of a corporation.

Limited liability partnerships are distinct from limited partnerships in some countries, which may allow all LLP partners to have limited liability, while a limited partnership may require at least one unlimited partner and allow others to assume the role of a passive and limited liability investor. As a result, in these countries, the LLP is more suited for businesses in which all investors wish to take an active role in management.

There is considerable confusion between LLPs as constituted in the U.S. and those introduced in the UK in 2001 and adopted elsewhere as the UK LLP is, despite its name, specifically legislated as a corporate body rather than as a partnership. In Nigeria, limited liability partnerships have legal personality. However, one must register a partnership first before it can gain the status of limited liability partnership.

National Variations

Canada

All provinces, except Yukon, Prince Edward Island and Nunavut, have permitted LLPs for lawyers and accountants. In British Columbia, the Partnership Amendment Act, 2004 (Bill 35) permitted LLPs for lawyers and other professionals as well as businesses.

China

In China, the LLP is known as a Special general partnership. The organizational form is restricted to knowledge-based professions and technical service industries. The structure shields co-partners from liabilities due to the willful misconduct or gross negligence of one partner or a group of partners.

Germany

The German *Partnerschaftsgesellschaft* or PartG is an association of non-commercial professionals, working together. Though not a corporate entity, it can sue and be sued, own property and act under the partnership's name. The partners, however, are jointly and severally liable for all the partnership's debts, except when only some partners' misconduct caused damages to another party — and then only if professional liability insurance is mandatory. Another exception possible since 2012 is a Partnerschaftsgesellschaft mbB (mit beschränkter Berufshaftung) where all liabilities from professional misconduct are limited by the partnerships capital.

The *Partnerschaftsgesellschaft* is not subject to corporate or business tax, only its partners' respective income is taxed.

Greece

An LLP is an approximate equivalent to the Greek ΕΠΕ (*Etería Periorisménis Evthínis* Company of Limited Liability). In an ΕΠΕ the partners own personal shares that can be sold by a partner only when all other partners agree. The business management can be exercised either directly by the board of partners or by a General Manager. In the aspect of liability, an ΕΠΕ is identical to an LLP.

Hungary

In Hungary, LLP is equivalent to the Hungarian "Betéti Társaság" (literally: "Deposit Partnership", legally styled as "Bt.") which must have at least two members: at least one must have unlimited liability and at least one must have limited liability. BTs have no legal personhood under Hungarian law.

India

The Limited Liability Partnership Act 2008 was published in the official Gazette of India on 9 January 2009 and has been notified with effect from 31 March 2009. However, the Act, has been notified with limited sections only. The rules have been notified in the official gazette on 1 April 2009. The first LLP was incorporated in the first week of April 2009.

LLP is different from limited partnership. It operates like a limited partnership, but in a LLP each member is protected from personal liability, except to the extent of their capital contribution in the LLP.

1. In India, for all purposes of taxation (service tax or any other stipulated tax payment), an LLP is treated like any other partnership firm.
2. be limited to their agreed contribution in the LLP.
3. Further, no partner would be liable on account of the independent or unauthorized actions of other partners, thus allowing individual partners to be shielded from joint liability created by another partner's wrongful business decisions or misconduct.
4. LLP shall be a body corporate and a legal entity separate from its partners. It will have perpetual succession. Indian Partnership Act, 1932 shall not be applicable to LLPs and there shall not be any upper limit on number of partners in an LLP unlike an ordinary partnership firm where the maximum number of partners can not exceed 20, LLP Act makes a mandatory statement where one of the partner to the LLP should be an Indian.
5. Provisions have been made for corporate actions like mergers, amalgamations etc.
6. While enabling provisions in respect of winding up and dissolutions of LLPs have been made, detailed provisions in this regard would be provided by way of rules under the Act.
7. The Act also provide LP.
8. The Registrar of Companies (Roc) shall register and control LLPs also.
9. The governance of LLPs shall .

Characteristics

1. Separate legal entity : Like a company LLP also has a separate legal entity. So the partners and the LLP in are distinct from each other. This is like a company where members are different from the company.
2. No requirement of minimum capital : In case of companies there should be a minimum amount of capital that should be brought by the members or owners who want to form it. But to start an LLP there is no requirement of minimum capital.
3. Minimum number of members: To start a limited liability partnership at least two members are required initially. However, there is no limit on the maximum number of partners.
4. No requirement of compulsory audit: All the companies, whether private or public, irrespective of their share capital, are required to get their accounts audited. But in case of LLP, there

is no such mandatory requirement. A limited liability partnership is required to get the audit done only if:

a. If the contributions of the LLP exceeds Rs. 25 lakhs, or b. If the annual turnover of the LLP exceeds Rs. 40 lakhs

Benefits

1. It is more flexible to organize the internal structure of LLP. Comparatively it is complex to organize the internal structure of a company.
2. There is no maximum limit for the no. of partners in LLP. In the private limited company shareholders are limited to the extent of 200 shareholders.
3. Raising and utilization of funds depends on the partners will. Funds can be bought and utilized only as per the norms listed under the Companies Act, 2013.
4. LLP is exempt of Dividend Distribution Tax (DDT). Company has to pay DDT on dividend distribution.

Demerits

LLPs as well have some limitations within. Some of them can be summarized as below.

1. Any act of the partner without the other partner, may bind the LLP
2. LLP cannot raise money from public.
3. Angel investor or venture capital firm does not prefer LLP.

Registration Process

- Obtain digital signature for the partners.
- Apply for the DIN (Director Identification Number) which is necessary to become a partner in the LLP.
- Apply for the name approval for the LLP registration.
- Issued the Certificate of Incorporation which is the proof for the registration.
- File LLP agreements and open a current bank account.

Japan

Limited liability partnerships were introduced to Japan in 2006 during a large-scale revamp of the country's laws governing business organizations. Japanese LLPs may be formed for any purpose (although The purpose must be clearly stated in the partnership agreement and cannot be general), have full limited liability and are treated as pass-through entities for tax purposes. However, each partner in an LLP must take an active role in the business, so the model is more suitable for joint ventures and small businesses than for companies in which investors plan to take passive roles. Japanese LLPs may *not* be used by lawyers or accountants, as these professions are required to do business through an unlimited liability entity.

A Japanese LLP is not a corporation, but rather exists as a contractual relationship between the partners, similarly to an American LLP. Japan also has a type of corporation with a partnership-styled internal structure, called a godo kaisha, which is closer in form to a British LLP or American limited liability company.

Kazakhstan

The concept of LLP exists in Kazakhstan law. All partners in a Kazakhstan LLP have limited liability, and they are liable for the debts of the partnership to the extent of the value of their corresponding participatory interests in the partnership. The names for LLP in Kazakhstan are "ШС" (which stands for *Zhawapkershiligi shektewli seriktestik*) in Kazakh and "ТОО" (which stands for *Tovarishchestvo s ogranichennoy otvyetstvyennost'yu*) in Russian. This is the most popular business form in Kazakhstan. Almost any private business may be incorporated as an LLP (notable exceptions are banks, airlines, insurance companies, and mortgage companies, which must be incorporated in the form of a joint stock company). An LLP in Kazakhstan is a corporate body, and in fact, is an LLC. Partners cannot conduct business on its own, and it's the corporate body that conducts the business. There is also a concept of "simple partnership" in Kazakhstan law, which corresponds more to the general concept of partnership, but it is not widely used and is not well developed in Kazakhstan.

Poland

A close equivalent to limited liability partnerships under Polish law is the *spółka partnerska*, where all partners are jointly and severely liable for partnership's debts apart from those arising from another partner's misconduct or negligence. This partnership type is only addressed to representatives of some "high risk" occupations, such as lawyers, medicine doctors, tax advisers, accountants, brokers, sworn translators etc.

Romania

An LLP is equivalent to the Romanian law vehicle known as a Societate civilă profesională cu răspundere limitată.

Singapore

LLPs are formed under the Limited Liability Partnerships Act 2005. This legislation draws on both the US and UK models of LLP, and like the latter establishes the LLP as a body corporate. However, for tax purposes it is treated like a general partnership, so that the partners rather than the partnership are subject to tax (tax transparency).

United Kingdom

In the United Kingdom LLPs are governed by the Limited Liability Partnerships Act 2000 (in

Great Britain) and the Limited Liability Partnerships Act (Northern Ireland) 2002 in Northern Ireland. A UK limited liability partnership is a corporate body - that is to say, it has a continuing legal existence independent of its members, as compared to a Partnership which may (in England and Wales, does not) have a legal existence dependent upon its membership.

A UK LLP's members have a collective ("Joint") responsibility, to the extent that they may agree in an "LLP agreement", but no individual ("several") responsibility for each other's actions. As with a limited company or a corporation, members in an LLP cannot, in the absence of fraud or wrongful trading, lose more than they invest.

In relation to tax, however, a UK LLP is similar to a partnership, namely, it is tax-transparent, that is to say it pays no UK corporation tax or capital gains tax. Instead, LLP income and/or gains are distributed gross to partners as self-employed persons, rather than as PAYE employees. Partners receiving income and/or gains from an LLP are liable for their own taxation.

It is a unique entity in its synthesis of collective and individual rights and responsibilities and its flexibility — there is in fact no requirement for the LLP agreement even to be in writing because simple partnership-based regulations apply by way of default provisions.

It has to date been closely replicated by Japan and by the financial centres of Dubai and Qatar. It is perhaps closest in nature to a limited liability company in the United States of America although it may be distinguished from that entity by the fact that the LLC, while having a legal existence independent of its members is not technically a corporate body because its legal existence is time limited and therefore not "continuing."

The LLP structure is commonly used by accountants to retain the tax structure of traditional partnerships whilst adding some limited liability protection. LLPs are also becoming more common among firms in the legal profession such as solicitors although they are permitted to use a limited company structure.

United States

Example of a LLP-Office in the State of Georgia (U.S.)

In the United States, each individual state has its own law governing their formation. Limited liability partnerships emerged in the early 1990s: while only two states allowed LLPs in 1992, over forty had adopted LLP statutes by the time LLPs were added to the Uniform Partnership Act in 1996.

The limited liability partnership was formed in the aftermath of the collapse of real estate and energy prices in Texas in the 1980s. This collapse led to a large wave of bank and savings and loan failures. Because the amounts recoverable from the banks were small, efforts were made to recover assets from the lawyers and accountants that had advised the banks in the early 1980s. The reason was that partners in law and accounting firms were subject to the possibility of huge claims which would bankrupt them personally, and the first LLP laws were passed to shield innocent members of these partnerships from liability.

Although found in many business fields, the LLP is an especially popular form of organization among professionals, particularly lawyers, accountants, and architects. In some U.S. states, namely California, New York, Oregon, and Nevada, LLPs can only be formed for such professional uses. Formation of an LLP typically requires filing certificates with the county and state offices. Although specific rules vary from state to state, all states have passed variations of the Revised Uniform Partnership Act.

The liability of the partners varies from state to state. Section 306(c) of the Revised Uniform Partnership Act (1997)(RUPA) (a standard statute adopted by a majority of the states) grants LLPs a form of limited liability similar to that of a corporation:

An obligation of a partnership incurred while the partnership is a limited liability partnership, whether arising in contract, tort, or otherwise, is solely the obligation of the partnership. A partner is not personally liable, directly or indirectly, by way of contribution or otherwise, for such an obligation solely by reason of being or so acting as a partner.

However, a sizable minority of states only extend such protection against negligence claims, meaning that partners in an LLP can be personally liable for contract and intentional tort claims brought against the LLP. While Tennessee and West Virginia have otherwise adopted RUPA, their respective adoptions of Section 306 depart from the uniform language, and only a partial liability shield is provided.

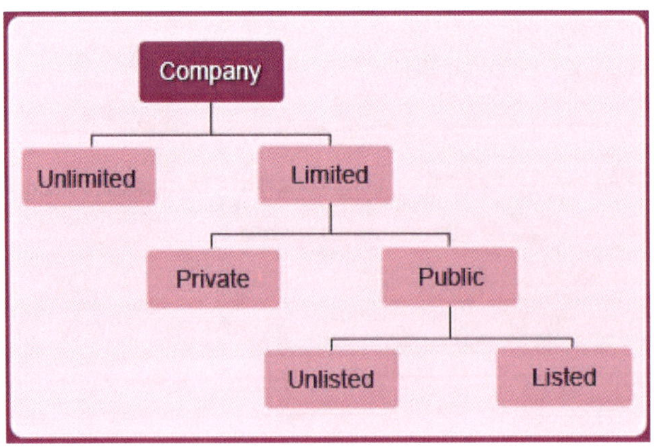

As in a partnership or limited liability company (LLC), the profits of an LLP are allocated among the partners for tax purposes, avoiding the problem of "double taxation" often found in corporations.

Some US states have combined the LP and LLP forms to create limited liability limited partnerships.

Company / Corporation

Company form of business organisation is a voluntary association of persons to carry on business. Normally, it is given a legal status and is subject to certain legal regulations. It is an association of persons who generally contribute money for some common purpose. The money so contributed is the capital of the company.

- The persons who contribute capital are its members. The proportion of capital to which each member is entitled is called his share, therefore members of a joint stock company are known as shareholders and the capital of the company is known as share capital.
- The companies are governed by the Indian Companies Act, 1956. The Act defines a company as an artificial person created by law, having separate entity, with perpetual succession and a common seal.

Advantages:

- Unlimited life.
- Professional Management.
- Limited liability.
- Ease of raising capital.
- High possibility of wealth maximization.

Disadvantages:

- Dividend Tax burden.
- High cost of set-up and report filing.
- More regulation.

Private Company Limited by Guarantee

In British and Irish company law, a company limited by guarantee (LBG) is an alternative type of corporation used primarily for non-profit organisations that require legal personality. A company limited by guarantee does not usually have a share capital or shareholders, but instead has members who act as guarantors. The guarantors give an undertaking to contribute a nominal amount (typically very small) in the event of the winding up of the company.

A company limited by guarantee can distribute its profits to its members, if allowed to by its articles of association, but then it would not be eligible for charitable status. Limited companies can convert to a Community Interest Company (CIC) which feature an asset lock which prevents the extraction of profits.

Like a private company limited by shares, a company limited by guarantee must include the suffix "Limited" in its name, except in circumstances specifically excluded by law. One condition of this exclusion is that the company does not distribute profits. Until 1981, it was possible in the United Kingdom to form a company limited by guarantee with share capital. Under section 5 of the Companies Act 2006, new companies cannot be formed as a company limited by guarantee with a share capital.

When incorporating multi-stakeholder organisations, this form is sometimes preferred over the industrial and provident society because company law allows multiple classes of member with separate voting constituencies.

Uses

Common uses of companies limited by guarantee include clubs, membership organisations, including students' unions, residential property management companies, sports associations (such as the PGA European Tour), workers' co-operatives, other social enterprises, non-governmental organizations (NGOs) and charities (such as Oxfam), and at least one political party (the UK Independence Party). The railway infrastructure provider Network Rail, domain name registry Nominet UK, England and Wales Cricket Board and IXPs LINX (London Internet Exchange), and LONAP (London Access Point) are also companies limited by guarantee. Australia also has companies limited by guarantee, Cricket Australia being one example.

Commercial Enterprises

One of the largest companies limited by guarantee is Bupa, the healthcare company, which has 32 million customers in more than 190 countries and which employs more than 84,000 people around the world.

The Anglo-Canadian law firm of Gowling WLG, formed in 2016, is structured as an English private company limited by guarantee, in which the two limited liability partnerships of Gowling WLG (Canada) LLP and Gowling WLG (UK) LLP are members and provide legal services; the structure is similar to the Swiss Verein structure used by several other major international law firms.

Private Company Limited by Shares

A private company limited by shares is a class of private limited company incorporated under the laws of England and Wales, Scotland, certain Commonwealth countries or the Republic of Ireland. It has shareholders with limited liability and its shares may not be offered to the general public, unlike those of a public limited company (plc).

"Limited by shares" means that the liability of the shareholders to creditors of the company is limited to the capital originally invested, i.e. the nominal value of the shares and any premium paid in return for the issue of the shares by the company. A shareholder's personal assets are thus protected in the event of the company's insolvency, but any money invested in the company may be lost.

A limited company may be "private" or "public". A private limited company's disclosure requirements are lighter, but its shares may not be offered to the general public and therefore cannot be traded on a public stock exchange. This is the major difference between a private limited company and a public limited company. Most companies, particularly small companies, are private.

Private companies limited by shares are usually required to have the suffix "Limited" (often written "Ltd" or "Ltd.") or "Incorporated" ("Inc.") as part of their name, though the latter cannot be used in the UK or the Republic of Ireland. In the Republic of Ireland "Teoranta" ("Teo.") may be used instead, largely by Gaeltacht companies. "Cyfyngedig" ("Cyf.") may be used by Welsh companies in a similar fashion.

Company Officers

In the United Kingdom, every company must have formally appointed company officers. By statute, a private company must have at least one director and until April 2008 also had to have a secretary. The company's articles of association may require more than one director. At least one director must be an individual, not another company.

Anybody can be a director, subject to certain exceptions. A person who is yet to be discharged from bankruptcy or who has been banned from being a company director by the court will be prohibited, except in certain cases. For example, if the bankrupted person had requested details of share transactions because there was sufficient equity within the business/es that had not been dealt with sufficiently by the court, they are technically not bankrupt and are permitted to start a company. In addition, a person may not be a director of a limited company if he or she is unable to consent to their appointment. As of October 2008, the minimum age required to give this consent is 16 years of age. This change was applied retroactively, with any directors under the age of 16 being removed from the register upon the implementation of the (Companies Act 2006). This was already the case in Scotland, under the Age of Legal Capacity (Scotland) Act 1991.

No formal qualifications are required to be a company director or secretary, but the company must comply with many laws and regulations, regardless of such qualifications or the lack of them.

Certain non-British nationals are restricted as to the work they may undertake in the UK, depending upon their visas, work permits, national insurance payments center location and tax details, training, English language and professional indemnity insurances.

As of October 2008 (Companies Act 2006), it is no longer necessary to obtain a court order to withhold a director's address, as a "service address" can be supplied as well, with the residential address being held as protected information at Companies House.

Share Capital

When a limited company is formed it must issue one or more subscriber shares to its initial members. It may increase capitalisation by issue of further shares. The issued share capital of the company is the total number of shares existing in the company multiplied by the nominal value of each share.

A company incorporated in England and Wales can be created with any number of shares of any nominal value, expressed in any currency. For example, there may be 10,000 shares with a nominal value of 1p, or 100 shares of £1 each. In each case the share capital would be £100.

Unissued shares can be issued at any time by the directors using a Form SH01 - Return of Allotment of Shares (Pursuant to Companies Act, 2006) subject to prior authorisation by the shareholders.

Shares in a private company are usually transferred by private agreement between the seller and the buyer, as they may not be offered to the general public. A stock transfer form is required to register the transfer with the company. The articles of association of private companies often place restrictions on the transfer of shares.

Company Accounts

A company's first accounts must start on the day of incorporation. The first financial year must end on the accounting reference date, or a date up to seven days either side of this date. Subsequent accounts start on the day following the year-end date of the previous accounts. They end on the next accounting reference date or a date up to seven days either side.

To help companies meet this filing requirement, Companies House sends a pre-printed "shuttle" form to its registered office several weeks before the anniversary of incorporation. This will show the information that has already been given to Companies House. If a company's accounts are delivered late there is an automatic penalty. This is between £100 and £1,000 for a private company.

The first accounts of a private company must be delivered:

- within 9 months of the end of the accounting reference period; or
- if the accounting reference period is more than 12 months, within 22 months of the date of incorporation, or three months from the end of the accounting reference period, whichever is longer.

A company may change its accounting reference date by sending Form 225 to the Registrar.

Registered Office

Every company must have a registered office, which does not need to be its usual business address. It is sometimes the address of the company's lawyers or accountants, for example. All official letters and documentation from the government departments (including Inland Revenue and Companies House) will be sent to this address, and it must be shown on all official company documentation. The registered office can be anywhere in England and Wales (or Scotland if the company is registered there).

Formation

To incorporate a company in the UK the following documents, together with the registration fee (£40 as of August 2012), must be sent to the Registrar of Companies:

- Form IN01
- The articles of association
- The memorandum of association

The memorandum of association states the name of the company, the registered office and the company objectives. The objective of a company may simply be stated as being to carry out business as a general commercial company. The memorandum delivered to the Registrar must be signed by each subscriber in front of a witness who must attest the signature.

The articles of association govern the company's internal affairs. The company's articles delivered to the Registrar must be signed by each subscriber in front of a witness who must attest the signature.

Form IN01 states the first directors, the first secretary, and the address of the registered office. Each director must give his or her name, address, date of birth, and occupation. Each officer appointed, and each subscriber (or their agent), must sign and date the form.

In other jurisdictions companies must make similar applications to the relevant registrar, such as the Companies Registration Office, Ireland in the Republic of Ireland, or the Registrar of Companies in India.

Companies House offers a registration service on their website using a system called business link (costing £15 as of August 2015).

Redundant Companies

Private companies that have not traded or otherwise carried on business for at least three months may apply to the Registrar to be struck off the register. Alternatively, the company may be voluntarily liquidated.

Converting to a Public Limited Company

A private company limited by shares, or an unlimited company with a share capital, may re-register as a public limited company (PLC). A private company must pass a special resolution that it be so re-registered and deliver a copy of the resolution together with an application form 43(3)(e) to the Registrar.

Limited Liability Company

A limited liability company (LLC) is the United States-specific form of a private limited company. It is a business structure that combines the pass-through taxation of a partnership or sole proprietorship with the limited liability of a corporation. An LLC is not a corporation; it is a legal form of a company that provides limited liability to its owners in many jurisdictions. LLCs do not need to be organized for profit. In certain U.S. states (for example, Texas), businesses that provide professional services requiring a state professional license, such as legal or medical services, may not be allowed to form an LLC but may be required to form a very similar entity called a professional limited liability company (PLLC).

Overview

A Limited Liability Company (LLC) is a hybrid business entity having certain characteristics of both a corporation and a partnership or sole proprietorship (depending on how many owners there are). An LLC, although a business entity, is a type of unincorporated association and is not a corporation. The primary characteristic an LLC shares with a corporation is limited liability, and the primary characteristic it shares with a partnership is the availability of pass-through income taxation. It is often more flexible than a corporation, and it is well-suited for companies with a single owner.

In the absence of express statutory guidance, most American courts have held that LLC members are subject to the same common law alter ego piercing theories as corporate shareholders. However, it is more difficult to pierce the LLC veil because LLCs do not have many formalities to maintain. So long as the LLC and the members do not commingle funds, it would be difficult to pierce this veil. Membership interests in LLCs and partnership interests are also afforded a significant level of protection through the charging order mechanism. The charging order limits the creditor of a debtor-partner or a debtor-member to the debtor's share of distributions, without conferring on the creditor any voting or management rights. Limited liability company members may, in certain circumstances, also incur a personal liability in cases where distributions to members render the LLC insolvent.

Flexibility and Default Rules

The other phrase "unless otherwise provided for in the operating agreement" (or its equivalent) is found throughout all existing LLC statutes and is responsible for the flexibility the members of the LLC have in deciding how their LLC will be governed (provided it does not go outside legal bounds). State statutes typically provide automatic or "default" rules for how an LLC will be governed unless the operating agreement provides otherwise.

Similarly, the phrase "unless otherwise provided for in the by laws" is also found in all corporation law statutes but often refers only to a narrower range of matters.

The limited liability company ("LLC") has grown to become one of the most prevalent business forms in the entire United States. As the LLC's popularity has swelled, unforeseen issues have emerged in these new statutes—particularly around single-member LLCs in Florida, New York, California, Colorado, and Georgia, where personal asset protection has been subverted.

Effective August 1, 2013, the Delaware Limited Liability Company Act provides that the managers and controlling members of a limited liability company owe fiduciary duties of care and loyalty to the limited liability company and its members. Under the amendment (prompted by the Delaware

Supreme Court's decision in *Gatz Properties, LLC v. Auriga Capital Corp*, November 2012), parties to an LLC remain free to expand, restrict, or eliminate fiduciary duties in their LLC agreements (subject to the implied covenant of good faith and fair dealing).

Under 6 Del. C. Section 18-101(7), a Delaware LLC operating agreement can be written, oral or implied. It sets forth member capital contributions, ownership percentages, and management structure. Like a prenuptial agreement, an operating agreement can avoid future disputes between members by addressing buy-out rights, valuation formulas, and transfer restrictions. A written LLC operating agreement should be signed by all of its members.

Income Tax

For U.S. federal income tax purposes, an LLC is treated by default as a pass-through entity. If there is only one member in the company, the LLC is treated as a "disregarded entity" for tax purposes, and an individual owner would report the LLC's income or loss on Schedule C of his or her individual tax return. Thus, income from the LLC is taxed at the individual tax rates. The default tax status for LLCs with multiple members is as a partnership, which is required to report income and loss on IRS Form 1065. Under partnership tax treatment, each member of the LLC, as is the case for all partners of a partnership, annually receives a Form K-1 reporting the member's distributive share of the LLC's income or loss that is then reported on the member's individual income tax return. On the other hand, income from corporations is taxed twice, once at the corporate entity level and again when distributed to shareholders, thus more tax savings often result if a business formed as an LLC rather than a corporation.

An LLC with either single or multiple members may elect to be taxed as a corporation through the filing of IRS Form 8832. After electing corporate tax status, an LLC may further elect to be treated as a regular C corporation (taxation of the entity's income prior to any dividends or distributions to the members and then taxation of the dividends or distributions once received as income by the members) or as an S corporation (entity level income and loss passes through to the members). Some commentators have recommended an LLC taxed as a S-corporation as the best possible small business structure. It combines the simplicity and flexibility of an LLC with the tax benefits of an S-corporation (self-employment tax savings).

Advantages

- Choice of tax regime. An LLC can elect to be taxed as a sole proprietor, partnership, S corporation or C corporation (as long as they would otherwise qualify for such tax treatment), providing for a great deal of flexibility.
- A limited liability company with multiple members that elects to be taxed as partnership may specially allocate the members' distributive share of income, gain, loss, deduction, or credit via the company operating agreement on a basis other than the ownership percentage of each member so long as the rules contained in Treasury Regulation (26 CFR) 1.704-1 are met. S corporations may not specially allocate profits, losses and other tax items under US tax law.
- Limited liability, meaning that the owners of the LLC, called "members", are protected from some or all liability for acts and debts of the LLC depending on state shield laws.

- In the United States, an S corporation has a limited number of stockholders, and all of them must be U.S. citizens; an LLC may have an unlimited number of members, and there is no citizenship restrictions.
- Much less administrative paperwork and record keeping than a corporation.
- Pass-through taxation (i.e., no double taxation), unless the LLC elects to be taxed as a C corporation.
- Using default tax classification, profits are taxed personally at the member level, not at the LLC level.
- LLCs in most states are treated as entities separate from their members. However, in some jurisdictions such as Connecticut, case law has determined that owners were not required to plead facts sufficient to pierce the corporate veil and LLC members can be personally liable for operation of the LLC.
- LLCs in some states can be set up with just one natural person involved.
- Less risk of being "stolen" by fire-sale acquisitions (more protection against "hungry" investors).
- For real estate companies, each separate property can be owned by its own, individual LLC, thereby shielding not only the owners, but their other properties from cross-liability.

Disadvantages

Although there is no statutory requirement for an operating agreement in most jurisdictions, members of a multiple member LLC who operate without one may run into problems. Unlike state laws regarding stock corporations, which are very well developed and provide for a variety of governance and protective provisions for the corporation and its shareholders, most states do not dictate detailed governance and protective provisions for the members of a limited liability company. Thus, in the absence of such statutory provisions, the members of an LLC must establish governance and protective provisions pursuant to an operating agreement or similar governing document.

- It may be more difficult to raise financial capital for an LLC as investors may be more comfortable investing funds in the better-understood corporate form with a view toward an eventual IPO. One possible solution may be to form a new corporation and merge into it, dissolving the LLC and converting into a corporation.
- Many jurisdictions—including Alabama, California, Kentucky, New York, Pennsylvania, Tennessee, and Texas—levy a franchise tax or capital values tax on LLCs. In essence, this franchise or business privilege tax is the fee the LLC pays the state for the benefit of limited liability. The franchise tax can be an amount based on revenue, an amount based on profits, or an amount based on the number of owners or the amount of capital employed in the state, or some combination of those factors, or simply a flat fee, as in Delaware.
    - Effective in Texas for 2007 the franchise tax is replaced with the Texas Business

Margin Tax. This is paid as: tax payable = revenues minus some expenses with an apportionment factor. In most states, however, the fee is nominal and only a handful charge a tax comparable to the tax imposed on corporations.

- In California, both foreign and domestic LLCs, corporations, and trusts, whether for-profit or non-profit—unless the entity is tax exempt—must at least pay a minimum income tax of $800 per year to the Franchise Tax Board; and no foreign LLC, corporation or trust may conduct business in California unless it is duly registered with the California Secretary of State.

- The District of Columbia considers LLCs to be taxable entities, thus eliminating the benefit of pass-through taxes—subjecting members to double taxation. Typically, LLCs will choose to be taxed as a partnership to avoid double taxation, which occurs in corporations. This allows companies to distribute their income among members who then report it on their personal tax returns.
- Renewal fees may also be higher. Maryland, for example, charges a stock or nonstock corporation $120 for the initial charter, and $100 for an LLC. The fee for filing the annual report the following year is $300 for stock-corporations and LLCs. The fee is zero for non-stock corporations. In addition, certain states, such as New York, impose a publication requirement upon formation of the LLC which requires that the members of the LLC publish a notice in newspapers in the geographic region that the LLC will be located that it is being formed. For LLCs located in major metropolitan areas (e.g., New York City), the cost of publication can be significant.
- The management structure of an LLC may not be clearly stated. Unlike corporations, they are not required to have a board of directors or officers. (This could also be seen as an advantage to some.)
- Taxing jurisdictions outside the US are likely to treat a US LLC as a corporation, regardless of its treatment for US tax purposes—for example a US LLC doing business outside the US or as a resident of a foreign jurisdiction. This is very likely where the country (such as Canada) does not recognize LLCs as an authorized form of business entity in that country.
- The principals of LLCs use many different titles—e.g., member, manager, managing member, managing director, chief executive officer, president, and partner. As such, it can be difficult to determine who actually has the authority to enter into a contract on the LLC's behalf.

Variations

- A Professional Limited Liability Company (PLLC, P.L.L.C., or P.L.) is a limited liability company organized for the purpose of providing professional services. Usually, professions where the state requires a license to provide services, such as a doctor, chiropractor, lawyer, accountant, architect, landscape architect, or engineer, require the formation of a PLLC. However, some states, such as California, do not permit LLCs to engage in the practice of a licensed profession. Exact requirements of PLLCs vary from state to state. Typically, a PLLC's members must all be professionals practicing the same profession. In addition, the limitation of personal liability of members does not extend to professional malpractice claims.

- A Series LLC is a special form of a Limited liability company that allows a single LLC to segregate its assets into separate series. For example, a series LLC that purchases separate pieces of real estate may put each in a separate series so if the lender forecloses on one piece of property, the others are not affected.
- An L3C is a for-profit, social enterprise venture that has a stated goal of performing a socially beneficial purpose, not maximizing income. It is a hybrid structure that combines the legal and tax flexibility of a traditional LLC, the social benefits of a nonprofit organization, and the branding and market positioning advantages of a social enterprise.
- An Anonymous Limited Liability Company is a LLC where ownership information is not made publicly available by the state where the LLC is registered. This is done by using a third-party to act as the organizer and registered agent of the LLC. Level of anonymity varies with different states.

International Equivalents

Companies with limited liability exist in business law worldwide. However, the limited liability company is a specific legal structure defined by the laws of U.S. states, with quite distinct characteristics. Many other countries have similar structures.

Albania and Kosovo

In Albania and Kosovo a limited liability company is a commercial company founded by persons of physical or judicial status, who are not liable for the company and personally bear losses only up to the outstanding contribution agreements. Partners' contributions constitute the registered capital of a limited liability company. Each partner has his quota in the company in proportion to the contribution of the capital so the registered capital of the company is divided between the partners based on the proportional ratio of their contribution. In Albania a limited liability company may not have a capital of less than 100 lek. In Kosovo a company does not need to provide proof for payment of capital.

Argentina

Although not an exact equivalent, the Argentine variant of the LLC is called *Sociedad de Responsabilidad Limitada (S.R.L.)* and it limits the liability of its members up to their capital contribution in the company. The equity is divided into equal stakes (can not be called "shares"), each one of which represents a percentage of the company and that can not be traded on the stock exchange. Their by-laws are regulated by law N° 19550 and the commercial partnership is limited to a maximum of 50 partners.

Bosnia and Herzegovina

Bosnian and Herzegovinian legislation, similarly to that in Serbia, Montenegro, Macedonia contemplates LLCs. Companies using this structure append the abbreviation d.o.o. to their company name. A shareholder or member in a d.o.o. is only personally liable up to the value of the member's investment in the company.

Brazil

The corporate structure in Brazilian law most similar to the American LLC is the *Sociedade Limitada* ("Ltda."), under the new Brazilian Civil Code of 2002. The *sociedade limitada* is the new name of the *sociedade por quotas de responsabilidade limitada*, and it can be organized as *empresária* or *simples*, under this new code, roughly corresponding to the form types of *comercial* ("commercial") and *civil* ("non commercial") of the Commercial Code. A new law in Brazil has made it legal to obtain an LLC by a sole-proprietor called *Empresa Individual de Responsabilidade Limitada* (*Eireli* for short). The main requirement is a capital of 100 times the current minimum wage, R$ 78.800,00 (US$26.267.00) as of 2015.

Bulgaria

Bulgarian legislation contemplates LLCs as (*Druzhestvo s ogranichena otgovornost*; Limited liability company). Companies working under this structure append the abbreviation (OOD) to their name. In case of an LLC with individual owner it is contemplated as (*Ednolichno druzhestvo s ogranichena otgovornost*; One-man/ Single-member limited liability company) and abbreviated as (EOOD).

Chile

Chilean law contemplates a certain form of LLC known as "Sociedad de Responsabilidad Limitada" (Limited Liability Association). Also (LLC) These companies are regulated by law N° 3.918. Among their most important characteristics we can say that:

- They can pursue a commercial or non-commercial purpose (Sociedad Comercial de Responsabilidad Limitada / Sociedad Civil de Responsabilidad Limitada).
- They must be formed by two or more partners and can hold up to a maximum of fifty.
- Their equity is divided into "cuotas" (not shares) each one of which represents a percentage of the company.
- They can be managed by one or more managers (external if need be), or by a board of directors.
- Their by-laws can't be modified, nor their partners be changed, without the consent of all the other partners.
- In tax considerations, they differ from the LLC's because they pay a corporate tax for their income, amount that can be deducted by their owners as a credit against the taxes they pay.

Chilean law also contemplates a very special kind of individual owner LLC called *Empresa Individual de Responsabilidad Limitada* (Limited Liability Individual Company), which uses the E.I.R.L. abbreviation.

Colombia

Colombian legislation contemplates a very similar structure as mentioned above in the Chilean case. The *Ltda.* abbreviation is also used in Colombia.

Croatia

In Croatia, a private limited liability company is termed *društvo s ograničenom odgovornošću* (literal: limited liability company), abbreviated *d.o.o.*. A public limited liability company is termed a *dioničko društvo* (literal: joint stock company) abbreviated *d.d.*.

Czech Republic

Czech legislation contemplates LLCs as *společnost s ručením omezeným* (*s.r.o.* or *spol. s r.o.*). An *s.r.o.* is not technically comparable to an LLC because the profits are still subject to double taxation. Czech law does not offer a possibility to start up a limited company without the possibility of avoiding double taxation.

Denmark

The Danish form of the LLC is the *kommanditselskab* (K/S). There is no minimum capital requirements. In a K/S there are two types of shareholders, the *komplementar* which is fully liable, and the *kommanditist* which liability is limited. The K/S is a tax-transparent company, which means the income "passes through" the company directly to the shareholders.

Dominican Republic

Dominican Republic legislation contemplates LLCs as *Sociedad de Responsabilidad Limitada*, also known by their abbreviation *S.R.L.;; S.R.L.s award limited liability to their members up to their contribution in the company (i.e., contribution of capital). This type of company began after the law number 479 of the year 2008.*

Estonia

In Estonia, a limited liability company is referred to as *osaühing* (OÜ). The type of entity is also required to be identified in the name. An OÜ is taxed as a corporation. The minimum capital required by law is €2,500.

Finland

Although not an exact equivalent, the Finnish version of the LLC is the Oy (osakeyhtiö) or in Swedish Ab (aktiebolag). An Oy is taxed as a corporation. The minimum capital required by law is €2,500.

Germany

Because of its hybrid characteristics it is very difficult to determine the German equivalent. On one hand it is possible to consider it as a kind of *Gesellschaft mit beschränkter Haftung* (GmbH) because it has aspects of a corporation; on the other hand it could be considered to be a kind of *Kommanditgesellschaft* (KG), which is the German equivalent of a limited partnership. Based on the literal translation of the word "company", an LLC should be considered to be a kind of KG without any liable partner. The German equivalent that comes closest to LLC, is GmbH & Co KG, a nested Kommanditgesellschaft (KG) where a Gesellschaft mit beschränkter Haftung (GmbH) takes the role of the fully liable partner. For the purpose of taxation, the Bundesfinanzministerium (German Federal Ministry of Finance) gives detailed guidelines of the circumstances under which an LLC is to be considered to be a "corporation" or as a "limited partnership". It is useful to note, however, that the original LLC statutes of Wyoming and other US states were more or less explicitly modeled after the GmbH.

Greece

A limited liability company (LLC) in Greece is synonymous to an EPE (ΕΠΕ).

Hong Kong

In Hong Kong, the Limited Company is the most commonly incorporated type of company and bears the characteristics of a Limited Liability Company. The core characteristics of a Hong Kong Limited Company include: i) it requires a minimum of one shareholder and one director (can be the same person), ii) a Hong Kong company requires a company secretary resident in HK, iii) foreign ownership is allowed, iv) company shareholders have limited liability and v) the company must have registered HK address.

Entrepreneurs who register a company in Hong Kong can choose a Hong Kong offshore company. This company structure is basically a HK Limited Company but all business is conducted outside of Hong Kong. The advantage of this structure is that all business income that is sourced outside of Hong Kong is tax exempt.

Hungary

Hungarian legislation contemplates LLCs as *Korlátolt felelősségű társaság*. Companies working under this structure append the abbreviation *Kft.* to their name. Hungarian LLCs are required to have a 3 million HUF (Hungarian Forint) (approx. 11,000 USD) starting capital. The time of formation by the new electronic formation option has been reduced from 2 weeks to 2 hours, additional cost of formation is around 100,000 HUF (approx. 540 USD). Kft.s can be formed by the cooperation of lawyers.

The Hungarian Kft. is the most common form of doing business in Hungary. As being part of the European Union (EU), Hungarian Kft.s can now obtain an EU VAT registration number for doing business across the EU. The Hungarian EU-VAT reg. number starts with "HU". This way the existence of the subject company, VAT issues and the cross-check is available on the common EU website for companies.

Iceland

According to Icelandic legislation, there are two types of LLC forms, private and public held limited liability forms. Private LLC is abbreviated "Ehf." The minimum capital of 500,000 Icelandic krónas (kr.). Public LLC is abbreviated "Hf." with minimum capital of 4,000,000 kr and goes to LLC.

India

Commonly used business forms in India are:

(a) Public and Private Limited Companies - Incorporated entities with limited liabilities. These are very similar to "Corporations" under U.S law.

(b) Limited Liability Partnerships (LLPs) - Incorporated entities with limited liability. The LLPs are organized as partnerships - they do not have a Board of Directors as such. LLP has lesser compliance requirements compared to Private limited companies. There is no maximum limit for the no. of partners in LLP. In the private limited company shareholders are limited to the extent of 200 shareholders.

The above entities are treated as taxable entities ("persons"), and as such are liable to tax on their incomes. These entities do not offer "pass-through" taxation benefits, unlike LLCs in the USA.

India vide Limited Liability Partnership Act, 2008 introduced concept of LLP and it got implemented in 2009. 2 persons are required to Incorporate LLP in India and they are called designated partners. This form is very organised in India and controlled under Ministry of Corporate Affairs. There is no specific minimum capital requirement. Foreign Direct Investment too allowed in LLP. Essential part is one of the 2 promoters must be Indian Resident.

Iran

As of 2015, there are seven types of companies which can be registered under Iran's company registration law. One of these seven types of companies and partnerships refers to LLPs. Like many other countries, two persons are required to form an LLP in Iran. Each person has his/her own shares and is responsible for business liability equivalent to his/her share percentage. LLPs in Iran are named according to the format illustrated by the following example: "Sherkat Ba Masooliyate Mahdood" translates as "Sherkat Company" + "Mahdood Limited" + "Masooliyat Liability".

Italy

The Italian Civil Code, approved in 1942 and as amended by the Government Act 6/2003 and furthers modifications, mainly provides three forms of limited liability company:

- *Società per azioni* (S.p.A.): the minimum required starting capital for an SpA is €50,000. The capital is divided into shares (azioni) that can be transferred by endorsement or bought and sold on stock exchange. Only SpAs can be quoted in stock exchange market, issue corporate bonds, and other financial instruments. SpA form and a higher capital are required by law to operate in protected businesses (i.e. banks, leasing companies, etc.).
- *Società a responsabilità limitata* (Srl): the minimum required starting capital for an Srl

is €10,000. Its capital is divided into stakes (quote) which can be bought or sold just by notarial act. Srls can issue corporate bonds but are subject to many limitations. Similar to the Srl is the Società Cooperativa a Responsabilità Limitata (Scarl) whose scope is not making profit but give benefits to stakes' holders.

- *Società in accomandita per azioni* (Sapa): the minimum required starting capital for a Sapa is €120,000 divided into shares. Sapas have a mixed liability scheme, where standard shareholders have limited liability while managing shareholders have full liability. Except this, SAPAs are exactly like SPAs even if uncommon.

Companies append the corresponding abbreviation to their company names.

Japan

Japan passed legislation in 1996 creating a new type of business organization, godo kaisha (J-LLC), a close variant of the American LLC. Japanese Tax authority does not consider J-LLC (Godo-Kaisha) a pass-through entity, but as a taxable entity.

Macedonia, Republic of

Macedonian legislation contemplates LLCs as (*Drushtvo so ogranichena odgovornost*). Companies working under this structure append the abbreviation *∂.o.o.* (*d.o.o.*) to their name. The minimum required starting capital for a d.o.o. is €5,000.

Mexico

Mexican legislation contemplates LLCs as *Sociedades de Responsabilidad Limitada*, also known for their abbreviation "S. de R.L.". S. de R.L.'s award limited liability to its members up to their contribution in the company (i.e., contribution of capital) and also act as pass-through or flow-through entities whereby profits are "passed-through" to its members, avoiding double taxation. This type of company is widely used by foreign investors in Mexico because of its "pass-through" modality and its "check the box" capability under the IRC (Internal Revenue Code of the U.S.).

Moldova

Moldovan legislation contemplates LLCs as *Societate cu Răspundere Limitată*, abbreviated "S.R.L.", and are regulated member(s)-founder(s), and other non-founder members, minimum one member-founder and maximum total of 50 members, at least one of them must be the founder of the company, but all of the 50 could be also founders.

Netherlands

The Dutch General Partnership, also known as VOF ("Vennootschap onder Firma"), is formed by at least two members, through a contract registered at the Chamber of Commerce (Trade Register). VOF partners are jointly and severally liable for the obligations of the VOF, meaning that if the assets owned by this partnership are not sufficient, creditors are entitled to claim the personal assets of the partners. Each partner will pay an income tax on their own share of profits, being treated as an independent person. Therefore, partners have their own tax allowances and deductions.

Norway

In Norway, the closest to an LLC is probably the *kommandittselskap* (KS). In a K/S there are two types of participants, one *komplementar* which is fully liable, and one or more *kommandittist*, with limited liability. There are minimum capital requirements. The KS is a tax-transparent company, which means the income "passes through" the company directly to the shareholders.

Pakistan

In Pakistan, LLCs are known as private companies that end (Local Liability Company) with Pvt. Ltd. They should have at least Rs. 100,000 as their minimum paid up capital.

The Securities and Exchange Commission of Pakistan (SECP) has made it mandatory for all listed companies to file their documents, returns, accounts and applications through the commission's eServices online filing facility, earlier, this requirement was only applicable to the companies, which had been incorporated through eServices online filing facility.

Peru

There is no direct equivalent of an LLC in Peru, but some similar corporate forms include:

- *Sociedad anónima cerrada* (SAC), a corporation which must have at least two and not more than twenty shareholders; its shares may not be offered to the public and cannot be traded on the stock exchange.
- *Sociedad comercial de responsabilidad limitada* (SRL), a commercial partnership divided in equal participations which may not be called "shares". It must have at least two and not more than twenty partners.
- *Sociedad civil de responsabilidad limitada* (S civil de RL), a professional partnership of at least two and not more than thirty individuals, with co-owner participation in the form of capital, of professional contribution, or of any combination of both.
- *Empresa individual de responsabilidad limitada* (EIRL), a legal entity with one single owner.

The capital for any of the above entities is freely determined by its statutes. There is no minimum requirement except for entities with certain types of activities, mainly in the financial markets, and then irrespective of their type.

Poland

In Poland, a limited liability company is referred to literally as "company with limited liability" (*spółka z ograniczoną odpowiedzialnością*, legally abbreviated as *sp. z o.o.* (or sometimes *Sp. z o.o.* in particular names). Informally, in the Polish speaking slang, it is abbreviated as *spółka zoo* (pronounced with a long "o", as in "tow."). However, *sp. z o.o.* has a (separate from its owners) legal personality, which gives it the ability to do certain actions under law, and it is considered a "corporation".

The minimum start capital is 5,000 PLN (since 2009; until then, 50,000 PLN).

Portugal

In Portugal, LLCs are called "*Sociedades de Responsabilidade Limitada*", that is, "company of limited responsibility", usually abbreviated *Lda.*. They are tax subject, and company shares cannot be sold in a public market, since 2006 the transference of them is not required to be done in the presence of a civil law notary, except if the company owns buildings, in the same way other major properties have to be sold. Nonetheless, the responsibility of the partners is limited to the capital share they hold, and the minimum capital required by law for a *Lda.* of €5000. (In 2006 the PS Government, led by José Socrates, did reduce the minimum capital to €1, but in 2011 the new PSD Government, led by Pedro Passos Coelho, reinstated the €5000 minimum capital.) The capital is not required to be deposited at the time of the registration of the company, instead the share holders have until 31 December of the year the registry was made.

Romania

Romania recognizes the limited liability company since 1990 under the name of *societate cu răspundere limitată* (S.R.L.), in which the owners are personally liable for the company obligations within the limit of their contribution to social capital. The minimum start capital is 200 RON which currently amounts to less than €50.

Russia

In Russia and certain other former Soviet countries, an entity with a somewhat similar structure is known as Общество с ограниченной ответственностью (Obshchestvo s ogranichennoy otvetstvennostyu) (lit., "company with limited liability"), usually abbreviated OOO, or in some CIS countries as OcOO.

Although a Russian limited liability company shares the same name with an American LLC, it is different in many ways. Most importantly, a Russian LLC is not tax transparent: the company is taxed at the corporate level, and then, upon distribution of dividends, shareholders pay income tax (personal or corporate).

A limited liability company is the most popular form of legal undertaking in Russia for simple shareholding structures.

The minimum capital required is 10,000 Russian rubles.

Serbia

Serbian legislation contemplates LLCs as *društvo sa ograničenom odgovornošću*. Companies working under this structure append the abbreviation *d.o.o.* or *DOO* to their name same as in Croatia. As in the Czech Republic, a *d.o.o.* is not technically comparable to an LLC because the profits are still subject to double taxation.

Slovakia

In Slovakia, the law contemplates *spoločnosť s ručením obmedzeným* (abbreviation *spol. s r. o.* or *s. r. o.*) or as the rough equivalent of a limited liability company. It is very popular form of business organization due to ensurance of limited liability in exchange for a relatively small investment into the registered capital. From one to 50 associates can found it through a founding agreement with minimum registered capital of €5000, minimum €750 per person, in money or other property. (105–153 of Act. No 513/1991 Coll. – Commercial Code as amended.)

Slovenia

Slovenian legislation contemplates LLCs as *družba z omejeno odgovornostjo*. Companies working under this structure append the abbreviation *d. o. o.* to their name. The minimum required starting capital for a *d. o. o.* is €7,500. Due to the high cost and complicated bookkeeping of a real corporation, this is a more widespread form.

Spain

In Spain, LLCs are called *Sociedad de responsabilidad limitada* (SRL), "company of limited responsibility", or *sociedad limitada* (SL), or "limited partnership". They are tax subject, and company shares cannot be sold in a public market, the transference of them having to be done compulsorily in the presence of a civil law notary, in the same way other major properties have to be sold. Nonetheless, the responsibility of the partners is limited to the capital share they hold, and the minimum capital required by law for a *S.L.* is at least €3,000.

Sweden

Sweden has no equivalent of an LLC. The closest company form is the *handelsbolag* (lit.: "trade company"). The Swedish AB (*aktiebolag*; lit.: "share company"), like the *handelsbolag*, is a tax subject and is more similar to a US C Corporation than an LLC. The minimum capital required by law in a private company, *privat aktiebolag*, is SEK 50,000, although this may be in the form of assets as well as capital. It should be noted that the AB structure requires shareholders, a Board of Directors, and regular meetings of both, together with complete accounts once per year. Depending on the size of the AB, the accounts may have to be audited. Creation or purchase "off-the-shelf" of an AB is relatively cheap and tax effective, but liquidation of a created *aktiebolag* can be an expensive and time-consuming operation. Creation of public limited liability companies, or *publikt aktiebolag*, which can raise capital from the public, requires a minimum capitalization of SEK 500,000, however the overall regulation of public companies in Sweden, especially regarding accounting methods and taxes, is thorough and detailed.

Switzerland

The Swiss Code of Obligations provides for different kinds of companies with limited liability, the two most commonly used are:

Swiss Limited Liability Company: The terms for this kind of company used in the three official languages of the Swiss Confederation are as follows: In German *Gesellschaft mit beschränkter Haftung* (abbreviation: *GmbH*), in French *Société à responsabilité limitée* (abbreviation: *S.à r.l.* or *SARL*) and in Italian *Società a Garanzia Limitata* (abbreviation: *SaGL*). A Swiss LLC is similar to an LLC with respect to various matters, including the following: Members may also be natural persons, corporations, partnerships or other LLCs, the liability of a member of a Swiss LLC to pay for the LLC's obligations is limited to its capital contribution, a Swiss LLC may be either member-managed or manager-managed, and, unless otherwise provided for in the operating agreement, the members' right to control or manage a Swiss LLC is proportionate to their individual membership interest. The membership interests in a Swiss LLC have to be registered and, thus, they may only be issued in the name of a member but not to the bearer.

Swiss Corporation (in English common law context usually translated as *company limited by shares*): The terms for this kind of company used in the three official languages of the Swiss Confederation are as follows: In German *Aktiengesellschaft* (abbreviation: *AG*), in French *Société Anonyme* (abbreviation: *SA*) and in Italian *Società Anonima* (abbreviation: *SA*). A Swiss corporation is with respect to various matters different from an LLC (including a Swiss LLC): Most important is that a Swiss corporation may, neither by default nor by exercising any respective option provided by the Swiss law, be member-managed like an LLC, as the respective mandatory provisions of Swiss law provide that the board of directors has certain non-transferable duties. Furthermore, the shares of a Swiss corporation may also be issued to the bearer (bearer shares) and, thus, not only in the name of a holder (registered shares), which, however, applies to the membership interests in a Swiss LLC, which may only be registered.

Tajikistan

In Tajikistan, the same as in Russia, an entity with a somewhat similar structure is known as "Ҷамъияти дорои масъулияти маҳдуд", Chamiyti Doroi Masuliyti Machdud.

Turkey

Minimum capital should be 10,000 TL. That capital could be the minimum total capital of company. Number of founding shareholders (real persons or legal entities) could be minimum 1 and maximum 50. All or some of the shareholders could be foreign nationals. There is no issued stock certificates and all shareholders liability is limited to their registered capital amount. 1/4 of capital should be blocked in a Bank until procedure of registration ends.

Ukraine

This type of entity has existed in Ukraine since the 1990s. In Ukrainian, (abbreviated – ТОВ, ТзОВ), in transliteration "Tovarystvo z Obmezhenoyu Vidpovidalnistyu," that is, "company with limited liability".

United Arab Emirates

A Limited Liability Company (LLC) is the most common type of registration in the UAE and is recommended where the purpose of the entity is to make sales within the region. However, it should be noted that 100% foreign ownership of such an entity is not permitted. Under the UAE Commercial Companies Law (CCL), foreign investors are permitted to hold up to 49 per cent equity ownership in UAE companies and 51 per cent of the equity must be held at all times by one or more UAE nationals. In accordance with Article (218) of the CCL a Limited Liability Company can be formed by a minimum of 2 and a maximum of 50 shareholders whose liability is limited to their shares in the capital of the company. Recent amendments to Article (217) of the CCL that came into force in June 2009 removed the requirement for minimum share capital (previously AED 300,000 in Dubai and AED 150,000 in other Emirates) allowing founders of a limited liability company the freedom to determine the company's share capital which could be less than the earlier prescribed bottom line. Shares of an LLC are not open for subscription by the public. Despite the split in shareholdings, profits may be divided in other ratios agreed upon, taking into consideration efforts of foreign partners in management, provision of technology or expertise. Responsibility for the management of a LLC can be vested in the foreign partner or UAE national partners or a third party. A LLC must appoint a minimum of one manager and up to a maximum of five managers for the business. Managers must be appointed by a Memorandum of Association or by a management contract, for a fixed term or an unlimited term. Unless the Memorandum of Association states otherwise, the manager has full powers of administration and management of the LLC. LLC is not allowed to practice its activities in the UAE without a Trade License and Commercial Registration Certificate.

United Kingdom

The new form of limited liability partnership (LLP), created in 2000, is similar to a US LLC in being tax neutral: member partners are taxed at the partner level, but the LLP itself pays no tax. It is treated as a body corporate for all other purposes including VAT. Otherwise, all companies, including limited companies and US LLCs, are treated as bodies corporate subject to United Kingdom corporation tax if the profits of the entity belong to the entity and not to its members.

United States

A limited liability company (LLC) is a relatively new business structure authorized by state statutes. The LLC is chiefly inspired by the GmbH ("Company with limited liability"), a type of business organization in Germany, and by the *limitada*, a type of business organization available in many Latin American countries.

In the United States, the first limited liability company act appeared in Wyoming in 1977 as special interest legislation for an oil company. In 1980, the Internal Revenue Service issued a private letter ruling to an LLC formed under the Wyoming LLC Act, indicating that the IRS would treat the LLC as a partnership for federal tax purposes. However, later that year, the IRS proposed regulations that would deny partnership classification to any business entity in which no member bore personal responsibility for the entity's liabilities. In 1982, Florida adopted an LLC act modeled on Wyoming's LLC Act. Due to uncertainty over the tax treatment of LLCs, no other states introduced LLC legislation until after 1988. In 1988, the IRS issued a revenue ruling stating that it would treat a Wyoming-style LLC as a partnership for tax purposes. By 1996, nearly every state had enacted an LLC statute. The National Conference of Commissioners on Uniform State Laws adopted the Uniform Limited Liability Company Act in 1996 and revised it in 2006.

A potential disadvantage specific to the United States is that LLCs are not considered to be corporations for the purposes of federal civil procedure; they are instead treated as partnerships. This affects the applicability of diversity jurisdiction in cases involving LLCs, barring application of diversity jurisdiction when even one member of the LLC is a citizen of the same state as one of the opposing parties. Should one member of an LLC be a citizen of a state of which one of the opposing parties is a citizen, any case between the LLC and those parties must be heard in that state's courts; corporations enjoy a more complete legal personhood that only denies diversity jurisdiction when the opposing party is a citizen of the state in which the corporation is incorporated (most commonly Delaware for large corporations, which has a small population) or has its principal place of business.

AOL was set up as an LLC during its ownership by Time Warner from 2001 to 2008. There is a similar setup for BMW's American subsidiary, BMW of North America, LLC. Chrysler has been an LLC since restructuring during the auto industry bailout of 2009, owned by Fiat Chrysler Automobiles N.V..

Unlimited Company

An unlimited company or private unlimited company is a hybrid company (corporation) incorporated with or without a share capital (and similar to its limited company counterpart) but where the legal liability of the members or shareholders is not limited: that is, its members or shareholders have a joint, several and non-limited obligation to meet any insufficiency in the assets of the company to enable settlement of any outstanding financial liability in the event of the company's formal liquidation. The joint, several and non-limited liability of the members or shareholders of the company to meet any insufficiency in the assets of the company (to settle its outstanding liabilities if any exist) applies only upon the formal liquidation of the company. Therefore, prior to any such formal liquidation of the company, any creditors or security holders of the company may have recourse only to the assets of the company, not those of its members or shareholders.

Until such an event occurs (formal liquidation), an unlimited company is similar with its counterpart, the limited company, in which its members or shareholders have no direct liability to the creditors or security holders of the company during its normal course of business or existence.

Unlimited companies are found in the United Kingdom, Ireland, Hong Kong, Pakistan, Nigeria, India, Australia, New Zealand and other jurisdictions where the company law is derived from English law. They can also be found in Germany, France, Macao, Czech Republic and in two jurisdictions in Canada (Alberta and Nova Scotia), where they are called unlimited liability corporations. In the United Kingdom, they are formed or incorporated by registration under the Companies Act 2006.

An unlimited company has the benefit and status of incorporation same as its limited company counterpart. Situations for which an unlimited company will be preferred to an alternative business model or its limited company counterpart include these:

- secrecy concerning financial affairs is desired, effectively shielding and protecting its financial affairs from its competitors and making them non-public information including shareholder dividend payments: a United Kingdom unlimited company, unlike its limited company counterpart, is generally not required to publish or make public its company financial statements (file its annual financial accounts at Companies House).
- the company is trading in an area where limited liability is not acceptable, vital or practical.
- extending, in general, a greater assurance and confidence to creditors and trade financial transactions, in contrast to its *limited company* counterpart.
- there is a low risk of insolvency.

- the company or its trading activities has or generates sufficient capital, funds or financing without need to approach general lenders such as high-street retail banks.
- developing more advantageous company and business capital strategies in an ever increasing irreversible trend of bank disintermediation by companies and their management.
- a focused higher standard of board of directors and executive management behaviour (or probity) and business model for risk management.
- a flow-through entity is required for United States federal tax purposes, under the entity classification rules.

Once formed or incorporated, an unlimited company can, in some jurisdictions, also re-register and designate itself to limited company status at any time with few formalities, the same also extending to a limited company, which may at any time re-register and designate itself to an unlimited company status.

Notable Unlimited Companies

The unlimited company is not very common or well known or promoted form of company incorporation (due to the narrow focus of generic company formation registration agents) and is not always required under company law to add or state the word Unlimited or its abbreviations (Unltd., or Ultd.) at the ending of its legal company name, making it not easily recognisable without first reviewing its *certificate of incorporation* or government registry status. Notable examples in the United Kingdom include these:

- the UK subsidiary of the international retail clothing group C&A (UK company number 00524665),
- Land Rover (UK company number 04019301), formerly Unlimited until 4 October 2013,
- GlaxoSmithKline Services Unlimited (UK company number 01047315) part of GlaxoSmithKline plc,
- The Equitable Life Assurance Society (UK company number 00037038),
- Credit Suisse International (UK company number 02500199), the United Kingdom investment banking arm of Credit Suisse,
- publishing company of acclaimed British author Ian McEwan (UK company number 07473219), and
- C. Hoare & Co (UK company number 00240822), England's oldest privately owned bank.

Other notable global trading companies such as Mobil Producing Nigeria Unlimited (a subsidiary of Exxon Mobil) and Texaco Overseas (Nigeria) Petroleum Company Unlimited (part of the merged Chevron and Texaco petroleum conglomerates) exist in Nigeria, amongst others. In the USA, another notable example is the American Express Company, which once was a publicly traded unlimited liability company, re-incorporating itself to a limited liability company status only in 1965.

In Ireland, local subsidiaries of a number of American companies have registered as unlimited companies to shield their finances from public view. Janssen Pharmaceutical, a subsidiary of its

US parent company Johnson & Johnson re-registered as an unlimited company to avoid the requirement to file annual financial accounts at the Companies Registration Office (CRO) Ireland, thereby effectively also protecting a portion of Johnson & Johnson's financial information. Apple Computer's Irish division did the same.

Specific Countries

United States

In the United States, a similar *unlimited* entity exists in the form of a joint-stock company (JSC). This type of joint stock association exists in New York and Texas, among other states. The JSC exists in Texas under the Texas Joint-Stock Company / Revocable Living Trust model, which would present the following differences from a general partnership:

1. Has all the corporate characteristics, except limited liability of shareholders.
2. Formed by private contract creating a separate entity.
3. Recognized by a specific Texas State Statute, but not regulated by the Uniform Partnership Act.
4. A shareholder cannot bind other shareholder concerning liability, etc.

Despite the fact that shareholders are severably liable for the company's liabilities (as with general partnerships), Texas Joint-Stock Companies have frequently been inappropriately promoted in asset protection schemes as "alternatives" to limited partnerships and LLCs.

Co-operative Society

Any ten persons can form a co-operative society. It functions under the Co-operative Societies Act, 1912 and other State Co-operative Societies Acts. A co-operative society is entirely different from all other forms of organisation discussed above in terms of its objective. The co-operatives are formed primarily to render services to its members.

Every member has a right to take part in the management of the society. Each member has one vote. Generally the members elect a committee known as the Executive Committee to look after the day to day administration and the said committee is responsible to the general body of members.

- The liability of the members is limited to the extent of capital contributed by them.
- Registration of a society under the Co-operative Societies Act is a must. Once it is registered, it becomes a body corporate and enjoys certain privileges just like a joint stock company.

Some of the privileges are:

- The society enjoys perpetual succession.
- It has its own common seal.
- It can own property in its name.

- It can enter into contract with others.
- It can sue others in court of law.

Generally it also provides some service to the society. The main objectives of co-operative society are:

a) rendering service rather than earning profit,

b) mutual help instead of competition, and

c) self help in place of dependence.

On the basis of objectives, various types of co-operatives are formed :

- Consumer co-operatives.
- Producers co-operatives.
- Marketing co-operatives.
- Housing Co-operatives.
- Credit Co-operatives.
- Forming Co-operatives.

Advantages:

- Democratic management.
- Assistance from the government.
- Elimination of middlemen's profit.
- Fairly stable life.

Disadvantages:

- Limited capital.
- Lack of managerial talent.
- Lack of motivation.
- Lack of secrecy.
- Dependence on the government.

Stakeholder

Stakeholder is a person who has a legitimate interest in an entity.

- Investors.
- Management of enterprise.

- Creditors / Lenders.
- Government.
- Employees.

Consumers Local Community

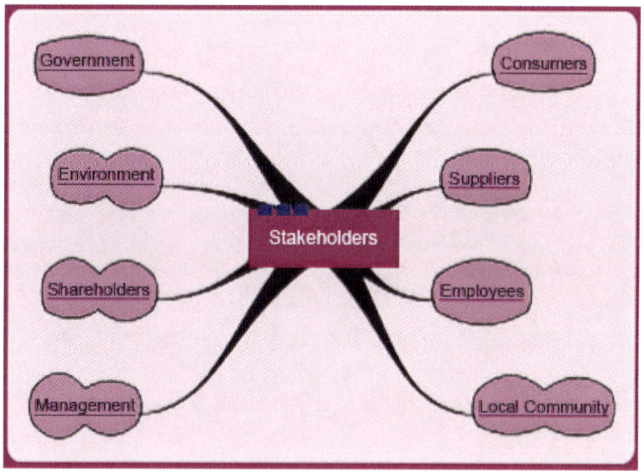

Investor

Investor study the Financial Statement of the company before deciding upon whether to buy or not a business or shares.

If they intend to buy, then the fair value of business or shares is also determined on the basis of the detailed analysis of the Financial Statement.

Prospective investors make use of financial statements to assess the viability of investing in a business.

Management

Managers are the main users of the Financial Statement. They use the financial statement

- To make the inter firm and inter period comparison.
- To study trends in sales, expenses etc.
- To understand the relationship among various items of financial statement.
- To know movement of funds through Fund Flow Analysis.

Creditors/ Lenders

Creditor or Lender study the Financial statement of the borrower before advancing credit or loan. Thereafter also the creditors and lenders analysis the Financial statement to find out whether the business is solvent (in position to repay the loan).

Government

The amounts payable by concern by way of taxes levied by Government such as Income Tax, Sales Tax, Excise etc. are examined on the basis of the data in Financial Statement.

Employees

Employees also use Financial Statements in making collective bargaining agreements with the management, in the case of labour union or for individuals in discussing their compensation, promotion and rankings.

References

- Al-Debei, M. M., & Avison, D. (2010). Developing a unified framework of the business model concept. European Journal of Information Systems, 19(3), 359-376
- George,G and Bock AJ. 2012. Models of opportunity: How entrepreneurs design firms to achieve the unexpected. Cambridge University Press, ISBN 978-0-521-17084-0
- "The beginning of the end for IAS 39 - Issue of IFRS 9 regarding Classification and Measurement of Financial Assets". Deloitte & Touche. November 2009. Retrieved 2011-06-03
- Mackrael, Kim (8 July 2015). "Gowlings Law Firm to Combine With U.K.'s Wragge Lawrence Graham". The Wall Street Journal. Retrieved 24 February 2016
- Karl M. Popp & Ralf Meyer (2010). Profit from Software Ecosystems: Business Models, Ecosystems and Partnerships in the Software Industry. Norderstedt, Germany: BOD. ISBN 3-8391-6983-6
- "An optimist sees the opportunity in every difficulty: is IFRS 9 an opportunity or a difficulty?". Ernst & Young. December 2010. Retrieved 2011-06-03
- Lee, G. K. and R. E. Cole. 2003. Internet Marketing, Business Models and Public Policy. Journal of Public Policy and Marketing 19 (Fall) 287-296
- Vitasek, Kate. Vested Outsourcing: Five Rules that will Transform Outsourcing" (New York: Palgrave Macmillan, 2012) ISBN 978-1-137-29719-8
- "FASB Exposure Draft: Recognition and Measurement of Financial Assets and Financial Liabilities". Financial Accounting Standards Board. April 12, 2013. p. 174. Retrieved 2013-06-11
- Mishkin, Frederic S. (2007). The Economics of Money, Banking, and Financial Markets (Alternate Edition). Boston: Addison Wesley. p. 8. ISBN 0-321-42177-9

- "Exposure Draft: Leases". Financial Accounting Standards Board. August 17, 2010. p. 29. Archived from the original on 2011-04-08. Retrieved 2011-06-03
- Ferri Fernando, D'Andrea Alessia, Grifoni Patrizia (2012). IBF: An Integrated Business Framework for Virtual Communities in Journal of electronic commerce in organizations; IGI Global, Hershey (Stati Uniti d'America)
- T.H. Greco. Money: Understanding and Creating Alternatives to Legal Tender, White River Junction, Vt: Chelsea Green Publishing (2001). ISBN 1-890132-37-3
- "Project Update: Leases—Joint Project of the FASB and the IASB". Financial Accounting Standards Board. August 1, 2012. Retrieved 2012-08-02
- D'Eprio, Peter & Pinkowish, Mary Desmond (1998). What Are the Seven Wonders of the World? First Anchor Books, p.192
- Wray, L. Randall (2012). Modern money theory: a primer on macroeconomics for sovereign monetary systems. Houndmills, Basingstoke, Hampshire: Palgrave Macmillan. pp. 45–50. ISBN 978-0230368897
- Gergen, Chris; Gregg Vanourek (December 3, 2008). "The 'pay as you can' cafe". The Washington Times. Retrieved 2009-03-10
- Daas, D., Hurkmans, T., Overbeek, S. and Bouwman, H. 2012. Developing a decision support system for business model design. Electronic Markets - The International Journal on Networked Business, published Online 29. Dec. 2012
- O'Sullivan, Arthur; Sheffrin, Steven M. (2003). Economics: Principles in Action. Upper Saddle River, New Jersey: Pearson Prentice Hall. p. 258. ISBN 0-13-063085-3
- Milton Friedman; Anna Jacobson Schwartz (1971). Monetary History of the United States, 1867–1960. Princeton, N.J: Princeton University Press. ISBN 0-691-00354-8
- The Federal Reserve. 'Monetary Policy and the Economy". (PDF) Board of Governors of the Federal Reserve System, (2005-07-05). Retrieved 2007-05-15

2

Accounting: Recording Financial Transactions and Standards

All transactions are recorded in a journal to find the accounts which have been affected. A journal forms the basis of recording financial transactions. A few distinct forms of journals are special journal and sales journal. After the transactions are recorded, they are sorted through preparation of accounts called a ledger. In order to completely understand financial transactions and accounting standards, it is necessary to understand the processes related to it. The following section elucidates the varied processes and mechanisms associated with this area of study.

General Journal

The journal is where double entry bookkeeping entries are recorded by debiting one or more accounts and crediting another one or more accounts with the same total amount. The total amount debited and the total amount credited should always be equal, thereby ensuring the accounting equation is maintained. In accounting and bookkeeping, a journal is a record of financial transactions in order by date.

A journal is also named the *book of original entry*, from when transactions were written in a journal prior to manually posting them to the accounts in the general ledger or subsidiary ledger. Manual systems usually had a variety of journals such as a sales journal, purchases journal, cash receipts journal, cash disbursements journal, and a general journal. Depending on the business's accounting information system, specialized journals may be used in conjunction with the general journal for record-keeping. In such case, use of the general journal may be limited to non-routine and adjusting entries.

A general journal entry includes the date of the transaction, the titles of the accounts debited and credited, the amount of each debit and credit, and an explanation of the transaction also known as a Narration.

Journal

The transactions are first recorded in the book to show which accounts are effected. This book is called as "Journal".

Recording of transaction in journal is termed as journalizing the entries.

- Entries are recorded chronologically to maintain the records in an orderly manner.
- Journal entries are very important and form basis for all further records.

Specimen of Journal

Date	Particulars	L.F.	Debit (Amt)	Credit (Amt)

An entry in journal may appear as follows for the following transaction

1.11.2010 Goods sold for cash of **₹ 5,000**

5.11.2010 Cash deposited in Bank **₹ 3,000**

Journal Entries

Date	Particulars	L.F.	Debit (Amt)	Credit (Amt)
1.11. 2010	Cash A/c....Dr.		5,000	
	To Sales A/c (Being Goods sold on cash)			5,000
5.11.2010	Bank A/c...Dr.		3,000	
	To Cash A/c (Being cash deposited in bank)			3,000

Sales Journal

A sales journal is a specialized accounting journal used in an accounting system to keep track of the sales of items that customers have purchased on account by charging a receivable on the debit side of an accounts receivable account and crediting revenue on the credit side. It differs from the cash receipts journal in that the latter will serve to book sales when cash is received. The sales journal is used to record all of the company sales on credit. Most often these sales are made up of inventory sales or other merchandise sales. Notice that only credit sales of inventory and merchandise items are recorded in the sales journal. Cash sales of inventory are recorded in the cash receipts journal. Both cash and credit sales of non-inventory or merchandise are recorded in the general journal.

Special Journals

Special Journals are designed to facilitate the process of journalizing and posting transactions. They are used for the most frequent transactions in a business. For example, in merchandising businesses, companies acquire merchandise from vendors, and then in turn sell the merchandise to individuals or other businesses. Sales and purchases are the most common transactions for the merchandising businesses. A business such as a retail store will record the following transactions many times a day for sales on account and cash sales.

Description	Debit	Credit
Accounts Receivable	XXX	
Sales		XXX
Sales Tax Payable		XXX

Description	Debit	Credit
Cash	XXX	
Sales		XXX
Sales Tax Payable		XXX

In order to save time for journalizing the entries, and posting the entries to the general ledgers and subledgers, Special Journals are used instead. An accountant can be specialized in a type of journal entry and several accountants can work each on 1 or more different types of journal entries only thereby using a better division of labour.

Types of Special Journals

The types of Special Journals that a business uses are determined by the nature of the business. Special journals are designed as a simple way to record the most frequently occurring transactions. There are four types of Special Journals that are frequently used by merchandising businesses: Sales journals, Cash receipts journals, Purchases journals, and Cash payments journals.

Sales Journal

Sales journals record transactions that involve sales purely on credit. Source documents here would probably be invoices. Provides a chronological record of all credit sales made in the life of a business. Credit sales are transactions where the goods are sold and payment is received at a later date. The source documents for the Sales journal are copies of all invoices given to the debtors.

Double entry Accounting is achieved by:

- Debit – debtors account with value of sales (increasing a current asset)
- Credit – sales account with total amount (increasing income)

Choose credit sales journal if this stock is then on-sold to customers who will pay later. The people/organizations here are known as debtors. Collectively, all these accounts that are to be paid to us by our customers are known as assets.

date	details	folio #	invoice #	amount
date sale was made	who did you sell it to		sequential - #order	

Cash Receipts Journal

A cash receipts journal (CRJ) records transactions that involve payments received with cash. Source documents would probably be receipts and cheque butts. The CRJ records the cash inflow of a business. Discount allowed is an expense as the discount allowed is the cost to the seller of obtaining an inflow of cash from a debtor weeks earlier than would be the case.

date	details	receipt #	discount allowed	sales	debtors	Other	BANK
date sale was made	who you received payment from				people who are also in sales journal	other types of income description	amount into bank

Expense Journals

Purchases Journal

Purchases Journals record transactions that involve purchases purely on credit. Source documents are invoices. For instance, the purchase of inventory on credit is recorded in the purchases journal.

date	details	folio #33	invoice #	amount
date sale was made	name of supplier		not sequential	

Cash Payments Journal

Cash Payments Journals record transactions that involve expenditures paid with cash. Source documents are likely receipts and cheque butts. The CPJ records the cash outflow of a business. If the owner of a business withdraws cash from the business an entry is made in the CPJ. Discount received is the cash discount received by a purchaser, it is an income item for the purchaser.

date	details	cheque #	discount received	purchases	creditors	Other	BANK
date payment was made	who you paid				people who are also in purchases journal	other types of expenses description	amount out of bank

Source Documents

When a transaction occur between a business and an external party, a source document will usually be created. Source documents are business forms that provide evidence of each transaction and give the details that are entered later into one of the journals in a computer accounting system. Some computer systems, such as payroll systems, also generate transactions that are recorded in one or more journals, but without paper source documents.

- *Receipt* when a business receives money or cheques over the shop counter it will usually issue a receipt. A receipt is a document that acknowledges that money or cheques have been received.
- *Check book stub*
- *Invoice* includes business name (sellers) and address, invoice number, ABN, buyer details, date, description of goods purchased, quantity, unit price, amount (per item x quantity), total price and GST. An invoice is a document that records the details of a credit sale of inventory. The origin of the invoice is either delivered with the goods or sent separately to the customer. A number of copies are kept by the seller.
- *Delivery note* is a document that sets out the type and quantity of the inventory delivered to the purchaser. When the inventory arrives at the premises of the purchaser, the delivery note is signed by the purchaser and is evidence that the goods ordered have been delivered. A copy is kept by the seller.
- *Purchase order*
- *Purchase requisition*

- *Credit note* is a document issued by a seller that acknowledges that a customer is entitled to receive a reduction in the amount owing on goods purchased on credit.

Folio Number: Every page of a journal is numbered. This number is known as a folio number. The folio number is used as a cross reference between the journal and the ledger accounts. The use of folio numbers makes it easy to refer back from the ledger account to the journal entry or forward from the journal entry to the ledger account. In addition, folio numbers are a check that all journal entries have been recorded in the ledger system.

Each ledger account has a folio number column. The name and page of the journal from which the ledger entry came is recorded in the folio number column.

Each journal has a folio number column. The number of the ledger account to which the journal entry was posted is recorded in the folio number column of the journal.

Cash money, eftpos, cheques, credit cards. Receipts and payments.

Credit sale of inventory on credit Purchases.

Cash Journals record items sold or purchased with cash and they also record income received (debtor payment, interest) and daily expenses. If the transaction is of a cash nature, you must be convinced that money/cheque/credit card was also exchanged at the time that the good or service was exchanged.

Credit Journals record purchases or sales on credit. If the transaction is of a credit nature, you will assume that the cash will be exchanged after the exchange of the good or service. At this stage, these will only be concerned with your firm acquiring stock and the selling of that stock to customers who will pay later.

Format of Special Journals

In the General Journal, transactions are recorded in several lines, and each transaction is posted to the general ledger separately. For example, if fifty sales on account were made during one day, fifty ledger postings would have to be made to three general ledger accounts: Accounts Receivable, Sales, and Sale Tax Payable. In special journal, transactions are recorded in a single line, and the format of the journal made it possible to post only the total amount for each account to the general ledger. For example, if fifty sales on account were made during one day, only the total amount for Accounts Receivable, Sales, and Sales Tax Payable were posted to the general ledger. Thus the posting process is more efficient. Figure shows the example formats of the Special Journals.

Sales Journal

Date	Sale No.	To Whom Sold	Post. Ref.	Accounts Receivable Debit	Sales Credit	Sales Tax Payable Credit
April 1	900	A. Smith		$1,000.00	$940.00	$60.00
April 1	901	B. Johnson		$2,000.00	$1,880.00	$120.00
April 1	902	C. Chang		$1,000.00	$940.00	$60.00
April 4	904	D. Garcia		$1,000.00	$940.00	$60.00

Cash Receipt Journal

Date	Account Credited	Post Ref.	General Credit	Accounts Receivable Credit	Sales Credit	Sales Tax Payable Credit	Cash Debit
May 1	B. Johnson			$1,000			$1,000
May 3	C. Chang			$1,000			$1,000
May 5	A. Smith			$1,000			$1,000
May 8	Interest Receivable			$400			$400

Purchases Journal

Date	Invoice No.	From Whom Purchased	Post Ref.	Purchased Debit / Accounts Payable Credit
June 2	6321	BCD Corp.		$12,000
June 5	12D	Telecom8 Inc		$800
June 21	412	Furniture-X		$2,000

Cash Payments Journal

Date	Check No.	Account Debited	Post Ref.	General Debit	Accounts Payable Debit	Purchases Credit	Cash Credit
July 1	1254	Rent Expense		$1,200			$1,200
July 2	1255	BCD Corp.			$1,200		$1,200
July 2	1256	Furniture-X			$1,200		$1,200

Ledger

A ledger is the principal book or computer file for recording and totaling economic transactions measured in terms of a monetary unit of account by account type, with debits and credits in separate columns and a beginning monetary balance and ending monetary balance for each account.

Overview

The ledger is a permanent summary of all amounts entered in supporting journals which list individual transactions by date. Every transaction flows from a journal to one or more ledgers. A company's financial statements are generated from summary totals in the ledgers.

Ledgers include:

- Sales ledger, records accounts receivable. This ledger consists of the financial transactions made by customers to the company.
- Purchase ledger records money spent for purchasing by the company.
- General ledger representing the five main account types: assets, liabilities, income, expenses, and Capital.

- Distributed ledger, sometimes called a shared ledger, is a consensus of replicated, shared, and synchronized digital data geographically spread across multiple sites, countries, and/ or institutions.

For every debit recorded in a ledger, there must be a corresponding credit so that the debits equal the credits in the grand totals.

Etymology

Ledger from 1828

The term *ledger* stems from the English dialect forms *liggen* or *leggen*, meaning "to lie or lay" (Dutch: *liggen* or *leggen*, German: *liegen* or *legen*); in sense it is adapted from the Dutch substantive *legger*, properly "a book laying or remaining regularly in one place". Originally, a ledger was a large volume of scripture or service book kept in one place in church and openly accessible. According to Charles Wriothesley's *Chronicle* (1538), "The curates should provide a booke of the bible in Englishe, of the largest volume, to be a ledger in the same church for the parishioners to read on."

In application of this original meaning the commercial usage of the term is for the "principal book of account" in a business house.

After recording transaction in journal, recorded entries are classified and grouped by preparation of accounts, is known as "ledger". It is also known as principal books of accounts.

Specimen of Ledger

Dr. ABC Account Cr.

Date	Particulars	J.F.	Amt	Date	Particulars	J.F.	Amt

- A ledger account has two sides debit and credit.
- Separate account is opened in ledger book for different set of transaction.
- It is practice to use word 'To' and 'By' while posting transaction on debit and credit side of account.
- To ascertain the balance in any account, what is done is to total the sides and ascertain the difference; the difference is balance.

Case 1: Ram & Co.

Prepare ledger accounts for Ram & Co from the following details:

Opening balances:

Cash A/c	Rs. 1,500
Creditors A/c	Rs. 800
Debtors A/c	Rs. 1,200
Capital A/c	Rs. 1,900

Transactions:

- 2 Apr. Purchased goods of Rs. 3,000 on credit.
- 4 Apr. Cash sales of Rs. 2,400.
- 7 Apr. Goods sold on credit Rs. 1,250.
- 15 Apr. Paid cash of Rs. 250 for expenses.
- 18 Apr. cash received from debtors Rs. 1,200.
- 22 Apr. paid cash to creditors Rs. 800.

In the books of Ram & Company

Dr. Cash A/c Cr.

Date	Particulars	J.F.	Amt	Date	Particulars	J.F.	Amt
01-Apr	To balance b/d		1,500	15-Apr	By Expenses A/c		250
04-Apr	To Sales A/c		2,400	22-Apr	By Creditors A/c		800
18-Apr	To Debtors A/c		1,200	30-Apr	By Balance C/d		4,050
	Total		**5,100**		**Total**		**5,100**
01-May	To balance b/d		4,050				

Dr. Purchase A/c Cr.

Date	Particulars	J.F.	Amt	Date	Particulars	J.F.	Amt
02-Apr	To Creditors A/c		3,000	30-Apr	By Balance C/d		3,000
	Total		**3,000**		**Total**		**3,000**
01-May	To balance b/d		3,000				

Dr. Sales A/c Cr.

Date	Particulars	J.F.	Amt	Date	Particulars	J.F.	Amt
30-Apr	To Balance C/d		3,650	04-Apr	By Cash A/c		2,400
				07-Apr	By Debtors A/c		1,250
	Total		**3,650**		**Total**		**3,650**
				01-May	By Balance b/d		3,650

Dr.			Debtors A/c				Cr.
Date	Particulars	J.F.	Amt	Date	Particulars	J.F.	Amt
01-Apr	To Balance b/d		1,200	18-Apr	By Cash A/c		1,200
07-Apr	To Sales A/c		1,250	30-Apr	By Balance c/d		1,250
	Total		**2,450**		**Total**		**2,450**
01-May	To Balance b/d		1,250				

Dr.			Creditors A/c				Cr.
Date	Particulars	J.F.	Amt	Date	Particulars	J.F.	Amt
22-Apr	To Cash A/c		800	01-Apr	By Balance b/d		800
30-Apr	To Balance c/d		3,000	02-Apr	By Purchase A/c		3,000
	Total		**3,800**		**Total**		**3,800**
				01-May	By Balance b/d		3,000

Dr.			Expenses A/c				Cr.
Date	Particulars	J.F.	Amt	Date	Particulars	J.F.	Amt
15-Apr	To Cash A/c		250	30-Apr	By Balance C/d		250
	Total		**250**		**Total**		**250**
01-May	To Balance b/d		250				

Dr.			Capital A/c				Cr.
Date	Particulars	J.F.	Amt	Date	Particulars	J.F.	Amt
30-Apr	To Balance c/d		1,900	01-Apr	By Balance b/d		1,900
	Total		**1,900**		**Total**		**1,900**
				01-May	To Balance b/d		1,900

Subsidiary Books

- In case of large business organisation numerous transactions takes place with respect to purchase, sales, cash etc. Journalization of each of these transactions separately is laborious and time-consuming.

To solve this problem subsidiary books are prepared.

- Subsidiary book is a book of original entry generally maintained by large organisation wherein cash and cash transactions are directly recorded avoiding cumbersome process of Journalization without sacrificing the fundamental principle of double entry book keeping system.

Normally, the following subsidiary books are used in business :-

- Cash book: To record cash, bank and discount transactions.
- Purchase book: To record transaction relating to credit purchases of goods in trade.

- Sales book: To record transaction relating to credit sales.
- Purchase return book: To record transaction relating to purchase return.
- Sales return book: To record transaction relating to sales return.
- Bills receivable book: To record the receipts of the promissory notes or hundies.
- Bills payable book: To record the issue of the promissory notes or hundies.
- Journal proper: To record other transactions for which no specific book is maintained, and for recording entries to rectify mistakes in books of accounts.

Mercantilism

An imaginary seaport painted by Claude Lorrain around 1639, at the height of mercantilism

Mercantilism was an economic theory and practice that was dominant in Western Europe during the 15th to the mid-18th centuries. Mercantilism is a form of economic nationalism. Its goal is to enrich and empower the nation and state to the maximum degree, by acquiring and retaining as much economic activity as possible within the nation's borders. Manufacturing and industry, particularly of goods with military applications, was prioritized. Mercantilism sought to ensure the nation produced as much volume and variety of output as possible, so as to limit its dependence upon foreign suppliers. Economic autarky was a critical element of mercantilism. These aims were primarily accomplished by:

1. Imposing high tariffs on the importation of finished goods; and imposing low, or no, taxes on the importation of raw materials or exotic products.
2. Imposing low, or no taxes on the export of finished goods; and imposing high taxes on the exportation of raw materials.
3. Seeking new markets for domestic manufactured products, so as to artificially increase the demand for domestic production.

These policies generally resulted in a positive balance of trade, which led to the accumulation of precious metals, which is how accounts used to be balanced.

Historically, such policies sometimes led to war and may have motivated colonial expansion. Indeed, with the establishment of overseas colonies by northern Europe powers early in the 17th century, mercantile theory gained a new and wider significance, in which its aim and ideal became both national and imperialistic. While it has been noted that both the United States under the American System, and Imperial China under the Canton System, pursued de facto mercantile policies, they did not engage in significant colonial activities. High tariffs, especially on manufactured goods, are an almost universal feature of mercantilist policy. Other policies have included:

- forbidding colonies to trade with other nations
- monopolizing markets with staple ports
- banning the export of gold and silver, even for payments
- forbidding trade to be carried in foreign ships, for example, the Navigation Acts.
- subsidies on exports
- promoting manufacturing and industry through research or direct subsidies
- maximizing the use of domestic resources
- restricting domestic consumption through non-tariff barriers to trade.

Mercantilism has been linked to bullionism ever since Adam Smith made the accusation. However, due to the fact that no author self-consciously used the label to refer to their own thoughts mercantilist authors can only be identified retrospectively. There are exceptions, for example, Antoine de Montchrestien, the "godfather" of French mercantilism, wrote:

it is not the abundance of gold and silver, the quantity of pearls and diamonds, which makes states opulent... it is the supply of things necessary for life and suitable for clothing.

John Maynard Keynes observed that the accumulation of gold may have served an important purpose in states before the advent of fiat money, since it increased liquidity in currency-starved early modern markets. The core of mercantile policy was a coherent national industrial policy, which was aimed at generating as much material wealth within the nation as possible. Doing so, it was thought, was the best way to increase the state's military and political power.

The term "mercantile system" was used by its foremost critic, Adam Smith, but "mercantilism" had been used earlier by Mirabeau.

Many nations applied the theory, one prime example being France which was the most important state economically in Europe at the time. King Louis XIV followed the guidance of Jean Baptiste Colbert, his controller general of finances (1665–83). It was determined that the state should rule in the economic realm as it did in the diplomatic, and that the interests of the state as identified by the king were superior to those of merchants and everyone else. The goal of mercantilist economic policies was to build up the state, especially in an age of incessant warfare, and the state should look for ways to strengthen the economy and weaken foreign adversaries.

Influence

Mercantilism was the dominant school of economic thought in Europe throughout the late Renaissance and early modern period (from the 15th to the 18th century). Mercantilism encouraged the many intra-European wars of the period and arguably fueled European expansion and imperialism—both in Europe and throughout the rest of the world—until the 19th century or early 20th century.

Evidence of mercantilistic practices appeared in early modern Venice, Genoa, and Pisa regarding control of the Mediterranean trade of bullion. However, as a codified school of economic theories, mercantilism's real birth was marked by the empiricism of the Renaissance, which first began to quantify large-scale trade accurately.

England began the first large-scale and integrative approach to mercantilism during the Elizabethan Era (1558–1603). An early statement on national balance of trade appeared in *Discourse of the Common Weal of this Realm of England*, 1549: "We must always take heed that we buy no more from strangers than we sell them, for so should we impoverish ourselves and enrich them." The period featured various but often disjointed efforts by the court of Queen Elizabeth to develop a naval and merchant fleet capable of challenging the Spanish stranglehold on trade and of expanding the growth of bullion at home. Queen Elizabeth promoted the Trade and Navigation Acts in Parliament and issued orders to her navy for the protection and promotion of English shipping. A systematic and coherent explanation of balance of trade was made public through Thomas Mun's argument *England's Treasure by Forraign Trade, or the Balance of our Forraign Trade is The Rule of Our Treasure*. It was written in the 1620s and published in 1664.

These efforts organized national resources sufficiently in the defense of England against the far larger and more powerful Spanish Empire, and in turn paved the foundation for establishing a global empire in the 19th century. The authors noted most for establishing the English mercantilist system include Gerard de Malynes and Thomas Mun, who first articulated the Elizabethan system, which in turn was then developed further by Josiah Child. Numerous French authors helped cement French policy around mercantilism in the 17th century. This French mercantilism was best articulated by Jean-Baptiste Colbert (in office, 1665–1683), though policy liberalised greatly under Napoleon.

In Europe, academic belief in mercantilism began to fade in the late 18th century, especially in Britain, in light of the arguments of Adam Smith and the classical economists. The repeal of the Corn Laws by Robert Peel symbolised the emergence of free trade as an alternative system.

Neomercantilism is a 20th-century economic policy that uses the ideas and methods of neoclassical economics. The new mercantilism has different goals and focuses on more rapid economic growth based on advanced technology. It promotes such policies as substitution state taxation, subsidies, expenditures, and general regulatory powers for tariffs and quotas, and protection through the formation of supranational trading blocs.

Theory

Most of the European economists who wrote between 1500 and 1750 are today generally considered mercantilists; this term was initially used solely by critics, such as Mirabeau and Smith, but was quickly adopted by historians. Originally the standard English term was "mercantile system". The word "mercantilism" was introduced into English from German in the early 19th century.

The bulk of what is commonly called "mercantilist literature" appeared in the 1620s in Great Britain. Smith saw the English merchant Thomas Mun (1571–1641) as a major creator of the mercantile system, especially in his posthumously published *Treasure by Foreign Trade* (1664), which Smith considered the archetype or manifesto of the movement. Perhaps the last major mercantilist work was James Steuart's *Principles of Political Economy*, published in 1767.

Mercantilist literature also extended beyond England. Italy and France produced noted writers of mercantilist themes, including Italy's Giovanni Botero (1544–1617) and Antonio Scrra (1580–?) and, in France, Jean Bodin, Colbert. Themes also existed in writers from the German historical school from List, as well as followers of the American system and British free-trade imperialism, thus stretching the system into the 19th century. However, many British writers, including Mun and Misselden, were merchants, while many of the writers from other countries were public officials. Beyond mercantilism as a way of understanding the wealth and power of nations, Mun and Misselden are noted for their viewpoints on a wide range of economic matters.

Merchants in Venice

The Austrian lawyer and scholar Philipp Wilhelm von Hornick, one of the pioneers of Cameralism, detailed a nine-point program of what he deemed effective national economy in his *Austria Over All, If She Only Will* of 1684, which comprehensively sums up the tenets of mercantilism:

- That every little bit of a country's soil be utilized for agriculture, mining or manufacturing.
- That all raw materials found in a country be used in domestic manufacture, since finished goods have a higher value than raw materials.
- That a large, working population be encouraged.
- That all export of gold and silver be prohibited and all domestic money be kept in circulation.
- That all imports of foreign goods be discouraged as much as possible.
- That where certain imports are indispensable they be obtained at first hand, in exchange for other domestic goods instead of gold and silver.
- That as much as possible, imports be confined to raw materials that can be finished [in the home country].
- That opportunities be constantly sought for selling a country's surplus manufactures to foreigners, so far as necessary, for gold and silver.
- That no importation be allowed if such goods are sufficiently and suitably supplied at home.

Other than Von Hornick, there were no mercantilist writers presenting an overarching scheme for the ideal economy, as Adam Smith would later do for classical economics. Rather, each mercantilist writer tended to focus on a single area of the economy. Only later did non-mercantilist scholars integrate these "diverse" ideas into what they called mercantilism. Some scholars thus reject the idea of mercantilism completely, arguing that it gives "a false unity to disparate events". Smith saw the mercantile system as an enormous conspiracy by manufacturers and merchants against consumers, a view that has led some authors, especially Robert E. Ekelund and Robert D. Tollison, to call mercantilism "a rent-seeking society". To a certain extent, mercantilist doctrine itself made a general theory of economics impossible. Mercantilists viewed the economic system as a zero-sum game, in which any gain by one party required a loss by another. Thus, any system of policies that benefited one group would by definition harm the other, and there was no possibility of economics being used to maximize the commonwealth, or common good. Mercantilists' writings were also generally created to rationalize particular practices rather than as investigations into the best policies.

Mercantilist domestic policy was more fragmented than its trade policy. While Adam Smith portrayed mercantilism as supportive of strict controls over the economy, many mercantilists disagreed. The early modern era was one of letters patent and government-imposed monopolies; some mercantilists supported these, but others acknowledged the corruption and inefficiency of such systems. Many mercantilists also realized that the inevitable results of quotas and price ceilings were black markets. One notion that mercantilists widely agreed upon was the need for economic oppression of the working population; laborers and farmers were to live at the "margins of subsistence". The goal was to maximize production, with no concern for consumption. Extra money, free time, and education for the lower classes were seen to inevitably lead to vice and laziness, and would result in harm to the economy.

Infinite Growth

The mercantilists saw a large population as a form of wealth which made possible the development of bigger markets and armies. The opposing doctrine of physiocracy predicted that mankind would outgrow its resources. The idea of mercantilism was to protect the markets, but it also helped to maintain the agriculture and those who were dependent upon it.

Scholars debate over why mercantilism dominated economic ideology for 250 years. One group, represented by Jacob Viner, sees mercantilism as simply a straightforward, common-sense system whose logical fallacies remained opaque to people at the time, as they simply lacked the required analytical tools.

The second school, supported by scholars such as Robert B. Ekelund, portrays mercantilism not as a mistake, but rather as the best possible system for those who developed it. This school argues that rent-seeking merchants and governments developed and enforced mercantilist policies. Merchants benefited greatly from the enforced monopolies, bans on foreign competition, and poverty of the workers. Governments benefited from the high tariffs and payments from the merchants. Whereas later economic ideas were often developed by academics and philosophers, almost all mercantilist writers were merchants or government officials.

Monetarism offers a third explanation for mercantilism. European trade exported bullion to pay for goods from Asia, thus reducing the money supply and putting downward pressure on prices and economic activity. The evidence for this hypothesis is the lack of inflation in the British economy until the Revolutionary and Napoleonic Wars, when paper money came into vogue.

A fourth explanation lies in the increasing professionalisation and technification of the wars of the era, which turned the maintenance of adequate reserve funds (in the prospect of war) into a more and more expensive and eventually competitive business.

Mercantilism developed at a time of transition for the European economy. Isolated feudal estates were being replaced by centralized nation-states as the focus of power. Technological changes in shipping and the growth of urban centres led to a rapid increase in international trade. Mercantilism focused on how this trade could best aid the states. Another important change was the introduction of double-entry bookkeeping and modern accounting. This accounting made extremely clear the inflow and outflow of trade, contributing to the close scrutiny given to the balance of trade. Of course, the impact of the discovery of America cannot be ignored. New markets and new mines propelled foreign trade to previously inconceivable volumes, resulting in "the great upward movement in prices" and an increase in "the volume of merchant activity itself".

Prior to mercantilism, the most important economic work done in Europe was by the medieval scholastic theorists. The goal of these thinkers was to find an economic system compatible with Christian doctrines of piety and justice. They focused mainly on microeconomics and on local exchanges between individuals. Mercantilism was closely aligned with the other theories and ideas that began to replace the medieval worldview. This period saw the adoption of the very Machiavellian realpolitik and the primacy of the *raison d'état* in international relations. The mercantilist idea of all trade as a zero-sum game, in which each side was trying to best the other in a ruthless competition, was integrated into the works of Thomas Hobbes. This dark view of human nature also fit well with the Puritan view of the world, and some of the most stridently mercantilist legislation, such as the Navigation Ordinance of 1651, was enacted by the government of Oliver Cromwell.

Jean-Baptiste Colbert's work in 17th-century France came to exemplify classical mercantilism. In the English-speaking world its ideas were criticized by Adam Smith with the publication of *The Wealth of Nations* and later by David Ricardo with his explanation of comparative advantage. Mercantilism was rejected by Britain and France by the mid-19th century. The British Empire embraced free trade and used its power as the financial centre of the world to promote the same. The Guyanese historian Walter Rodney describes mercantilism as the period of the worldwide development of European commerce, which began in the 15th century with the voyages of Portuguese and Spanish explorers to Africa, Asia, and the New World.

Policies

French finance minister and mercantilist Jean-Baptiste Colbert served for over 20 years.

Mercantilist ideas were the dominant economic ideology of all of Europe in the early modern period, and most states embraced it to a certain degree. Mercantilism was centred on England and France, and it was in these states that mercantilist polices were most often enacted.

France

Mercantilism arose in France in the early 16th century soon after the monarchy had become the dominant force in French politics. In 1539, an important decree banned the import of woolen goods from Spain and some parts of Flanders. The next year, a number of restrictions were imposed on the export of bullion.

Over the rest of the 16th century, further protectionist measures were introduced. The height of French mercantilism is closely associated with Jean-Baptiste Colbert, finance minister for 22 years in the 17th century, to the extent that French mercantilism is sometimes called Colbertism. Under Colbert, the French government became deeply involved in the economy in order to increase exports. Protectionist policies were enacted that limited imports and favored exports. Industries were organized into guilds and monopolies, and production was regulated by the state through a series of more than one thousand directives outlining how different products should be produced.

To encourage industry, foreign artisans and craftsmen were imported. Colbert also worked to decrease internal barriers to trade, reducing internal tariffs and building an extensive network of roads and canals. Colbert's policies were quite successful, and France's industrial output and economy grew considerably during this period, as France became the dominant European power. He was less successful in turning France into a major trading power, and Britain and the Netherlands remained supreme in this field.

New France

France imposed its mercantilist philosophy on its colonies in North America, especially New France. It sought to derive the maximum material benefit from the colony, for the homeland, with a minimum of imperial investment in the colony itself. The ideology was embodied in New France through the establishment under Royal Charter of a number of corporate trading monopolies including La Compagnie des Marchands, which operated from 1613 to 1621 and the Compagnie de Montmorency, from that date until 1627. It was in turn replaced by La Compagnie des Cent-Associés created in 1627, by King Louis XIII and the Communauté des habitants in 1643. These were the first corporations to operate in what is now Canada.

Great Britain

In England, mercantilism reached its peak during the Long Parliament government (1640–60). Mercantilist policies were also embraced throughout much of the Tudor and Stuart periods, with Robert Walpole being another major proponent. In Britain, government control over the domestic economy was far less extensive than on the Continent, limited by common law and the steadily increasing power of Parliament. Government-controlled monopolies were common, especially before the English Civil War, but were often controversial.

The Anglo-Dutch Wars were fought between the English and the Dutch for control over the seas and trade routes.

With respect to its colonies, British mercantilism meant that the government and the merchants became partners with the goal of increasing political power and private wealth, to the exclusion of other empires. The government protected its merchants—and kept others out—through trade barriers, regulations, and subsidies to domestic industries in order to maximize exports from and minimize imports to the realm. The government had to fight smuggling, which became a favorite American technique in the 18th century to circumvent the restrictions on trading with the French, Spanish, or Dutch. The goal of mercantilism was to run trade surpluses, so that gold and silver would pour into London. The government took its share through duties and taxes, with the remainder going to merchants in Britain. The government spent much of its revenue on a superb Royal Navy, which not only protected the British colonies but threatened the colonies of the other empires, and sometimes seized them. Thus the British Navy captured New Amsterdam (New York) in 1664. The colonies were captive markets for British industry, and the goal was to enrich the mother country.

British mercantilist writers were themselves divided on whether domestic controls were necessary. British mercantilism thus mainly took the form of efforts to control trade. A wide array of regulations were put in place to encourage exports and discourage imports. Tariffs were placed on imports and bounties given for exports, and the export of some raw materials was banned completely. The Navigation Acts expelled foreign merchants from England's domestic trade. The nation aggressively sought colonies and once under British control, regulations were imposed that allowed the colony to only produce raw materials and to only trade with Britain. This led to friction with the inhabitants of these colonies, and mercantilist policies (such as forbidding trade with other empires and controls over smuggling) were a major irritant leading to the American Revolution.

Mercantalism taught that trade was a zero-sum game, with one country's gain equivalent to a loss sustained by the trading partner. Overall, however, mercantilist policies had a positive impact on Britain helping turn it into the world's dominant trader and the global hegemon. De facto mercantile policies continued until the 1850s, when Britain began to embrace freer trade. For example, during the Industrial Revolution, Britain's average tariff on manufactured goods rose from 30% to 50%, peaking at 57% in the 1820s. This worked in concert with Britain's imperialistic expansion, which was motivated, in part, to acquire new markets for British manufactured goods—the quintessential mercantile paradigm. One domestic policy that had a lasting impact was the conversion of "waste lands" to agricultural use. Mercantilists believed that to maximize a nation's power, all land and resources had to be used to their utmost, and this era thus saw projects like the draining of The Fens.

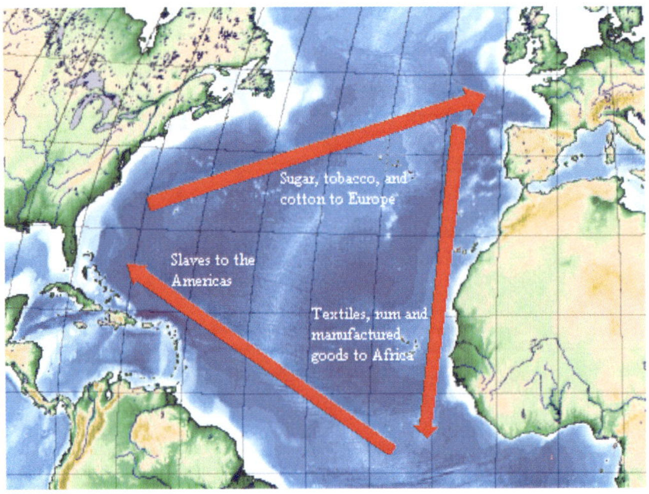

Mercantilism helped create trade patterns such as the triangular trade in the North Atlantic, in which raw materials were imported to the metropolis and then processed and redistributed to other colonies.

Other Countries

The other nations of Europe also embraced mercantilism to varying degrees. Perhaps the earliest coherent mercantile policy developed in the Italian city-state of Venice, which monopolized the Mediterranean pilgrim and spice trades. Venice prohibited the importation of finished products, and forced all Venetian naval traffic to make a stop in Venice, regardless of the cargoes final destination. This ensured that additional economic activity occurred within Venice. This enriched Venice at its consumers expense. The policy was summed up by a prominent Venetian merchant:

Nothing is better to increase and enrich the condition of our city than to give all liberty and occasion that commodities of our city be brought here and procured here rather than elsewhere, because this results in advantage both to the state and to private persons.

The Netherlands, which had become the financial centre of Europe by being its most efficient trader, had little interest in seeing trade restricted and adopted few mercantilist policies. Mercantilism became prominent in Central Europe and Scandinavia after the Thirty Years' War (1618–48), with Christina of Sweden, Jacob Kettler of Courland, and Christian IV of Denmark being notable proponents. The Habsburg Holy Roman Emperors had long been interested in mercantilist policies, but the vast and decentralized nature of their empire made implementing such notions difficult.

Some constituent states of the empire did embrace Mercantilism, most notably Prussia, which under Frederick the Great had perhaps the most rigidly controlled economy in Europe. During the economic collapse of the 17th century, Spain had little coherent economic policy, but French mercantilist policies were imported by Philip V with some success. Russia under Peter I (Peter the Great) attempted to pursue mercantilism, but had little success because of Russia's lack of a large merchant class or an industrial base.

Wars and Imperialism

Mercantilism was the economic version of warfare using economics as a tool for warfare by other means backed up by the state apparatus, and was well suited to an era of military warfare. Since the level of world trade was viewed as fixed, it followed that the only way to increase a nation's trade was to take it from another. A number of wars, most notably the Anglo-Dutch Wars and the Franco-Dutch Wars, can be linked directly to mercantilist theories. Most wars had other causes but they reinforced mercantilism by clearly defining the enemy, and justified damage to the enemy's economy.

Mercantilism fueled the imperialism of this era, as many nations expended significant effort to conquer new colonies that would be sources of gold (as in Mexico) or sugar (as in the West Indies), as well as becoming exclusive markets. European power spread around the globe, often under the aegis of companies with government-guaranteed monopolies in certain defined geographical regions, such as the Dutch East India Company or the British Hudson's Bay Company (operating in present-day Canada).

Criticisms

Adam Smith and David Hume were the founding fathers of anti-mercantilist thought. A number of scholars found important flaws with mercantilism long before Adam Smith developed an ideology that could fully replace it. Critics like Hume, Dudley North, and John Locke undermined much of mercantilism, and it steadily lost favor during the 18th century.

Much of Adam Smith's *The Wealth of Nations* is an attack on mercantilism.

In 1690, John Locke argued that prices vary in proportion to the quantity of money. Locke's *Second Treatise* also points towards the heart of the anti-mercantilist critique: that the wealth of the world is not fixed, but is created by human labor (represented embryonically by Locke's labor theory of value). Mercantilists failed to understand the notions of absolute advantage and comparative advantage (although this idea was only fully fleshed out in 1817 by David Ricardo) and the benefits of trade.

For instance, imagine that Portugal was a more efficient producer of wine than England, yet in England cloth could be produced more efficiently than it could in Portugal. Thus if Portugal specialized in wine and England in cloth, *both* states would end up *better off* if they traded. This is an example of the reciprocal benefits of trade (whether due to comparative or absolute advantage). In modern economic theory, trade is *not* a zero-sum game of cutthroat competition, because both sides can benefit.

Hume famously noted the impossibility of the mercantilists' goal of a constant positive balance of trade. As bullion flowed into one country, the supply would increase, and the value of bullion in that state would steadily decline relative to other goods. Conversely, in the state exporting bullion, its value would slowly rise. Eventually it would no longer be cost-effective to export goods from the high-price country to the low-price country, and the balance of trade would reverse. Mercantilists fundamentally misunderstood this, long arguing that an increase in the money supply simply meant that everyone gets richer.

The importance placed on bullion was also a central target, even if many mercantilists had themselves begun to de-emphasize the importance of gold and silver. Adam Smith noted that at the core of the mercantile system was the "popular folly of confusing wealth with money", that bullion was just the same as any other commodity, and that there was no reason to give it special treatment. More recently, scholars have discounted the accuracy of this critique. They believe Mun and Misselden were not making this mistake in the 1620s, and point to their followers Josiah Child and Charles Davenant, who in 1699 wrote, "Gold and Silver are indeed the Measure of Trade, but that the Spring and Original of it, in all nations is the Natural or Artificial Product of the Country; that is to say, what this Land or what this Labour and Industry Produces." The critique that mercantilism was a form of rent seeking has also seen criticism, as scholars such Jacob Viner in the 1930s pointed out that merchant mercantilists such as Mun understood that they would not gain by higher prices for English wares abroad.

The first school to completely reject mercantilism was the physiocrats, who developed their theories in France. Their theories also had several important problems, and the replacement of mercantilism did not come until Adam Smith published *The Wealth of Nations* in 1776. This book outlines the basics of what is today known as classical economics. Smith spent a considerable portion of the book rebutting the arguments of the mercantilists, though often these are simplified or exaggerated versions of mercantilist thought.

Scholars are also divided over the cause of mercantilism's end. Those who believe the theory was simply an error hold that its replacement was inevitable as soon as Smith's more accurate ideas were unveiled. Those who feel that mercantilism amounted to rent seeking hold that it ended only when major power shifts occurred. In Britain, mercantilism faded as the Parliament gained the monarch's power to grant monopolies. While the wealthy capitalists who controlled the House of Commons benefited from these monopolies, Parliament found it difficult to implement them because of the high cost of group decision making.

Mercantilist regulations were steadily removed over the course of the 18th century in Britain, and during the 19th century the British government fully embraced free trade and Smith's laissez-faire economics. On the continent, the process was somewhat different. In France, economic control remained in the hands of the royal family, and mercantilism continued until the French Revolution. In Germany mercantilism remained an important ideology in the 19th and early 20th centuries, when the historical school of economics was paramount.

Legacy

Adam Smith

Adam Smith rejected the mercantilist focus on production, arguing that consumption was paramount to production. He added that mercantilism was popular among merchants because it was what is now called rent seeking. However, John Maynard Keynes argued that encouraging production was just as important as encouraging consumption, and he favoured the "new mercantilism". Keynes also noted that in the early modern period the focus on the bullion supplies was reasonable. In an era before paper money, an increase in bullion was one of the few ways to increase the money supply. Keynes said mercantilist policies generally improved both domestic and foreign investment—domestic because the policies lowered the domestic rate of interest, and investment by foreigners by tending to create a favorable balance of trade.

Keynes and other economists of the 20th century also realized that the balance of payments is an important concern. Keynes also supported government intervention in the economy as necessity, as did mercantilism.

As of 2010, the word "mercantilism" remains a pejorative term, often used to attack various forms of protectionism. The similarities between Keynesianism (and its successor ideas) and mercantilism have sometimes led critics to call them neo-mercantilism. Paul Samuelson, writing within a Keynesian framework, wrote of mercantilism, "With employment less than full and Net National Product suboptimal, all the debunked mercantilist arguments turn out to be valid."

Some other systems that copy several mercantilist policies, such as Japan's economic system, are also sometimes called neo-mercantilist. In an essay appearing in the 14 May 2007 issue of *Newsweek*, business columnist Robert J. Samuelson wrote that China was pursuing an essentially neo-mercantilist trade policy that threatened to undermine the post–World War II international economic structure.

Murray Rothbard, representing the Austrian School of economics, describes it this way:

Mercantilism, which reached its height in the Europe of the seventeenth and eighteenth centuries, was a system of statism which employed economic fallacy to build up a structure of imperial state power, as well as special subsidy and monopolistic privilege to individuals or groups favored by the state. Thus, mercantilism held exports should be encouraged by the government and imports discouraged.

John Maynard Keynes

In specific instances, protectionist mercantilist policies also had an important and positive impact on the state that enacted them. Adam Smith, for instance, praised the Navigation Acts, as they greatly expanded the British merchant fleet and played a central role in turning Britain into the world's naval and economic superpower from the 18th century onward. Some economists thus feel that protecting infant industries, while causing short-term harm, can be beneficial in the long term.

System of Accounting

Accounting system is followed majorly in two ways :

- Cash.
- Mercantile.

Cash System

Definition and Explanation:

- It is a system in which accounting entries are made only when cash is received or paid. No entry is made when a payment or receipt is merely due.
- Government system of accounting is mostly on the cash system.

For example :

- The salary for December 2010 has not been paid till 5th Jan. 2011. Under cash basis, Salary expense for the month of December will not be recorded as payment has not been made.

Mercantile System

Definition and Explanation:

- It is a system in which accounting entries are made on the basis of amount having become due for payment or receipt.
- This system recognizes the fact that if a transaction or an event occurred, its consequences cannot be avoided and therefore, should be brought into book in order to present a meaningful picture of profit earned or loss suffered.
- The mercantile system is also known as the accrual system.

Difference Between Cash and Mercantile System of Accounting

- Under cash basis accounting, Revenues are recognized and earned only when cash is received irrespective of when and how the services were performed or goods delivered.

To put it in different terms, the cash basis of accounting takes into consideration all those incomes/gains that have been received and expenses/losses that have been paid during the accounting period in consideration.

Under accrual or mercantile basis accounting, Revenues are recognized and earned when they are realized or realizable irrespective of when the cash is received.

To put it in different terms, the accrual basis of accounting, records all incomes/gains and expenses/ losses pertaining to the accounting period under consideration, irrespective of receipt or payment.

Preparation of Financial Statement

Particulars	Amount (₹)
Cash	5,600
Trade debtors	8,400
Rent	5,500
Salaries	12,000
Trade Creditors	18,700
Insurance	4,000
Petty Expenses	3,000
Opening Stock	20,000
Sales	2,65,000
Purchases	1,80,000
Capital	1,05,900
Motor Vehicle	65,000
Machinery	54,000
Office Expenses	2,950
Repairs & Maintenance	5,000
Electricity exps.	2,550

Prepare Profit & Loss A/c and Balance Sheet from the above trial balance.

Solution

Trading & Profit & Loss A/c for the year ended 31st March ....

Particulars	₹	Particulars	₹
Opening Stock	20,000	Sales	2,65,000
Purchases	1,80,000		
Gross Profit	65,000		
Total	**2,65,000**	**Total**	**2,65,000**

Particulars	₹	Particulars	₹
Rent	5,500	Gross Profit b/d	65,000
Salaries	12,000		
Insurance	4,000		
Petty Exps.	3,000		
Office Exps.	2,950		
Repairs & Maintenance	5,000		
Electricity Exp.	2,250		
Net Profit	30,300		

Balance Sheet as on 31st March ....

Liabilities	₹	Assets	₹
Capital	1,05,900	Motor Vehicle	65,000
Net Profit	30,300	Machinery	54,000
Trade Creditors	8,400	Trade debtors	20,000
		Cash	5,600
	1,44,600		**1,44,600**

Share Capital

A corporation's share capital (or capital stock in US English) is the portion of a corporation's equity that has been obtained by the issue of shares in the corporation to a shareholder, usually for cash.

In a strict accounting sense, share capital is the nominal value of issued shares (that is, the sum of their par values, as indicated on share certificates). If the allocation price of shares is greater than their par value, e.g. as in a rights issue, the shares are said to be sold at a premium (variously called *share premium, additional paid-in capital* or *paid-in capital in excess of par*). Commonly, the share capital is the total of the aforementioned nominal share capital and the premium share capital. Conversely, when shares are issued below par, they are said to be issued at a discount or part-paid.

Sometimes shares are allocated in exchange for non-cash consideration, most commonly when company A acquires company B for shares. Here the share capital is increased to the par value of the new shares, and the merger reserve is increased to the balance of the price of company B.

Besides its meaning in accounting, described above, "share capital" may also describe the number and types of shares that compose a company's share structure. For an example of the different meanings: a company might have an "outstanding share capital" of 500,000 shares (the "structure" usage); it has received for them a total of 2 million dollars, which in the balance sheet is the "share capital" (the accounting usage).

The legal aspects of share capital are mostly dealt with in a jurisdiction's corporate law system. An example of such an issue is that when a company allocates new shares, it must do so in a way that does not inequitably dilute existing shareholders without their agreement.

- Total capital of the company is divided into a number of small indivisible units of a fixed amount and each such unit is called a share.
- As the total capital of the company is divided into shares, the capital of the company is called 'share capital'.
- The fixed value of a share, printed on the share certificate is called nominal/ par/ face value of a share.
- A company can issue shares at a price different from the face value of a share; this is issue price of share.
- Types of shares Shares issued by a company are divided into two categories:
    - Preference Shares:

      The shares which are assured of preferential dividend at a fixed rate during the life of company and carry a preferential right over other shareholders to be paid first in case of winding up of company.
    - Equity Shares

      Equity shares are those shares, which are not preference shares. It means that they do not enjoy any preferential rights in the matter of payment of dividend or repayment of capital.

Issue of Share Capital

- The shares can be issued by company either for cash or for the consideration other than cash.
- A public company issues a prospectus inviting general public to subscribe for its shares. On the basis of prospectus, application are deposited in a scheduled bank by the interested parties along with the amount payable at the time of application in cash which is called as application money.
- Company reserves the right to reject or accept an application fully or partially. Successful applicants become shareholders of the company and are required to pay the second installment which is known as allotment money.
- Subsequent installments, if any, to be called by the company are known as calls.
- Journal Entries for issues of shares for cash
    - On the receipt of the application money
      Bank A/c...... Dr.
      To Shares Application money

- On the allotment of share
  Share Allotment A/c.....Dr.
  Share Application A/c...Dr.
  To Share Capital A/c
  To Securities Premium A/c
  (if shares are issued at premium)

- On the receipt of allotment money
  Bank A/c.....Dr.
  To Share Allotment A/c

- On the call being made
  Share call A/c.....Dr.
  To Share Capital A/c

- On receipt of call money
  Bank A/c......Dr.
  To Share Call A/c

- If call money is received from shareholders even before making call
  Bank A/c....Dr.
  To Calls in Advance A/c

- If money is not received from shareholders on any call
  Calls in Arrears A/c....Dr.
  To Share Allotment A/c
  To Share Call A/c

The Articles of Association of a company usually empower the director to charge interest at a stipulated rate on calls in arrears. According to Table A of Companies Act 1956 interest at the rate of 5% p.a. is to be charged on unpaid calls from the due date of the call up to the actual payment.

JE for interest receivable on call in arrears
Shareholders A/c....Dr.
To Interest on Calls in Arrears A/c

For receipt of interest
Interest on Calls in Arrears A/c...Dr.
Shareholders A/c

According to Table A of Companies Act 1956 interest at the rate of 6% p.a. is to be paid on calls in advance from the actual payment up to due date of the call.

JE for Interest due
Interest on Calls in Arrears A/c...Dr.
To Shareholders A/c

Payment of interest
Shareholders A/c ...Dr.
Interest on Calls in Advance A/c

Issued Shares

Issued shares is a term of law and finance for the number of shares of a corporation which have been allocated (allotted) and are subsequently held by shareholders. The act of creating new issued shares is called *issuance, allocation* or *allotment*. Allotment is simply the creation of shares and their transfer to a subscriber. After allotment, a subscriber becomes a shareholder, though usually that also requires formal entry in the members register.

The number of shares that can be issued is limited to the total authorized shares. Issued shares are those shares which the board of directors and/or shareholders have agreed to allocate. Issued shares are the sum of outstanding shares held by shareholders; and treasury shares are shares which had been issued but have been repurchased by the corporation, and which generally have no voting rights or rights to dividends.

The issued shares of a corporation form the equity capital of the corporation, and some corporations are required by law to have a minimum value of equity capital, while others may not need any or just a nominal number. The value of the issued shares are determined at the time they are issued and the value does not change, in relation to the issuing corporation after that time.

Shares are most commonly issued fully paid, in which case the liability of the shareholders is limited to the amount paid on the shares; but they may also be issued partly paid, with unlimited liability, subject to guarantee, or some other form.

Basic Formulae

- Shares authorized = Shares issued + Shares unissued
- Shares issued = Shares outstanding + Treasury shares

Capital Surplus

Capital surplus, also called share premium, is an account which may appear on a corporation's balance sheet, as a component of shareholders' equity, which represents the amount the corporation raises on the issue of shares in excess of their par value (nominal value) of the shares (common stock).

This is called Additional paid in capital in US GAAP terminology but, additional paid in capital is not limited to share premium. It is a very broad concept and includes tax related and conversion related adjustments.

Taken together, common stock (and sometimes preferred stock) issued and paid plus capital surplus represent the total amount actually paid by investors for shares when issued (assuming no subsequent adjustments or changes).

Shares for which there is no par value will generally not have any form of capital surplus on the balance sheet; all funds from issuing shares will be credited to common stock issued.

Some other scenarios for triggering a capital surplus include when the Government donates a piece of land to the company.

The capital surplus/share premium account (SPA) is generally not distributable, but may be used to:

- write off the expenses/commission relating to the issue of those shares, or
- make a bonus share issue of fully paid-up shares.

It may also be used to account for any gains the firm may derive from selling treasury stock, although this is less commonly seen.

Capital surplus is also a term used by economists to denote capital inflows in excess of capital outflows on a country's balance of payments.

Background

Many firms authorize shares with some nominal par value, often the smallest unit of currency commonly in use (such as one penny or $0.01), in many jurisdictions due to legal requirements. The firm may then sell these shares for a much higher price (as the par value is a largely archaic and fictional concept).

Any premium received over the par value is credited to capital surplus.

Share Premium Reserve Account

According to Companies Act 2006 s.610 in the United Kingdom the share premium account may be put only to certain specified uses. However UK company law in this connection was significantly relaxed in 2008 by permitting the share premium account to be converted into share capital and then the share capital to be reduced (effectively allowing the elimination of the share premium account by a two-stage process).

Under companies ordinance 1984 (Nepal) s.84:

(1) If a company issues shares at a premium, whether for cash or otherwise, a sum equal to the aggregate amount or value of the premiums on those shares shall be transferred to an account called "the share premium account".

(2) The share premium account may be applied by the company in paying up unissued shares to be allotted to members as fully paid bonus shares, or in writing off- (a) the company's preliminary expenses; or (b) the expenses of, or the commission paid or discount allowed on, any issue of shares or debentures of the company, or (c) in providing for the premium payable on redemption of debentures of the company.

(3) Subject to this, the provisions of this Act relating to the reduction of a company's share capital apply as if the share premium account were part of its paid up share capital.

A company's SPA is a part of creditors' buffer.

Assets:

Cash: $450

Liabilities:

Nil

Shareholders' equity:

Common stock: $100

Preference stock: $25

Share premium: $325

SPA = Number of new shares issued x (issue price - par value)

Preferred Stock

Preferred stock (also called preferred shares, preference shares or simply preferreds) is a type of stock which may have any combination of features not possessed by common stock including properties of both an equity and a debt instrument, and is generally considered a hybrid instrument. Preferred stocks are senior (i.e., higher ranking) to common stock, but subordinate to bonds in terms of claim (or rights to their share of the assets of the company) and may have priority over common stock (ordinary shares) in the payment of dividends and upon liquidation. Terms of the preferred stock are described in the articles of association.

Like bonds, preferred stocks are rated by the major credit-rating companies. The rating for preferreds is generally lower than for bonds because preferred dividends do not carry the same guarantees as interest payments from bonds and because preferred-stock holders' claims are junior to those of all creditors.

Features

Preferred stock is a special class of shares which may have any combination of features not possessed by common stock. The following features are usually associated with preferred stock:

- Preference in dividends
- Preference in assets, in the event of liquidation
- Convertibility to common stock.
- Callability (ability to be redeemed before it matures), at the option of the corporation
- Nonvoting

Preference in Dividends

In general, preferred stock has *preference* in dividend payments. The preference does not assure the payment of dividends, but the company must pay the stated dividends on preferred stock before paying any dividends on common stock.

Preferred stock can be *cumulative* or *noncumulative*. A cumulative preferred requires that if a company fails to pay a dividend (or pays less than the stated rate), it must make up for it at a later time. Dividends accumulate with each passed dividend period (which may be quarterly, semi-annually or annually). When a dividend is not paid in time, it has "passed"; all passed dividends on a cumulative stock make up a dividend in arrears. A stock without this feature is known as a noncumulative, or *straight*, preferred stock; any dividends passed are lost if not declared.

Other Features or Rights

- Preferred stock may or may not have a fixed liquidation value (or par value) associated with it. This represents the amount of capital which was contributed to the corporation when the shares were first issued.
- Preferred stock has a claim on liquidation proceeds of a stock corporation equal to its par (or liquidation) value, unless otherwise negotiated. This claim is senior to that of common stock, which has only a residual claim.
- Almost all preferred shares have a negotiated, fixed-dividend amount. The dividend is usually specified as a percentage of the par value or as a fixed amount (for example, Pacific Gas & Electric 6% Series A Preferred). Sometimes, dividends on preferred shares may be negotiated as *floating*; they may change according to a benchmark interest-rate index (such as LIBOR).
- Some preferred shares have special voting rights to approve extraordinary events (such as the issuance of new shares or approval of the acquisition of a company) or to elect directors, but most preferred shares have no voting rights associated with them; some preferred shares gain voting rights when the preferred dividends are in arrears for a substantial time. This is all variable on the rights assigned to the preferred shares at the time of incorporation.

The above list (which includes several customary rights) is not comprehensive; preferred shares (like other legal arrangements) may specify nearly any right conceivable. Preferred shares in the U.S. normally carry a call provision, enabling the issuing corporation to repurchase the share at its (usually limited) discretion.

Types

In addition to straight preferred stock, there is diversity in the preferred stock market. Additional types of preferred stock include:

- *Prior preferred stock*—Many companies have different issues of preferred stock outstanding at one time; one issue is usually designated highest-priority. If the company has only enough money to meet the dividend schedule on one of the preferred issues, it makes the payments on the prior preferred. Therefore, prior preferreds have less credit risk than other preferred stocks (but usually offers a lower yield).
- *Preference preferred stock*—Ranked behind a company's prior preferred stock (on a seniority basis) are its preference preferred issues. These issues receive preference over all other classes of the company's preferred (except for prior preferred). If the company issues more than one issue of preference preferred, the issues are ranked by seniority. One issue is designated first preference, the next-senior issue is the second and so on.
- *Convertible preferred stock*—These are preferred issues which holders can exchange for a predetermined number of the company's common-stock shares. This exchange may occur at any time the investor chooses, regardless of the market price of the common stock. It is a one-way deal; one cannot convert the common stock back to preferred stock. A variant of

this is the *anti-dilutive convertible preferred* recently made popular by investment banker Stan Medley who structured several variants of these preferred for some forty plus public companies. In the variants used by Stan Medley the preferred share converts to either a percentage of the company's common shares or a fixed dollar amount of common shares rather than a set number of shares of common. The intention is to ameliorate the bad effects investors suffer from rampant shorting and dilutive efforts on the OTC markets.

- *Cumulative preferred stock*—If the dividend is not paid, it will accumulate for future payment.
- *Exchangeable preferred stock*—This type of preferred stock carries an embedded option to be exchanged for some other security.
- *Participating preferred stock*—These preferred issues offer holders the opportunity to receive extra dividends if the company achieves predetermined financial goals. Investors who purchased these stocks receive their regular dividend regardless of company performance (assuming the company does well enough to make its annual dividend payments). If the company achieves predetermined sales, earnings or profitability goals, the investors receive an additional dividend.
- *Perpetual preferred stock*—This type of preferred stock has no fixed date on which invested capital will be returned to the shareholder (although there are redemption privileges held by the corporation); most preferred stock is issued without a redemption date.
- *Putable preferred stock*—These issues have a "put" privilege, whereby the holder may (under certain conditions) force the issuer to redeem shares.
- *Monthly income preferred stock*—A combination of preferred stock and subordinated debt.
- *Non-cumulative preferred stock*—Dividends for this type of preferred stock will not accumulate if they are unpaid; very common in TRuPS and bank preferred stock, since under BIS rules preferred stock must be non-cumulative if it is to be included in Tier 1 capital.
- *Supervoting stock*—a "class of stock that provides its holders with larger than proportionate voting rights compared with another class of stock issued by the same company." It enables a limited number of stockholders to control a company. Usually, the purpose of the super voting shares is to give key company insiders greater control over the company's voting rights, and thus its board and corporate actions. The existence of super voting shares can also be an effective defense against hostile takeovers, since key insiders can maintain majority voting control of their company without actually owning more than half of the outstanding shares.

Usage

Preferred stocks offer a company an alternative form of financing—for example through pension-led funding; in some cases, a company can defer dividends by going into arrears with little penalty or risk to its credit rating, however, such action could have a negative impact on the company meeting the terms of its financing contract. With traditional debt, payments are required; a missed payment would put the company in default.

Occasionally companies use preferred shares as means of preventing hostile takeovers, creating preferred shares with a poison pill (or forced-exchange or conversion features) which are exercised upon a change in control. Some corporations contain provisions in their charters authorizing the issuance of preferred stock whose terms and conditions may be determined by the board of directors when issued. These "blank checks" are often used as a takeover defense; they may be assigned very high liquidation value (which must be redeemed in the event of a change of control), or may have great super-voting powers.

When a corporation goes bankrupt, there may be enough money to repay holders of preferred issues known as "senior" but not enough money for "junior" issues. Therefore, when preferred shares are first issued their governing document may contain protective provisions preventing the issuance of new preferred shares with a senior claim. Individual series of preferred shares may have a senior, pari-passu (equal), or junior relationship with other series issued by the same corporation.

Users

Preferred shares are more common in private or pre-public companies, where it is useful to distinguish between the control of and the economic interest in the company. Government regulations and the rules of stock exchanges may either encourage or discourage the issuance of publicly traded preferred shares. In many countries, banks are encouraged to issue preferred stock as a source of Tier 1 capital. On the other hand, the Tel Aviv Stock Exchange prohibits listed companies from having more than one class of capital stock.

A company may issue several classes of preferred stock. It may undergo several rounds of financing, with each round receiving separate rights and having a separate class of preferred stock. Such a company might have "Series A Preferred," "Series B Preferred," "Series C Preferred" and common stock.

In the United States there are two types of preferred stocks: *straight* preferreds and *convertible* preferreds. Straight preferreds are issued in perpetuity (although some are subject to call by the issuer, under certain conditions) and pay a stipulated rate of interest to the holder. Convertible preferreds—in addition to the foregoing features of a straight preferred—contain a provision by which the holder may convert the preferred into the common stock of the company (or, sometimes, into the common stock of an affiliated company) under certain conditions (among which may be the specification of a future date when conversion may begin, a certain number of common shares per preferred share or a certain price per share for the common stock).

There are income-tax advantages generally available to *corporations* investing in preferred stocks in the United States.

But for *individuals*, a *straight* preferred stock, a hybrid between a bond and a stock, bears some disadvantages of each type of securities without enjoying the advantages of either. Like a bond, a straight preferred does not participate in future earnings and dividend growth of the company, or growth in the price of the common stock. However, a bond has greater security than the preferred and has a maturity date at which the principal is to be repaid. Like the common, the preferred has less security protection than the bond. However, the potential increase in the market price of the common (and its dividends, paid from future growth of the company) is lacking for the preferred. One advantage of the preferred to its issuer is that the preferred receives better equity credit at rating agencies than straight debt (since it is usually perpetual). Also, certain types of preferred stock qualify as Tier 1 capital; this allows financial institutions to satisfy regulatory requirements without diluting common shareholders. Through preferred stock, financial institutions are able to gain leverage while receiving Tier 1 equity credit.

If an investor paid par ($100) today for a typical straight preferred, such an investment would give a current yield of just over six percent. If, in a few years, 10-year Treasuries were to yield more than 13 percent to maturity (as they did in 1981) these preferreds would yield at least 13 percent; since the rate of dividend is fixed, this would reduce their market price to $46, a 54-percent loss. The difference between straight preferreds and Treasuries (or any investment-grade Federal-agency or corporate bond) is that the bonds would move up to par as their maturity date approaches; however, the straight preferred (having no maturity date) might remain at these $40 levels (or lower) for a long time.

Advantages of straight preferreds may include higher yields and—in the U.S. at least—tax advantages; they yield about 2 percent more than 10-year Treasuries, rank ahead of common stock in case of bankruptcy and dividends are taxable at a maximum rate of 15% rather than at ordinary-income rates (as with bond interest).

Advantages of Preference Shares

1. No obligation for dividends: A company is not bound to pay a dividend on preference shares if its profits in a particular year are insufficient. It can postpone the dividend in case of cumulative preference shares also. No fixed burden is created on its finances.

2. No interference: Generally, preference shares do not carry voting rights.Therefore, a company can raise capital without dilution of control. Equity shareholders retain exclusive control over the company.

3. Trading on equity: The rate of dividend on preference shares is fixed. Therefore, with the rise in its earnings, the company can provide the benefits of trading on equity to the equity shareholders.

4. No charge on assets: Preference shares do not create any mortgage or charge on the assets of the company. The company can keep its fixed assets free for raising loans in future

5. Variety: Different types of preference shares can be issued depending on the needs of investors. Participating preference shares or convertible preference shares may be issued to attract bold and enterprising investors.

Country-by-country Perspectives

Canada

Preferred shares represent a significant portion of Canadian capital markets, with over C$11.2 billion in new preferred shares issued in 2016. Many Canadian issuers are financial organizations which may count capital raised in the preferred-share market as Tier 1 capital (provided that the shares issued are perpetual). Another class of issuer includes split share corporations. Investors in Canadian preferred shares are generally those who wish to hold fixed-income investments in a taxable portfolio. Preferential tax treatment of dividend income (as opposed to interest income) may, in many cases, result in a greater after-tax return than might be achieved with bonds.

Preferred shares are often used by private corporations to achieve Canadian tax objectives. For instance, the use of preferred shares can allow a business to accomplish an estate freeze. By transferring common shares in exchange for fixed-value preferred shares, business owners can allow future gains in the value of the business to accrue to others (such as a discretionary trust).

Germany

The rights of holders of preference shares in Germany are usually rather similar to those of ordinary shares, except for some dividend preference and no voting right in many topics of shareholders' meetings. Preference shares in German stock exchanges are usually indicated with *V*, *VA* or *Vz* (short for *Vorzugsaktie*)—for example, "BMW Vz"—in contrast to *St*, *StA* (short for *Stammaktie*) or *NA* (short for *Namensaktie*) for standard shares. Preference shares with multiple voting rights, e.g. at RWE or Siemens, have been abolished.

Preferred stock may comprise up to half of total equity. It is convertible into common stock, but its conversion requires approval by a majority vote at the stockholders' meeting. If the vote passes, German law requires consensus with preferred stockholders to convert their stock (which is usually encouraged by offering a one-time premium to preferred stockholders). The firm's intention to do so may arise from its financial policy (i.e. its ranking in a specific index). Industry stock indices usually do not consider preferred stock in determining the daily trading volume of a company's stock; for example, they do not qualify the company for a listing due to a low trading volume in common stocks.

United Kingdom

Perpetual non-cumulative preference shares may be included as Tier 1 capital. Perpetual cumulative preferred shares are Upper Tier 2 capital. Dated preferred shares (normally having an original maturity of at least five years) may be included in Lower Tier 2 capital.

United States

In the United States, the issuance of publicly listed preferred stock is generally limited to financial institutions, REITs and public utilities. Because in the U.S. dividends on preferred stock are not tax-deductible at the corporate level (in contrast to interest expense), the effective cost of capital raised by preferred stock is 35 percent greater than issuing the equivalent amount of debt at the same interest rate. This has led to the development of TRuPS: debt instruments with the same properties as preferred stock. With the passage of the Dodd-Frank Wall Street Reform and Consumer Protection Act in 2010, TRuPS will be phased out as a vehicle for raising Tier 1 capital by bank holding companies. Outstanding TRuPS issues will be phased out completely by 2015.

However, with a qualified dividend tax of 15 percent (compared to a top ordinary marginal tax rate of 35 percent), $1 of dividend income taxed at this rate provides the same after-tax income as approximately $1.30 in interest. The size of the preferred stock market in the United States has been estimated as $100 billion (as of early 2008), compared to $9.5 trillion for equities and US$4.0 trillion for bonds. The amount of new issuance in the United States was $34.1 billion in 2016.

Other countries

- In Nigeria preferred shares make up a small percentage of a company's stock with no voting rights except in cases were they are not paid dividends; owners of preferred shares are entitled to a greater percentage of company profits.
- *Czech Republic*—Preferred stock cannot be more than 50 percent of total equity.
- *France*—By a law enacted in June 2004 France allows the creation of preferred shares.
- *South Africa*—Dividends from preference shares are not taxable as income when held by individuals.
- *Brazil*—In Brazil, up to 50 percent of the capital stock of a company may be composed of preferred stock. The preferred stock will have at least one less right than the common stock (normally voting power), but will have a preference in receiving dividends.
- *Russia*—No more than 25% of capital may be preferred stock. Voting rights are limited, but if dividends are not fully paid, shareholders obtain full voting rights.

Common Stock

Common stock is a form of corporate equity ownership, a type of security. The terms voting share and ordinary share are also used frequently in other parts of the world; "common stock" being primarily used in the United States. They are known as Equity shares or Ordinary shares in the UK and other Commonwealth realms. This type of share gives the stockholder the right to share in the profits of the company, and to vote on matters of corporate policy and the composition of the members of the board of directors.

It is called "common" to distinguish it from preferred stock. If both types of stock exist, common/equity stockholders usually cannot be paid dividends until all preferred/preference stock dividends are paid in full; it is possible to have common stock that has dividends that are paid alongside the preferred stock.

In the event of bankruptcy, common stock investors receive any remaining funds after bondholders, creditors (including employees), and preferred stockholders are paid.

Common stockholders can also earn money through capital appreciation. Common shares may perform better than preferred shares or bonds over time, in part to accommodate the increased risk.

Shareholder Rights

Shareholder rights are more conceptual than technical or factual. Their most common source is in the statutory and case law of the jurisdiction in which the company was formed. Information about what people think of as shareholder rights can also be found in the corporate charter and governance documents, but companies do not actually have documentation outlining specific "Shareholder Rights." Some shareholders elect to enter into shareholder agreements that create new rights among the shareholders, and it is common for the company to be a party to that agreement.

Some common stock shares have voting rights on certain matters, such as electing the board of directors. However in the United States, a company can have both a "voting" and "non-voting" series of common stock, as with preferred stock, but not in countries which have laws against multiple voting and non-voting shares

Hypothetically speaking, holders of voting common stock can influence the corporation through votes on establishing corporate objectives and policy, stock splits, and electing the company's board of directors. In practice, it's questionable whether or not such actions can be organized or ruled in their favor. Some shareholders, including holders of common stock, also receive preemptive rights, which enable them to retain their proportional ownership in a company if it issues additional stock or other securities. There is no fixed dividend paid out to common/equity stockholders and so their returns are uncertain, contingent on earnings, company reinvestment, and efficiency of the market to value and sell stock.

Classification

Common/Equity stock is classified to differentiate it from preferred stock. Each is considered a "class" of stock, with different series of each issued from time to time such as Series B Preferred Stock. Nevertheless, using "Class B Common Stock" is a common label for a super-voting series of common stock.

Debenture

In corporate finance, a debenture is a medium to long-term debt instrument used by large companies to borrow money, at a fixed rate of interest. The legal term "debenture" originally referred to a document that either creates a debt or acknowledges it, but in some countries the term is now used interchangeably with bond, loan stock or note. A debenture is thus like a certificate of loan or a loan bond evidencing the fact that the company is liable to pay a specified amount with interest and although the money raised by the debentures becomes a part of the company's capital structure, it does not become share capital. Senior debentures get paid before subordinate debentures, and there are varying rates of risk and payoff for these categories.

Debentures are generally freely transferable by the debenture holder. Debenture holders have no rights to vote in the company's general meetings of shareholders, but they may have separate meetings or votes e.g. on changes to the rights attached to the debentures. The interest paid to them is a charge against profit in the company's financial statements.

Attributes

- A movable property
- Issued by the company in the form of a certificate of indebtedness
- Generally specifying the dates of redemption, repayment of principal and payment of interest

- May or may not create a charge on the assets of the company
- Corporations in the US often issue bonds of around $1,000, while government bonds are more likely to be $5,000

Debentures gave rise to the idea of the rich "clipping their coupons," which means that a bondholder will present their "coupon" to the bank and receive a payment each quarter (or in whatever period is specified in the agreement).

There are also other features that minimize risk, such as a "sinking fund," which means that the debtor must pay some of the value of the bond after a specified period of time. This decreases risk for the creditors, as a hedge against inflation, bankruptcy, or other risk factors. A sinking fund makes the bond less risky, and therefore gives it a smaller "coupon" (or interest payment). There are also options for "convertibility," which means a creditor may turn their bonds into equity in the company if it does well. Companies also reserve the right to call their bonds, which mean they can call it sooner than the maturity date. Often there is a clause in the contract that allows this; for example, if a bond issuer wishes to rebuy a 30-year bond at the 25th year, they must pay a premium. If a bond is called, it means that less interest is paid out.

Failure to pay a bond effectively means bankruptcy. Bondholders who have not received their interest can throw an offending company into bankruptcy, or seize its assets if that is stipulated in the contract.

Security in Different Jurisdictions

In the United States, debenture refers specifically to an unsecured corporate bond, i.e. a bond that does not have a certain line of income or piece of property or equipment to guarantee repayment of principal upon the bond's maturity. Where security is provided for loan stocks or bonds in the US, they are termed 'mortgage bonds'.

However, in the United Kingdom a debenture is usually secured.

In Canada, a debenture refers to a secured loan instrument where security is generally over the debtor's credit, but security is not pledged to specific assets. Like other secured debts, the debenture gives the debtor priority status over unsecured creditors in a bankruptcy; however debt instruments where security is pledged to specific assets (such as a bond) receive a higher priority status in a bankruptcy than do debentures.

In Asia, if repayment is secured by a charge over land, the loan document is called a mortgage; where repayment is secured by a charge against other assets of the company, the document is called a debenture; and where no security is involved, the document is called a note or 'unsecured deposit note'.

Convertibility

There are two types of debentures:

1. Convertible debentures, which are convertible bonds or bonds that can be converted into equity shares of the issuing company after a predetermined period of time. "Convertibility" is

a feature that corporations may add to the bonds they issue to make them more attractive to buyers. In other words, it is a special feature that a corporate bond may carry. As a result of the advantage a buyer gets from the ability to convert, convertible bonds typically have lower interest rates than non-convertible corporate bonds.

2. Non-convertible debentures, which are simply regular debentures, cannot be converted into equity shares of the liable company. They are debentures without the convertibility feature attached to them. As a result, they usually carry higher interest rates than their convertible counterparts.

Issue of Debentures

Issue of debentures can be categorized into the following:

1. Debenture issued at par and redeemable at par or at a discount.
2. Debenture issued at discount and redeemable at par or at a discount.
3. Debenture issued at premium and redeemable at par or at a discount.
4. Debenture issued at par and redeemable at premium.
5. Debenture issued at a discount and redeemable at premium.

Journal Entries in each of the above cases are discussed below:

1. Debenture issued at par and redeemable at par or at a discount
   For receipt of application money:
   Bank A/c......Dr.
      To Debenture Application Money A/c
      For transfer of application money to debenture account:
   Debenture Application A/c
      To Debenture A/c

2. Debenture issued at discount and redeemable at par or at a discount
   For receipt of application money:
   Bank A/c......Dr.
      To Debenture Application Money A/c
    For transfer of application money to debenture account:
   Debenture Application A/c
      To Debenture A/c

3. Debenture issued at discount and redeemable at par or at a discount
   For receipt of application money:
   Bank A/c......Dr.
      To Debenture Application Money A/c
    For transfer of application money to debenture account:
   Debenture Application A/c
   Discount on issue of debenture A/c
      To Debenture A/c

4. Debenture issued at premium and redeemable at par or at a discount
For receipt of application money:
Bank A/c......Dr.
To Debenture Application
Money A/c
For transfer of application money to debenture account:
Debenture Application A/c
To Debenture A/c
To Securities premium A/c

5. Debenture issued at par and redeemable at premium
For receipt of application money:
Bank A/c......Dr.
To Debenture Application
Money A/c
For transfer of application money to debenture account:
Debenture Application A/c
To Debenture A/c
Call made consequent upon allotment:
Debenture Allotment A/c
Loss on issue of Debenture A/c
To Debenture A/c
To Debenture redemption
Premium A/c

6. Debenture issued at a discount and redeemable at premium
For receipt of application money:
Bank A/c......Dr.
To Debenture Application Money A/c
For transfer of application money to debenture account:
Debenture Application A/c
To Debenture A/c
Call made consequent upon allotment:
Debenture Allotment A/c
Discount /Loss on issue of Debenture A/c (Discount + premium on redemption)
To Debenture A/c
To Debenture redemption
Premium A/c

7. Debenture issued at a premium and redeemable at premium
For receipt of application money:
Bank A/c......Dr.
To Debenture Application
Money A/c
For transfer of application money to debenture account:
Debenture Application A/c
To Debenture A/c

Call made consequent upon allotment:
Debenture Allotment A/c
Loss on issue of Debenture A/c (amount equal to premium on redemption)
To Debenture A/c
To Debenture redemption
Premium A/c

Redemption of Debentures

Redemption of debentures can be categorized into the following:

1. Debenture issued at par and redeemable at par.
2. Debenture issued at discount and redeemable at par.
3. Debenture issued at premium and redeemable at par.
4. Debenture issued at par and redeemable at premium.
5. Debenture issued at a discount and redeemable at premium.
6. Debenture issued at a premium and redeemable at premium.

Journal Entries in Each of the Above Cases are Discussed Below:

1. Debenture issued at par and redeemable at par
-Closing debenture account
Debenture A/c......Dr.
To Debenture holders A/c
-For payment of money to debenture holders:
Debenture holders A/c
To Bank A/c

2. Debenture issued at discount and redeemable at par
-For transfer of loss of discount to profit & loss account:
Profit & Loss A/c......Dr.
To Discount on issue of debenture A/c
the above entry may be repeated during the tenure of the debenture for writing off proportionate discount every year.
-Closing debenture account
Debenture A/c......Dr.
To Debenture holders A/c
-For payment of money to debenture holders:
Debenture holders A/c
To Bank A/c

3. Debenture issued at premium and redeemable at par
-Closing debenture account
Debenture A/c......Dr.
To Debenture holders A/c
-For payment of money to debenture holders:

Debenture holders A/c
To Bank A/c

4. Debenture issued at par and redeemable at premium
-For transfer of loss of premium to profit & loss account:
Profit & Loss A/c......Dr.
To Loss on issue of debenture A/c

the above entry may be repeated during the tenure of the debenture for writing off proportionate premium to be paid on redemption every year.
-Closing debenture and premium account
Debenture A/c......Dr.
Debenture redemption Premium A/c......Dr.
To Debenture holders A/c
-For payment of money to debenture holders:
Debenture holders A/c
To Bank A/c

5. Debenture issued at a discount and redeemable at premium
-For transfer of loss of discount and premium to profit & loss account:
Profit & Loss A/c......Dr.
To Discount / Loss on issue of debenture A/c (Discount + Premium)
-Closing debenture and premium account
Debenture A/c......Dr.
Debenture redemption Premium A/c......Dr.
To Debenture holders A/c
-For payment of money to debenture holders:
Debenture holders A/c
To Bank A/c

6. Debenture issued at a premium and redeemable at premium
-For transfer of loss of discount to profit & loss account:
Profit & Loss A/c......Dr.
To Loss on issue of debenture A/c (Premium on redemption)
-Closing debenture and premium account
Debenture A/c......Dr.
Debenture redemption Premium A/c......Dr.
To Debenture holders A/c
-For payment of money to debenture holders:
Debenture holders A/c
To Bank A/c

Purchase of Debenture

Debentures sometime are purchased in an open market and then cancelled on due date.

Example,

Company has issued 1000 9 % debentures for Rs. 100000. interest being payable half yearly The company purchases 100 debentures at Rs. 98 per debenture cum interest (interest for 6 months).

Journal Entries:

Own Debenture A/c....Dr. 9350

Interest A/c....Dr. 450

To Bank 9800

Suppose out of these debentures 40 debentures sold at Rs. 102 ex interest and remaining are cancelled at the end of 6 months from date of purchase.

Journal Entries:

Bank A/c...DR. 4080

To Own Debentures 4080

To Interest A/c 60

Own Debentures A/c...DR. 340

To Profit & Loss 340

(Profit on sale transferred to P & L A/c)

At the end of 6 months

9% debentures A/c....Dr. 6000

To Own Debenture 5610

To Capital Reserve 390

(Profit on cancellation transferred)

Accounting Principles

For communicating the results of business to outside world, it should be based on certain uniform and scientifically laid down principles or postulates.

Accounting principles mean those rules of conduct or procedures which are adopted by accountants universally while recording the accounting transactions to ensure uniformity, clarity and understanding while recording transactions.

Accounting Concepts

Accounting Concepts are those basic assumptions or conditions upon which accounting is based. Important accounting concepts are:

Business Entity Concept: – Entity is different from it's owner for accounting purposes.

Dual Aspect Concept: – Recording simultaneously debits credits.

Equity+ Liabilities = Assets

Cost Concept: – Assets are normally recorded basis of historical cost i.e. acquisition cost. Market value immaterial, except on concepts of revaluation.

Going Concern Concept: – Always on anticipation that a business will continue for long and will not be liquidated.

Accounting Period Concept: – Though business continues indefinitely, life of business sub-divided into accounting periods (generally of 1 year).

Money Measurement Concept: – Those transactions which are expressed in money terms are only recorded.

Realisation Concept: - Revenue is recognised only when, an agreement is reached or sale is made. Exceptions may be on certain businesses such on HP/sale on contract etc.

Constant Value Concept: - Assumption of constant value of currency e.g. rupee.

Accrual Concept: - Under this concept, the effects of transactions and other events are recognised on mercantile basis i.e. when they occur (and not as cash received or paid).

Consistency: – In order to achieve comparability of the financial statements of a enterprise through time, the accounting policies are followed consistently from the one period to another. A change in accounting policy is made only in certain exceptional circumstances.

Fundamental Accounting Assumptions are:

Going Concern, Consistency, and Accrual.

If nothing has been mentioned about fundamental accounting assumptions in the financial statements then it is assumed that they have already been followed in the preparation of financial statements.

However, if any of the above mentioned fundamental accounting assumption is not followed then this fact should be disclosed.

Exercise

Consider the following data pertaining to L Ltd.

Cost of the land purchased on 1st April 2010 Rs. 2,50,000.

Registration Charges Rs. 5,000.

Market Value as on 31st 2012 Rs.5,00,000.

While finalising the annual accounts, if the company values land at Rs. 5,00,000.

Which of the following concept is violated by L Ltd?

Cost, Accrual, Matching, Conservatism.

Accounting Standards

- Accounting Standards are written policy document issued by expert accounting body or by government or regulatory body covering the aspects of recognition, treatment, measurement, presentation and disclosure of accounting transaction and events in the financial statements.
- Accounting Standards (ASs) provide framework and standard accounting policies so that financial statements of different enterprises become comparable.
- The Accounting Standards seek to ensure that the financial statements of an enterprise should give a true and fair view of its financial position and working results.
- The Accounting Standards not only prescribe appropriate accounting treatment of complex business transactions but also foster greater transparency and market discipline.

Accounting Standards promote:

- Uniformity.
- Rationalization.
- Comparability.
- Transparency.

Generally Accepted Accounting Principles

Financial statements prepared and presented by a company typically follow an external standard that specifically guides their preparation. These standards vary across the globe and are typically overseen by some combination of the private accounting profession in that specific nation and the various government regulators. Variations across countries may be considerable making cross country evaluation of financial data challenging.

Publicly traded companies typically are subject to the most rigorous standards. Small and midsize businesses often follow more simplified standards, plus any specific disclosures required by their specific lenders and shareholders. Some firms operate on the cash method of accounting which can often be simple and straight forward. Larger firms most often operate on an accrual basis. Accounting standards prescribe in considerable detail what accruals must be made, how the financial statements are to be presented, and what additional disclosures are required.

Some important elements that accounting standards cover include: identifying the exact entity which is reporting, discussing any "going concern" questions, specifying monetary units, and reporting time frames.

Limitations

Accounting standards were largely written in the early 21st century. Massive *accounting irregularities* at large firms such as Worldcom and Enron illustrate that despite all the efforts widespread fraud can still occur, and even be missed by the outsidc auditors.

Benefits of Accounting Standards

The lack of transparent accounting standards in some nations has been cited as increasing the difficulty of doing business in them. In particular, the Asian financial meltdown in the late 1990s has been partially attributed due to the lack of detailed accounting standards. Giant firms in some Asian countries were able to take advantage of their poorly devised accounting standards to cover up immense debts and losses, which yielded a collective effect that eventually led the whole region into financial crisis.

Common Accounting Standards Around the Globe

- International Financial Reporting Standards

This standard is adopted in whole, or in large part, by many countries. Its acceptable in the U.S. (for a firm located outside of the U.S.) to report in this widely accepted format.

Accounting Standards by Nation

- China - Chinese Accounting Standards
- Canada - Generally Accepted Accounting Principles
- France - Generally Accepted Accounting Practice (*Plan Comptable Général*)
- Germany - Generally Accepted Accounting Practice (*Grundsätze ordnungsmäßiger Buchführung*)
- India - Indian Accounting Standards
- Nepal - Nepal Financial Reporting Standards
- Russia - Russian GAAP
- United Kingdom - Generally Accepted Accounting Practice (UK)
- United States - Generally Accepted Accounting Principles (United States) Domestic firms typically report in this format. Foreign firms that trade in the U.S. typically report in IFRS format.

Global Standardization and IFRS

Many countries use or are converging on the International Financial Reporting Standards (IFRS) that were established and are maintained by the International Accounting Standards Board. In some countries, local accounting principles are applied for regular companies but listed or large companies must conform to IFRS, so statutory reporting is comparable internationally.

All listed and grouped EU companies have been required to use IFRS since 2005, Canada moved in 2009, Taiwan in 2013, and other countries are adopting local versions.

In the United States, while *"...the SEC published a statement of continued support for a single set of high-quality, globally accepted accounting standards, and acknowledged that IFRS is best positioned to serve this role..."* progress is less evident.

Accounting Standards in India

The Institute of Chartered Accountants of India (ICAI) being apex accounting body in India, constituted the Accounting Standards Board (ASB) on 21st April, 1977, with a view to harmonies the diverse accounting policies and practices in use in India.

- While formulating accounting standards, the ASB takes into consideration the applicable laws, customs, usages and business environment prevailing in the country.
- The ASB also gives due consideration to International Financial Reporting Standards (IFRSs)/ International Accounting Standards (IASs) issued by IASB and tries to integrate them, to the extent possible, in the light of conditions and practices prevailing in India.

IND AS

In accordance with India's assurance to converge with IFRS, the Ministry of Corporate Affairs (MCA) issued a press release on 25 February 2011, notifying the Ind AS (Indian Accounting Standards).

Several of the requirements of Ind AS are considerably dissimilar from policies and practices presently followed by Indian companies. Further, while finalising the Ind AS, the Indian standard setters have examined individual IFRS and modified the requirements, wherever necessary, to suit Indian requirements. This has resulted in differences between Ind AS and equivalent requirements under IFRS (referred to as 'carve outs').

- Ind AS 101: First-time Adoption of Indian Accounting Standards.
- Ind AS 102: Share based Payment.
- Ind AS 103: Business Combinations.
- Ind AS 104: Insurance Contracts.
- Ind AS 105: Non current Assets Held for Sale and Discontinued Operations.
- Ind AS 106: Exploration for and Evaluation of Mineral Resources.
- Ind AS 107: Financial Instruments: Disclosures.
- Ind AS 108: Operating Segments.
- Ind AS 1: Presentation of Financial Statements.

- Ind AS 2: Inventories.
- Ind AS 7: Statement of Cash Flows.
- Ind AS 8: Accounting Policies, Changes in Accounting Estimates and Errors.
- Ind AS 10: Events after the Reporting Period.
- Ind AS 11: Construction Contracts.
- Ind AS 12: Income Taxes.
- Ind AS 16: Property, Plant and Equipment.
- Ind AS 17: Leases.
- Ind AS 18: Revenue.
- Ind AS 19: Employee Benefits.
- Ind AS 20: Accounting for Government Grants and Disclosure of Government Assistance.
- Ind AS 21: The Effects of Changes in Foreign Exchange Rate.
- Ind AS 23: Borrowing Costs.
- Ind AS 24: Related Party Disclosures.
- Ind AS 27: Consolidated and Separate Financial Statements.
- Ind AS 28: Investments in Associates.
- Ind AS 29: Financial Reporting in Hyperinflationary Economies.
- Ind AS 31: Interests in Joint Ventures.
- Ind AS 32: Financial Instruments: Presentation.
- Ind AS 33: Earnings per Share.
- Ind AS 34: Interim Financial Reporting.
- Ind AS 36: Impairment of Assets.
- Ind AS 37: Provisions, Contingent Liabilities and Contingent Assets.
- Ind AS 38: Intangible Assets.
- Ind AS 39: Financial Instruments: Recognition and Measurement.
- Ind AS 40: Investment Property.

International Financial Reporting Standards

International Financial Reporting Standards (IFRS) are designed as a common global language for business affairs so that company accounts are understandable and comparable across international boundaries. They are a consequence of growing international shareholding and trade and are particularly important for companies that have dealings in several countries. They are progressively replacing the many different national accounting standards. They are the rules to be followed by accountants to maintain books of accounts which are comparable, understandable, reliable and relevant as per the users internal or external.

IFRS, with the exception of *IAS 29 Financial Reporting in Hyperinflationary Economies* and *IFRIC 7 Applying the Restatement Approach under IAS 29*, are authorized in terms of the historical cost paradigm. IAS 29 and IFRIC 7 are authorized in terms of the units of constant purchasing power paradigm.

IFRS began as an attempt to harmonize accounting across the European Union but the value of harmonization quickly made the concept attractive around the world. However, it has been debated whether or not de facto harmonization has occurred. Standards that were issued by IASC (the predecessor of IASB) are still within use today and go by the name International Accounting Standards (IAS), while standards issued by IASB are called IFRS. IAS were issued between 1973 and 2001 by the Board of the International Accounting Standards Committee (IASC). On 1 April 2001, the new International Accounting Standards Board (IASB) took over from the IASC the responsibility for setting International Accounting Standards. During its first meeting the new Board adopted existing IAS and Standing Interpretations Committee standards (SICs). The IASB has continued to develop standards calling the new standards "International Financial Reporting Standards".

In the absence of a Standard or an Interpretation that specifically applies to a transaction, management must use its judgement in developing and applying an accounting policy that results in information that is relevant and reliable. In making that judgement, IAS 8.11 requires management to consider the definitions, recognition criteria, and measurement concepts for assets, liabilities, income, and expenses in the Framework.

Criticisms of IFRS are (1) that they are not being adopted in the US, (2) a number of criticisms from France and (3) that *IAS 29 Financial Reporting in Hyperinflationary Economies* had no positive effect at all during 6 years in Zimbabwe's hyperinflationary economy. The IASB offered responses to the first two criticisms, but has offered no response to the last criticism while IAS 29 was as of March 2014 being implemented in its original ineffective form in Venezuela and Belarus.

Objective of Financial Statements

Financial statements are a structured representation of the financial positions and financial performance of an entity. The objective of financial statements is to provide information about the financial position, financial performance and cash flows of an entity that is useful to a wide range of users in making economic decisions. Financial statements also show the results of the management's stewardship of the resources entrusted to it.

To meet this objective, financial statements provide information about an entity's:

a. assets;

b. liabilities;

c. equity;

d. income and expenses, including gains and losses;

e. contributions by and distributions to owners in their capacity as owners; and

f. cash flows.

This information, along with other information in the notes, assists users of financial statements in predicting the entity's future cash flows and, in particular, their timing and certainty.

The following are the general features in IFRS:

- Fair presentation and compliance with IFRS: Fair presentation requires the faithful representation of the effects of the transactions, other events and conditions in accordance with the definitions and recognition criteria for assets, liabilities, income and expenses set out in the Framework of IFRS.
- Going concern: Financial statements are present on a going concern basis unless management either intends to liquidate the entity or to cease trading, or has no realistic alternative but to do so.
- Accrual basis of accounting: An entity shall recognise items as assets, liabilities, equity, income and expenses when they satisfy the definition and recognition criteria for those elements in the Framework of IFRS.
- Materiality and aggregation: Every material class of similar items has to be presented separately. Items that are of a dissimilar nature or function shall be presented separately unless they are immaterial.
- Offsetting: Offsetting is generally forbidden in IFRS. However certain standards require offsetting when specific conditions are satisfied (such as in case of the accounting for defined benefit liabilities in IAS 19 and the net presentation of deferred tax liabilities and deferred tax assets in IAS 12).
- Frequency of reporting: IFRS requires that at least annually a complete set of financial statements is presented. However listed companies generally also publish interim financial statements (for which the accounting is fully IFRS compliant)for which the presentation is in accordance with IAS 34 *Interim Financing Reporting.*
- Comparative information: IFRS requires entities to present comparative information in respect of the preceding period for all amounts reported in the current period's financial statements. In addition comparative information shall also be provided for narrative and descriptive information if it is relevant to understanding the current period's financial statements. The standard IAS 1 also requires an additional statement of financial position (also called a third balance sheet) when an entity applies an accounting policy retrospectively or makes a retrospective restatement of items in its financial statements, or when it reclassifies items in its financial statements. This for example occurred with the adoption of the revised standard IAS 19 (as of 1 January 2013) or when the new consolidation standards IFRS 10-11-12 were adopted (as of 1 January 2013 or 2014 for companies in the European Union).
- Consistency of presentation: IFRS requires that the presentation and classification of items in the financial statements is retained from one period to the next unless:

a. it is apparent, following a significant change in the nature of the entity's operations or a review of its financial statements, that another presentation or classification would be more appropriate having regard to the criteria for the selection and application of accounting policies in IAS 8; or

b. an IFRS standard requires a change in presentation.

Qualitative Characteristics of Financial Information

Fundamental qualitative characteristics of financial information include:

- Relevance
- Faithful representation

Enhancing qualitative characteristics include:

- Comparability
- Verifiability
- Timeliness
- Understandability

Elements of Financial Statements

The elements directly related to the measurement of the statement of financial position include:

- Asset: An asset is a resource controlled by the entity as a result of past events and from which future economic benefits are expected to flow to the entity.
- Liability: A liability is a present obligation of the entity arising from the past events, the settlement of which is expected to result in an outflow from the entity of resources embodying economic benefits, i.e. assets.
- Equity: Nominal equity is the nominal residual interest in the nominal assets of the entity after deducting all its liabilities in nominal value.

The financial performance of an entity is presented in the statement of comprehensive income, which consists of the income statement (Statement of Profit/Loss) and the statement of other comprehensive income (usually presented in two separate statements). Financial performance includes the following elements (which are recognised in the income statement or other comprehensive income as required by the applicable IFRS standard):

- Revenues: increases in economic benefit during an accounting period in the form of inflows or enhancements of assets, or decrease of liabilities that result in increases in equity. However, it does not include the contributions made by the equity participants (for example owners, partners or shareholders).
- Expenses: decreases in economic benefits during an accounting period in the form of out-

flows, or depletions of assets or incurrences of liabilities that result in decreases in equity. However, these don't include the distributions made to the equity participants.

Results recognised in other comprehensive income are limited to the following specific circumstances:

- Remeasurements of defined benefit assets or liabilities (as defined in the standard IAS 19)
- Increases or decreases in the fair value of financial assets classified as available for sale (with the exception of impairment losses)(as defined in the standard IAS 39)
- Increases or decreases resulting from the application of a revaluation of property, plant and equipment or intangible assets
- Exchange differences resulting from the translation of foreign operations (subsidiary, associate, joint arrangement or branch of a reporting entity, the activities of which are conducted in a country or currency other than those of the reporting entity) according to the standard IAS 21
- the portion of the gain or loss on the hedging instrument in a cash flow hedge (or a hedge of a net investment in a foreign operation, as this is accounted similarly) that is determined to be an effective hedge

The statement of changes in equity consists of a reconciliation of the changes in equity in which the following information is provided:

- total comprehensive income for the period, showing separately the total amounts attributable to owners of the parent and to non-controlling interests;
- for each component of equity, the effects of retrospective application or retrospective restatement recognised in accordance with IAS 8; and
- for each component of equity, a reconciliation between the carrying amount at the beginning and the end of the period, separately disclosing changes resulting from:
    - profit or loss;
    - other comprehensive income; and
    - transactions with owners in their capacity as owners, showing separately contributions by and distributions to owners and changes in ownership interests in subsidiaries that do not result in a loss of control.

Statement of Cash Flows

- Operating cash flows: the principal revenue-producing activities of the entity and are generally calculated by applying the indirect method, whereby profit or loss is adjusted for the effects of transaction of a non-cash nature, any deferrals or accruals of past or future cash receipts or payments, and items of income or expense associated with investing or financing cash flows.
- Investing cash flows: the acquisition and disposal of long-term assets and other invest-

ments not included in cash equivalents. These represent the extent to which expenditures have been made for resources intended to generate future income and cash flows. Only expenditures that result in a recognised asset in the statement of financial position are eligible for classification as investing activities.

- Financing cash flows: activities that result in changes in the size and composition of the contributed equity and borrowings of the entity. These are important because they are useful in predicting claims on future cash flows by providers of capital to the entity.

Notes to the Financial Statements: These shall (a) present information about the basis of preparation of the financial statements and the specific accounting policies used; (b) disclose the information required by IFRSs that is not presented elsewhere in the financial statements; and (c) provide information that is not presented elsewhere in the financial statements, but is relevant to an understanding of any of them.

Recognition of Elements of Financial Statements

An item is recognized in the financial statements when:

- it is probable future economic benefit will flow to or from an entity.
- the resource can be reliably measured

In some cases specific standards add additional conditions before recognition is possible or prohibit recognition altogether.

An example is the recognition of internally generated brands, mastheads, publishing titles, customer lists and items similar in substance, for which recognition is prohibited by IAS 38. In addition research and development expenses can only be recognised as an intangible asset if they cross the threshold of being classified as 'development cost'.

Whilst the standard on provisions, IAS 37, prohibits the recognition of a provision for contingent liabilities, this prohibition is not applicable to the accounting for contingent liabilities in a business combination. In that case the acquirer shall recognise a contingent liability even if it is not probable that an outflow of resources embodying economic benefits will be required.

International Financial Reporting Standards (IFRS) are designed as a common global language for business affairs so that company accounts are understandable and comparable across international boundaries. They are a consequence of growing international.

Concepts of Capital and Capital Maintenance

Concepts of Capital

Par. 102. A financial concept of capital is adopted by most entities in preparing their financial statements. Under a financial concept of capital, such as invested money or invested purchasing power, capital is synonymous with the net assets or equity of the entity. Under a physical concept of capital, such as operating capability, capital is regarded as the productive capacity of the entity based on, for example, units of output per day.

Par. 103. The selection of the appropriate concept of capital by an entity should be based on the needs of the users of its financial statements. Thus, a financial concept of capital should be adopted if the users of financial statements are primarily concerned with the maintenance of nominal invested capital or the purchasing power of invested capital. If, however, the main concern of users is with the operating capability of the entity, a physical concept of capital should be used. The concept chosen indicates the goal to be attained in determining profit, even though there may be some measurement difficulties in making the concept operational.

Concepts of Capital Maintenance and the Determination of Profit

Par. 104. The concepts of capital in paragraph 102 give rise to the following two concepts of capital maintenance:

(a) Financial capital maintenance. Under this concept a profit is earned only if the financial (or money) amount of the net assets at the end of the period exceeds the financial (or money) amount of net assets at the beginning of the period, after excluding any distributions to, and contributions from, owners during the period. Financial capital maintenance can be measured in either nominal monetary units or units of constant purchasing power.

(b) Physical capital maintenance. Under this concept a profit is earned only if the physical productive capacity (or operating capability) of the entity (or the resources or funds needed to achieve that capacity) at the end of the period exceeds the physical productive capacity at the beginning of the period, after excluding any distributions to, and contributions from, owners during the period.

The concepts of capital in paragraph 102 give rise to the following three concepts of capital during low inflation and deflation:

- (A) Physical capital.
- (B) Nominal financial capital.
- (C) Constant item purchasing power financial capital.

The concepts of capital in paragraph 102 give rise to the following three concepts of capital maintenance during low inflation and deflation:

(1) Physical capital maintenance: optional during low inflation and deflation. Current Cost Accounting model prescribed by IFRS.

(2) Financial capital maintenance in nominal monetary units (Historical cost accounting): authorized by IFRS but not prescribed—optional during low inflation and deflation. (a) Historical cost accounting. Financial capital maintenance in nominal monetary units per se during inflation and deflation is a fallacy: it is impossible to maintain the real value of financial capital constant with measurement in nominal monetary units per se during inflation and deflation.

(3) Financial capital maintenance in units of constant purchasing power (Capital Maintenance in Units of Constant Purchasing Power): authorized by IFRS but not prescribed—optional during low inflation and deflation. Capital Maintenance in Units of Constant Purchasing

Power is prescribed during hyperinflation in IAS 29: i.e. the restatement of Historical Cost or Current Cost period-end financial statements in terms of the period-end monthly published Consumer Price Index. Only financial capital maintenance in units of constant purchasing power (Capital Maintenance in Units of Constant Purchasing Power) in terms of a daily index per se can automatically maintain the real value of financial capital constant at all levels of inflation and deflation in all entities that at least break even in real value—ceteris paribus—for an indefinite period of time. This would happen whether these entities own revaluable fixed assets or not and without the requirement of more capital or additional retained profits to simply maintain the existing constant real value of existing shareholders' equity constant. Financial capital maintenance in units of constant purchasing power requires the calculation and accounting of net monetary losses and gains from holding monetary items during low inflation and deflation. The calculation and accounting of net monetary losses and gains during low inflation and deflation have thus been authorized in IFRS since 1989.

Par. 105. The concept of capital maintenance is concerned with how an entity defines the capital that it seeks to maintain. It provides the linkage between the concepts of capital and the concepts of profit because it provides the point of reference by which profit is measured; it is a prerequisite for distinguishing between an entity's return on capital and its return of capital; only inflows of assets in excess of amounts needed to maintain capital may be regarded as profit and therefore as a return on capital. Hence, profit is the residual amount that remains after expenses (including capital maintenance adjustments, where appropriate) have been deducted from income. If expenses exceed income the residual amount is a loss.

Par. 106. The physical capital maintenance concept requires the adoption of the current cost basis of measurement. The financial capital maintenance concept, however, does not require the use of a particular basis of measurement. Selection of the basis under this concept is dependent on the type of financial capital that the entity is seeking to maintain.

Par. 107. The principal difference between the two concepts of capital maintenance is the treatment of the effects of changes in the prices of assets and liabilities of the entity. In general terms, an entity has maintained its capital if it has as much capital at the end of the period as it had at the beginning of the period. Any amount over and above that required to maintain the capital at the beginning of the period is profit.

Par. 108. Under the concept of financial capital maintenance where capital is defined in terms of nominal monetary units, profit represents the increase in nominal money capital over the period. Thus, increases in the prices of assets held over the period, conventionally referred to as holding gains, are, conceptually, profits. They may not be recognised as such, however, until the assets are disposed of in an exchange transaction. When the concept of financial capital maintenance is defined in terms of constant purchasing power units, profit represents the increase in invested purchasing power over the period. Thus, only that part of the increase in the prices of assets that exceeds the increase in the general level of prices is regarded as profit. The rest of the increase is treated as a capital maintenance adjustment and, hence, as part of equity.

Par. 109. Under the concept of physical capital maintenance when capital is defined in terms of the physical productive capacity, profit represents the increase in that capital over the period. All price changes affecting the assets and liabilities of the entity are viewed as changes in the measurement of the physical productive capacity of the entity; hence, they are treated as capital maintenance adjustments that are part of equity and not as profit.

Par. 110. The selection of the measurement bases and concept of capital maintenance will determine the accounting model used in the preparation of the financial statements. Different accounting models exhibit different degrees of relevance and reliability and, as in other areas, management must seek a balance between relevance and reliability. This Framework is applicable to a range of accounting models and provides guidance on preparing and presenting the financial statements constructed under the chosen model. At the present time, it is not the intention of the Board of IASC to prescribe a particular model other than in exceptional circumstances, such as for those entities reporting in the currency of a hyperinflationary economy. This intention will, however, be reviewed in the light of world developments.

Requirements

- a Statement of Financial Position
- a Statement of Comprehensive Income separate statements comprising an Income Statement and separately a Statement of Comprehensive Income, which reconciles Profit or Loss on the Income statement to total comprehensive income
- a Statement of Changes in Equity (SOCE)
- a Cash Flow Statement or Statement of Cash Flows
- notes, including a summary of the significant accounting policies

Comparative information is required for the prior reporting period (IAS 1.36). An entity preparing IFRS accounts for the first time must apply IFRS in full for the current and comparative period although there are transitional exemptions (IFRS1.7).

On 6 September 2007, the IASB issued a revised IAS 1 Presentation of Financial Statements. The main changes from the previous version are to require that an entity must:

- present all non-owner changes in equity (that is, 'comprehensive income') *either* in one Statement of comprehensive income or in two statements (a separate income statement and a statement of comprehensive income). Components of comprehensive income may *not* be presented in the Statement of changes in equity.
- present a statement of financial position (balance sheet) as at the beginning of the earliest comparative period in a complete set of financial statements when the entity applies the new standard.
- present a statement of cash flow.
- make necessary disclosure by the way of a note.

The revised IAS 1 is effective for annual periods beginning on or after 1 January 2009. Early adoption is permitted.

Criticisms of IFRS

In 2012 the US Securities and Exchange Commission Staff issued a 127-page report of potential issues with IFRS that would need to be addressed before adoption by the United States. The staff of the IFRS Foundation provided a detailed answer on the main criticisms in the SEC staff report.

A number of criticisms were voiced in the beginning of 2013 in the French media to which the IASB Board member Philippe Danjou responded in his document 'An Update on International Financial Reporting Standards (IFRSs).'

It is widely acknowledged that *IAS 29 Financial Reporting in Hyperinflationary Economies* had no positive effect during the six years it was implemented during hyperinflation in Zimbabwe. This led people to ask the purpose of IAS 29. As of March 2014, IAS 29 was being implemented in its original ineffective form in Venezuela and Belarus. It was suggested to the IASB in 2012 that IAS 29 should be corrected to require daily indexation which would result in effective constant purchasing power accounting and would stabilize the non-monetary economy during hyperinflation. The IASB has offered no response to date (March 2014) to this criticism and has not yet altered IAS 29 to require daily indexation.

Adoption

IFRS are used in many parts of the world, including the South Korea, European Union, India, Hong Kong, Australia, Malaysia, Pakistan, GCC countries, Russia, Chile, Philippines, South Africa, Singapore and Turkey, but not in the United States. Please refer to PricewaterhouseCoopers' "IFRS by country" publication for a detailed explanation of the level of IFRS adoption per country. 140 Jurisdiction profiles are available online.

It is generally expected that IFRS adoption worldwide will be beneficial to investors and other users of financial statements, by reducing the costs of comparing alternative investments and increasing the quality of information. Companies are also expected to benefit, as investors will be more willing to provide financing. Companies that have high levels of international activities are among the group that would benefit from a switch to IFRS. Companies that are involved in foreign activities and investing benefit from the switch due to the increased comparability of a set accounting standard. However, Ray J. Ball has expressed some skepticism of the overall cost of the international standard; he argues that the enforcement of the standards could be lax, and the regional differences in accounting could become obscured behind a label. He also expressed concerns about the fair value emphasis of IFRS and the influence of accountants from non-common-law regions, where losses have been recognized in a less timely manner.

To assess progress towards the goal of a single set global accounting standards, the IFRS Foundation has developed and posted profiles about the use of IFRSs in individual jurisdictions. These were based on information from various sources. The starting point was the responses provided by standard-setting and other relevant bodies to a survey that the IFRS Foundation conducted. Currently, profiles are completed for 124 jurisdictions, including all of the G20 jurisdictions plus 104 others. Eventually, the plan is to have a profile for every jurisdiction that has adopted IFRSs, or is on a programme toward adoption of IFRSs.

Australia

The Australian Accounting Standards Board (AASB) has issued 'Australian equivalents to IFRS' (A-IFRS), numbering IFRS standards as AASB 1–8 and IAS standards as AASB 101–141. Australian equivalents to SIC and IFRIC Interpretations have also been issued, along with a number of 'domestic' standards and interpretations. These pronouncements replaced previous Australian generally accepted accounting principles with effect from annual reporting periods beginning on or after 1 January 2005 (i.e. 30 June 2006 was the first report prepared under IFRS-equivalent standards for June year ends). To this end, Australia, along with Europe and a few other countries, was one of the initial adopters of IFRS for domestic purposes (in the developed world). It must be acknowledged, however, that IFRS and primarily IAS have been part and parcel of accounting standard package in the developing world for many years since the relevant accounting bodies were more open to adoption of international standards for many reasons including that of capability.

The AASB has made certain amendments to the IASB pronouncements in making A-IFRS, however these generally have the effect of eliminating an option under IFRS, introducing additional disclosures or implementing requirements for not-for-profit entities, rather than departing from IFRS for Australian entities. Accordingly, for-profit entities that prepare financial statements in accordance with A-IFRS are able to make an unreserved statement of compliance with IFRS.

The AASB continues to mirror changes made by the IASB as local pronouncements. In addition, over recent years, the AASB has issued so-called 'Amending Standards' to reverse some of the initial changes made to the IFRS text for local terminology differences, to reinstate options and eliminate some Australian-specific disclosure. There are some calls for Australia to simply adopt IFRS without 'Australianising' them and this has resulted in the AASB itself looking at alternative ways of adopting IFRS in Australia.

Brazil

Brazil has already adopted IFRS for all companies whose securities are publicly traded and for most financial institutions whose securities are not publicly traded, for both consolidated and separate (individual) company financial statements.

Canada

The use of IFRS became a requirement for Canadian publicly accountable profit-oriented enterprises for financial periods beginning on or after 1 January 2011. This includes public companies and other "profit-oriented enterprises that are responsible to large or diverse groups of shareholders."

European Union

In 2002 the European Union agreed that from 1 January 2005 International Accounting Standards / International Financial Reporting Standards would apply for the consolidated accounts of the EU listed companies.

In order to be approved for use in the EU, standards must be endorsed by the Accounting Regulatory Committee (ARC), which includes representatives of member state governments and is advised by a group of accounting experts known as the European Financial Reporting Advisory Group. As a result, IFRS as applied in the EU may differ from that used elsewhere.

Parts of the standard IAS 39: Financial Instruments: Recognition and Measurement were not originally approved by the ARC. IAS 39 was subsequently amended, removing the option to record financial liabilities at fair value, and the ARC approved the amended version. The IASB is working with the EU to find an acceptable way to remove a remaining anomaly in respect of hedge accounting. The World Bank Centre for Financial Reporting Reform is working with countries in the ECA region to facilitate the adoption of IFRS and IFRS for SMEs.

Whilst the IASB set the effective dates for the new consolidation standards IFRS 10 *Consolidated Financial Statements*, IFRS 11 *Joint Arrangements* and IFRS 12 *Disclosure of Interests in Other Entities* at 1 January 2013, the ARC decided to delay the mandatory effective date for the companies listed in the European Union by one year. The standards therefore only became effective on 1 January 2014.

The European Commission has launched a general analysis of the impacts of 8 years of use of international financial reporting standards (IFRSs) in the EU for preparers and users of financial statements from the private sector. The study will include an overall assessment of whether the Regulation 1606/2002 of the European Parliament and the Council ('IAS Regulation') has met the two-fold initial objectives of ensuring a high degree of transparency and comparability of the financial statements of European companies and an efficient functioning of the market, in comparison with the situation before IFRS implementation in 2005. It will also include a cost-benefit analysis and an assessment and analysis of the benefits and drawbacks brought by the IAS Regulation for different stakeholder groups.

Ghana

Ghana transitioned from the Ghana Accounting Standards (GAS) to adopt the IFRS on January 1, 2007. As of 2008 and beyond, a legislative injunction has been imposed on the Bank of Ghana to prepare financial statements in accordance with IFRS; thereby making it mandatory for all public entities in the country.

India

The Institute of Chartered Accountants of India (ICAI) has announced that IFRS will be mandatory in India for financial statements for the periods beginning on or after 1 April 2016 in a phased manner. There is a roadmap issued by MCA for adoption of IFRS.

Reserve Bank of India has stated that financial statements of banks need to be IFRS-compliant for periods beginning on or after 1 April 2011.

The ICAI has also stated that IFRS will be applied to companies above INR 1000 crore (INR 10 billion) from April 2011. Phase wise applicability details for different companies in India:

Phase 1: Opening balance sheet as at 1 April 2011*

i. Companies which are part of NSE Index – Nifty 50

ii. Companies which are part of BSE Index – Sensex 30

a. Companies whose shares or other securities are listed on a stock exchange outside India

b. Companies, whether listed or not, having net worth of more than INR 1000 crore (INR 10 billion)

Phasc 2: Opening balance sheet as at 1 April 2012*

Companies not covered in phase 1 and having net worth exceeding INR 500 crore (INR 5 billion)

Phase 3: Opening balance sheet as at 1 April 2014*

Listed companies not covered in the earlier phases * If the financial year of a company commences at a date other than 1 April, then it shall prepare its opening balance sheet at the commencement of immediately following financial year.

On 22 January 2010, the Ministry of Corporate Affairs issued the road map for transition to IFRS. It is clear that India has deferred transition to IFRS by a year. In the first phase, companies included in Nifty 50 or BSE Sensex, and companies whose securities are listed on stock exchanges outside India and all other companies having net worth of INR 10 billion will prepare and present financial statements using Indian Accounting Standards converged with IFRS. According to the press note issued by the government, those companies will convert their first balance sheet as at 1 April 2011, applying accounting standards convergent with IFRS if the accounting year ends on 31 March. This implies that the transition date will be 1 April 2011. According to the earlier plan, the transition date was fixed at 1 April 2010.

The press note does not clarify whether the full set of financial statements for the year 2011–12 will be prepared by applying accounting standards convergent with IFRS. The deferment of the transition may make companies happy, but it will undermine India's position. Presumably, lack of preparedness of Indian companies has led to the decision to defer the adoption of IFRS for a year. This is unfortunate that India, which boasts for its IT and accounting skills, could not prepare itself for the transition to IFRS over last four years. But that might be the ground reality.

Transition in Phases

Companies, whether listed or not, having net worth of more than INR 5 billion will convert their opening balance sheet as at 1 April 2013. Listed companies having net worth of INR 5 billion or less will convert their opening balance sheet as at 1 April 2014. Un-listed companies having net worth of Rs5 billion or less will continue to apply existing accounting standards, which might be modified from time to time. Transition to IFRS in phases is a smart move.

The transition cost for smaller companies will be much lower because large companies will bear the initial cost of learning and smaller companies will not be required to reinvent the wheel. However, this will happen only if a significant number of large companies engage Indian accounting firms to provide them support in their transition to IFRS. If, most large companies, which will comply with Indian accounting standards convergent with IFRS in the first phase, choose one of the international firms, Indian accounting firms and smaller companies will not benefit from the learning in the first phase of the transition to IFRS.

It is likely that international firms will protect their learning to retain their competitive advantage. Therefore, it is for the benefit of the country that each company makes judicious choice of the accounting firm as its partner without limiting its choice to international accounting firms. Public sector companies should take the lead and the Institute of Chartered Accountants of India (ICAI) should develop a clear strategy to diffuse the learning.

Size of Companies

The government has decided to measure the size of companies in terms of net worth. This is not the ideal unit to measure the size of a company. Net worth in the balance sheet is determined by accounting principles and methods. Therefore, it does not include the value of intangible assets. Moreover, as most assets and liabilities are measured at historical cost, the net worth does not reflect the current value of those assets and liabilities. Market capitalisation is a better measure of the size of a company. But it is difficult to estimate market capitalisation or fundamental value of unlisted companies. This might be the reason that the government has decided to use 'net worth' to measure size of companies. Some companies, which are large in terms of fundamental value or which intend to attract foreign capital, might prefer to use Indian accounting standards convergent with IFRS earlier than required under the road map presented by the government. The government should provide that choice.

Japan

The minister for Financial Services in Japan announced in late June 2011 that mandatory application of the IFRS should not take place from fiscal year-ending March 2015; five to seven years should be required for preparation if mandatory application is decided; and to permit the use of U.S. GAAP beyond the fiscal year ending 31 March 2016.

Montenegro

Montenegro gained independence from Serbia in 2006. Its accounting standard setter is the Institute of Accountants and Auditors of Montenegro (IAAM). In 2005, IAAM adopted a revised version of the 2002 "Law on Accounting and Auditing" which authorized the use of IFRS for all entities. IFRS is currently required for all consolidated and standalone financial statements, however, enforcement is not effective except in the banking sector. Financial statements for banks in Montenegro are, generally, of high quality and can be compared to those of the European Union. Foreign companies listed on Montenegro's two stock exchanges (Montenegro Stock Exchange and NEX Stock Exchange) are also required to apply IFRS in their financial statements. Montenegro does not have a national GAAP. Currently, no Montenegrin translation of IFRS exists, and because of this Montenegro applies the Serbian translation from 2010. IFRS for SMEs is not currently applied in Montenegro.

Nepal

In Nepal the Accounting Standards Board (ASB) is in charge of standard setting. Nepal closely models its Financial Reporting Standards (FRS) according to the IFRS, with appropriate changes made to suit the Nepalese context. It has issued Nepal Financial Reporting Standards in 2013. The 2013 version of standards almost resembles IFRS with slight modification.

Pakistan

All listed companies must follow all issued IAS/IFRS except the following:

IAS 39 and IAS 41: Implementation of these standards has been held in abeyancc by State Bank of Pakistan for Banks and DFIs

IFRS-1: Effective for the annual periods beginning on or after 1 January 2004. This IFRS is being considered for adoption for all companies other than banks and DFIs.

IFRS-9: Under consideration of the relevant Committee of the Institutes (ICAP & ICMAP). This IFRS will be effective for the annual periods beginning on or after 1 January 2013.

Russia

The government of Russia has been implementing a program to harmonize its national accounting standards with IFRS since 1998. Since then twenty new accounting standards were issued by the Ministry of Finance of the Russian Federation aiming to align accounting practices with IFRS. Despite these efforts essential differences between Russian accounting standards and IFRS remain. Since 2004 all commercial banks have been obliged to prepare financial statements in accordance with both Russian accounting standards and IFRS. Full transition to IFRS is delayed but starting 2012 new modifications making Russian GAAP converging to IFRS have been made. They notably include the booking of reserves for bad debts and contingent liabilities and the devaluation of inventory and financial assets.

Still, several differences between the two sets of account still remain. Major reasons for deviation between Russian GAAP and IFRS / US-GAAP (e.g. when the Russian affiliate of a larger group need to be consolidated to the mother company) are the following:

1. Booking of payables in the General Ledger according to national accounting standards can only be made upon receipt of the actual acceptance protocol (good's receipt). Indeed, in Russia, in contrast to IFRS and US-GAAP, the invoice (outgoing or incoming) is not an official tax or accounting document and does not trigger any booking. There is also no provision to book in the General Ledger any expense for goods and services that according to a contract are effectively received but for whom documents are still not exchanged.
2. There is no possibility under Russian GAAP to recognise the good-will as an intangible asset in the balance sheet of a company. This has a major consequence when a company is sold. Indeed, if a company (or part of it) is sold at a higher value than its book value (i.e. to account for the good-will value), the selling party need to pay tax at the relevant profit tax rate (20% in 2013) on the difference in value between selling and accounting value and the buyer has no possibility to amortize the cost and deduct it from present and future revenues.
3. There is no equivalent of IAS 37 in the Russian GAAP. Loans and monetary securities are not discounted, so the present value of such financial assets is not discounted for the relevant interest rates at the different maturities of the loans.

Singapore

In Singapore the Accounting Standards Committee (ASC) is in charge of standard setting. Singapore closely models its Financial Reporting Standards (FRS) according to the IFRS, with appropriate changes made to suit the Singapore context. Before a standard is enacted, consultations with the IASB are made to ensure consistency of core principles.

South Africa

All companies listed on the Johannesburg Stock Exchange have been required to comply with the requirements of International Financial Reporting Standards since 1 January 2005.

The IFRS for SMEs may be applied by 'limited interest companies', as defined in the South African Corporate Laws Amendment Act of 2006 (that is, they are not 'widely held'), if they do not have public accountability (that is, not listed and not a financial institution). Alternatively, the company may choose to apply full South African Statements of GAAP or IFRS.

South African Statements of GAAP are entirely consistent with IFRS, although there may be a delay between issuance of an IFRS and the equivalent SA Statement of GAAP (can affect voluntary early adoption).

Taiwan

Adoption scope and timetable

(1) Phase I companies: listed companies and financial institutions supervised by the Financial Supervisory Commission (FSC), except for credit cooperatives, credit card companies and insurance intermediaries:

A. They will be required to prepare financial statements in accordance with Taiwan-IFRS starting from 1 January 2013.

B. Early optional adoption: Firms that have already issued securities overseas, or have registered an overseas securities issuance with the FSC, or have a market capitalization of greater than NT$10 billion, will be permitted to prepare additional consolidated financial statements in accordance with Taiwan-IFRS starting from 1 January 2012. If a company without subsidiaries is not required to prepare consolidated financial statements, it will be permitted to prepare additional individual financial statements on the above conditions.

(2) Phase II companies: unlisted public companies, credit cooperatives and credit card companies:

A. They will be required to prepare financial statements in accordance with Taiwan-IFRS starting from 1 January 2019

B. They will be permitted to apply Taiwan-IFRS starting from 1 January 2013.

(3) Pre-disclosure about the IFRS adoption plan, and the impact of adoption

To prepare properly for IFRS adoption, domestic companies should propose an IFRS adoption plan and establish a specific taskforce. They should also disclose the related information from 2 years prior to adoption, as follows:

A. Phase I companies:

(A) They will be required to disclose the adoption plan, and the impact of adoption, in 2011 annual financial statements, and in 2012 interim and annual financial statements.

(B) Early optional adoption:

a. Companies adopting IFRS early will be required to disclose the adoption plan, and the impact of adoption, in 2010 annual financial statements, and in 2011 interim and annual financial statements.

b. If a company opts for early adoption of Taiwan-IFRS after 1 January 2011, it will be required to disclose the adoption plan, and the impact of adoption, in 2011 interim and annual financial statements commencing on the decision date.

B. Phase II companies will be required to disclose the related information from 2 years prior to adoption, as stated above.

Year Work Plan

2008

- Establishment of IFRS Taskforce

2009~2011

- Acquisition of authorization to translate IFRS
- Translation, review, and issuance of IFRS
- Analysis of possible IFRS implementation problems, and resolution thereof
- Proposal for modification of the related regulations and supervisory mechanisms
- Enhancement of related publicity and training activities

2012

- IFRS application permitted for Phase I companies
- Study on possible IFRS implementation problems, and resolution thereof
- Completion of amendments to the related regulations and supervisory mechanisms
- Enhancement of the related publicity and training activities

2013

- Application of IFRS required for Phase I companies, and permitted for Phase II companies

- Follow-up analysis of the status of IFRS adoption, and of the impact

2014

- Follow-up analysis of the status of IFRS adoption, and of the impact

2015

- Applications of IFRS required for Phase II companies

Expected Benefits

(1) More efficient formulation of domestic accounting standards, improvement of their international image, and enhancement of the global rankings and international competitiveness of our local capital markets;

(2) Better comparability between the financial statements of local and foreign companies;

(3) No need for restatement of financial statements when local companies wish to issue overseas securities, resulting in reduction in the cost of raising capital overseas;

(4) For local companies with investments overseas, use of a single set of accounting standards will reduce the cost of account conversions and improve corporate efficiency.

Above is quoted from Accounting Research and Development Foundation.

Turkey

The Banking Regulation and Supervision Agency and Capital Markets Board of Turkey translated IFRS into Turkish in 2002. Banks and Turkish companies listed on the Istanbul Stock Exchange are required to prepare IFRS reports since then. The Turkish Accounting Standards Board (called the Public Oversight Authority after 2011) also translated IFRS in 2005. The new Commercial Code came into force in 2012. The Public Oversight Authority is the only authorized board regarding auditing and financial reporting standards. Most businesses authorized by the Council of Ministers in addition to banks and Turkish companies listed on the Istanbul Stock Exchange are required to prepare IFRS reports since 2012.

Zimbabwe

Zimbabwe also adopted IFRS.

IASs

- IAS 1 Presentation of Financial Statements.
- IAS 2 Inventories.
- IAS 7 Cash Flow Statements.
- IAS 8 Accounting Policies, Changes in Accounting Estimates and Errors.

- IAS 10 Events After the Balance Sheet Date.
- IAS 11 Construction Contracts.
- IAS 12 Income Taxes.
- IAS 16 Property,Plant and Equipment.
- IAS 17 Leases.
- IAS 18 Revenue.
- IAS 19 Employee Benefits.
- IAS 20 Accounting for Government Grants and Disclosure of Government Assistance.
- IAS 21 The Effects of Changes in Foreign Exchange Rates.
- IAS 23 Borrowing Costs.
- IAS 24 Related Party Disclosures.
- IAS 26 Accounting and Reporting by Retirement Benefit Plans.
- IAS 27 Consolidated and Separate Financial Statements.
- IAS 28 Investments in Associates.
- IAS 29 Financial Reporting in Hyperinflationary Economies.
- IAS 31 Interests in Joint Ventures.
- IAS 32 Financial Instruments: Presentation.
- IAS 33 Earnings per Share.
- IAS 34 Interim Financial Reporting.
- IAS 36 Impairment of Assets.
- IAS 37 Provisions, Contingent Liabilities and Contingent Assets.
- IAS 38 Intangible Assets.
- IAS 39 Financial Instruments: Recognition and Measurement.
- IAS 40 Investment Property.
- IAS 41 Agriculture.

GAAP

- To avoid confusion and to achieve uniformity, accounting process is applied within the conceptual framework of 'Generally Accepted Accounting Principles' (GAAP).

- The Financial Statements of entity cannot be said to be showing a true and fair view, unless these Financial Statements have been drawn up on GAAP.
- GAAP consist of four components.
    - The requirements of law.
    - The judgments by courts of law.
    - Pronouncement by the governing bodies (Like ICAI, FASB in US).
    - Requirements of regulatory authority (Like RBI, SEBI, SEC in US).
- GAAPs are the backbone of the accounting information system, without which whole system cannot even stand erectly.
- GAAPs and Accounting Standard are considered as the theory base of accounting.

References

- Jerry J. Weygandt; Paul D. Kimmel; Donald E. Kieso (5 January 2010). Accounting Principles. John Wiley and Sons. p. 608. ISBN 978-0-470-57725-7. Retrieved 3 April 2012
- Heinkel, R. & Zechner, J. (1990), "The Role of Debt and Preferred Stock as a Solution to Adverse Investment Incentives", Journal of Financial and Quantitative Analysis, 25 (1): 1–24 [p. 2], doi:10.2307/2330885
- Wallace W. Kravitz (1 September 1999). Bookkeeping the Easy Way. Barron's Educational Series. pp. 119–120. ISBN 978-0-7641-1079-5. Retrieved 6 April 2012
- "Stammaktie, Vorzugsaktie, Inhaberaktie, Namensakti Die Arten von Aktien" (in German). 2004-03-24. Retrieved 6 May 2010
- Claudia B. Gilbertson; Mark W. Lehman (12 March 2008). Fundamentals of Accounting: Course 1. Cengage Learning. p. 242. ISBN 978-0-538-44826-0. Retrieved 6 April 2012
- Jan Bebbington; Rob Gray; Richard Laughlin (16 August 2001). Financial accounting: practice and principles. Cengage Learning EMEA. p. 6. ISBN 978-1-86152-771-4. Retrieved 6 April 2012
- "AcSB Confirms Changeover Date to IFRSs". Canadian Institute of Chartered Accountants. 13 February 2008. Retrieved 8 August 2009

3

Basics of Financial Statement

A financial statement is the formal record of the financial activities of a company or a person. Its purposes include balance sheet, statement of change in equity, income statement, profit and loss account and cash flow statement. The profit and loss account calculates the profit or loss incurred by a company or a person. Income can be defined as benefits made in terms of inflows, increase in asset or decrease in liability. The major components of financial statements and profit and loss account are discussed in this chapter.

Financial Statement

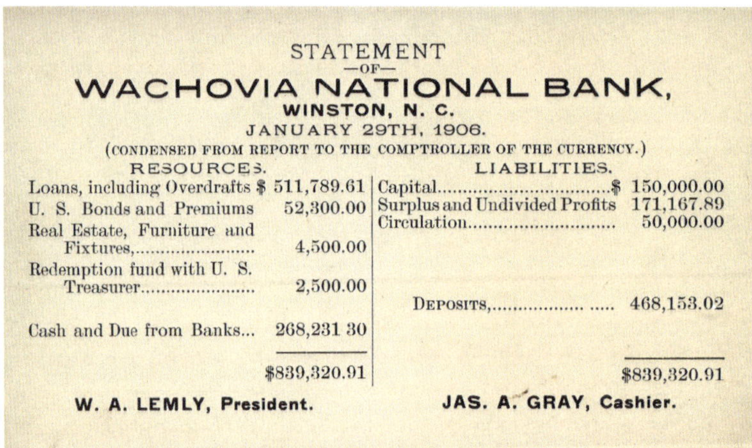

STATEMENT
—OF—
WACHOVIA NATIONAL BANK,
WINSTON, N. C.
JANUARY 29TH, 1906.
(CONDENSED FROM REPORT TO THE COMPTROLLER OF THE CURRENCY.)

RESOURCES.		LIABILITIES.	
Loans, including Overdrafts	$ 511,789.61	Capital	$ 150,000.00
U. S. Bonds and Premiums	52,300.00	Surplus and Undivided Profits	171,167.89
Real Estate, Furniture and Fixtures,	4,500.00	Circulation	50,000.00
Redemption fund with U. S. Treasurer	2,500.00	Deposits,	468,153.02
Cash and Due from Banks	268,231 30		
	$839,320.91		$839,320.91

W. A. LEMLY, President. JAS. A. GRAY, Cashier.

Historical financial statements

A financial statements (or financial report) is a formal record of the financial activities and position of a business, person, or other entity.

Relevant financial information is presented in a structured manner and in a form easy to understand. They typically include basic financial statements, accompanied by a management discussion and analysis:

1. A balance sheet, also referred to as a statement of financial position, reports on a company's assets, liabilities, and owners equity at a given point in time.
2. An income statement, also known as a statement of comprehensive income, statement of revenue & expense, P&L or profit and loss report, reports on a company's income, expenses, and profits over a period of time. A profit and loss statement provides information on the operation of the enterprise. These include sales and the various expenses incurred during the stated period.

3. A Statement of changes in equity, also known as equity statement or statement of retained earnings, reports on the changes in equity of the company during the stated period.

4. A cash flow statement reports on a company's cash flow activities, particularly its operating, investing and financing activities.

For large corporations, these statements may be complex and may include an extensive set of footnotes to the financial statements and management discussion and analysis. The notes typically describe each item on the balance sheet, income statement and cash flow statement in further detail. Notes to financial statements are considered an integral part of the financial statements.

Purpose for Business Entities

"The objective of financial statements is to provide information about the financial position, performance and changes in financial position of an enterprise that is useful to a wide range of users in making economic decisions." Financial statements should be understandable, relevant, reliable and comparable. Reported assets, liabilities, equity, income and expenses are directly related to an organization's financial position.

Financial statements are intended to be understandable by readers who have "a reasonable knowledge of business and economic activities and accounting and who are willing to study the information diligently." Financial statements may be used by users for different purposes:

- Owners and managers require financial statements to make important business decisions that affect its continued operations. Financial analysis is then performed on these statements to provide management with a more detailed understanding of the figures. These statements are also used as part of management's annual report to the stockholders.
- Employees also need these reports in making collective bargaining agreements (CBA) with the management, in the case of labor unions or for individuals in discussing their compensation, promotion and rankings.
- Prospective investors make use of financial statements to assess the viability of investing in a business. Financial analyses are often used by investors and are prepared by professionals (financial analysts), thus providing them with the basis for making investment decisions.
- Financial institutions (banks and other lending companies) use them to decide whether to grant a company with fresh working capital or extend debt securities (such as a long-term bank loan or debentures) to finance expansion and other significant expenditures.

Consolidated

Consolidated financial statements are defined as "Financial statements of a group in which the assets, liabilities, equity, income, expenses and cash flows of the parent (company) and its subsidiaries are presented as those of a single economic entity", according to International Accounting Standard 27 "Consolidated and separate financial statements", and International Financial Reporting Standard 10 "Consolidated financial statements".

Government

The rules for the recording, measurement and presentation of government financial statements may be different from those required for business and even for non-profit organizations. They may use either of two accounting methods: accrual accounting, or cost accounting, or a combination of the two (OCBOA). A complete set of chart of accounts is also used that is substantially different from the chart of a profit-oriented business.

Personal

Personal financial statements may be required from persons applying for a personal loan or financial aid. Typically, a personal financial statement consists of a single form for reporting personally held assets and liabilities (debts), or personal sources of income and expenses, or both. The form to be filled out is determined by the organization supplying the loan or aid.

Audit and Legal Implications

Although laws differ from country to country, an audit of the financial statements of a public company is usually required for investment, financing, and tax purposes. These are usually performed by independent accountants or auditing firms. Results of the audit are summarized in an audit report that either provide an unqualified opinion on the financial statements or qualifications as to its fairness and accuracy. The audit opinion on the financial statements is usually included in the annual report.

There has been much legal debate over who an auditor is liable to. Since audit reports tend to be addressed to the current shareholders, it is commonly thought that they owe a legal duty of care to them. But this may not be the case as determined by common law precedent. In Canada, auditors are liable only to investors using a prospectus to buy shares in the primary market. In the United Kingdom, they have been held liable to potential investors when the auditor was aware of the potential investor and how they would use the information in the financial statements. Nowadays auditors tend to include in their report liability restricting language, discouraging anyone other than the addressees of their report from relying on it. Liability is an important issue: in the UK, for example, auditors have unlimited liability.

In the United States, especially in the post-Enron era there has been substantial concern about the accuracy of financial statements. Corporate officers (the chief executive officer (CEO) and chief financial officer (CFO)) are personally responsible for fair financial reporting allowing those reading the report to have a good sense of the organization.

Standards and Regulations

Different countries have developed their own accounting principles over time, making international comparisons of companies difficult. To ensure uniformity and comparability between financial statements prepared by different companies, a set of guidelines and rules are used. Commonly referred to as Generally Accepted Accounting Principles (GAAP), these set of guidelines provide the basis in the preparation of financial statements, although many companies voluntarily disclose information beyond the scope of such requirements.

Recently there has been a push towards standardizing accounting rules made by the International Accounting Standards Board ("IASB"). IASB develops International Financial Reporting Standards that have been adopted by Australia, Canada and the European Union (for publicly quoted companies only), are under consideration in South Africa and other countries. The United States Financial Accounting Standards Board has made a commitment to converge the U.S. GAAP and IFRS over time.

Inclusion in Annual Reports

To entice new investors, public companies assemble their financial statements on fine paper with pleasing graphics and photos in an annual report to shareholders, attempting to capture the excitement and culture of the organization in a "marketing brochure" of sorts. Usually the company's chief executive will write a letter to shareholders, describing management's performance and the company's financial highlights.

In the United States, prior to the advent of the internet, the annual report was considered the most effective way for corporations to communicate with individual shareholders. Blue chip companies went to great expense to produce and mail out attractive annual reports to every shareholder. The annual report was often prepared in the style of a coffee table book.

Notes

Notes to financial statements (notes) are additional information added to the end of financial statements that help explain specific items in the statements as well as provide a more comprehensive assessment of a company's financial condition. Notes to financial statements can include information on debt, going concern criteria, accounts, contingent liabilities or contextual information explaining the financial numbers (e.g. to indicate a lawsuit).

The notes clarify individual statement line-items. For example, if a company lists a loss on a fixed asset impairment line in their income statement, notes could state the reason for the impairment by describing how the asset became impaired. Notes are also used to explain the accounting methods used to prepare the statements and they support valuations for how particular accounts have been computed.

In consolidated financial statements, all subsidiaries are listed as well as the amount of ownership (controlling interest) that the parent company has in the subsidiaries. Any items within the financial statements that are valuated by estimation are part of the notes if a substantial difference exists between the amount of the estimate previously reported and the actual result. Full disclosure of the effects of the differences between the estimate and actual results should be included.

Management Discussion and Analysis

Management discussion and analysis or MD&A is an integrated part of a company's annual financial statements. The purpose of the MD&A is to provide a narrative explanation, through the eyes of management, of how an entity has performed in the past, its financial condition, and its future prospects. In so doing, the MD&A attempt to provide investors with complete, fair, and balanced information to help them decide whether to invest or continue to invest in an entity.

The section contains a description of the year gone by and some of the key factors that influenced the business of the company in that year, as well as a fair and unbiased overview of the company's past, present, and future.

MD&A typically describes the corporation's liquidity position, capital resources, results of its operations, underlying causes of material changes in financial statement items (such as asset impairment and restructuring charges), events of unusual or infrequent nature (such as mergers and acquisitions or share buybacks), positive and negative trends, effects of inflation, domestic and international market risks, and significant uncertainties.

Moving to Electronic

Financial statements have been created on paper for hundreds of years. The growth of the Web has seen more and more financial statements created in an electronic form which is exchangeable over the Web. Common forms of electronic financial statements are PDF and HTML. These types of electronic financial statements have their drawbacks in that it still takes a human to read the information in order to reuse the information contained in a financial statement.

More recently a market driven global standard, XBRL (Extensible Business Reporting Language), which can be used for creating financial statements in a structured and computer readable format, has become more popular as a format for creating financial statements. Many regulators around the world such as the U.S. Securities and Exchange Commission have mandated XBRL for the submission of financial information.

The UN/CEFACT created, with respect to Generally Accepted Accounting Principles, (GAAP), internal or external financial reporting XML messages to be used between enterprises and their partners, such as private interested parties (e.g. bank) and public collecting bodies (e.g. taxation authorities). Many regulators use such messages to collect financial and economic information.

Financial statements are records that provide an information of an individual's, organization's, or business' financial status.

They are normally prepared general or specific purposes.

General purpose Financial Statement examples

- Balance Sheet.
- Profit and Loss A/c.

- Cash Flow Statement.
- Fund Flow Statement.
- Segment Revenue Report.

Specific purpose Financial Statement examples

- Departmental Budget.
- Computation prepared for Income Tax Purpose.

Balance Sheet

In financial accounting, a balance sheet or statement of financial position is a summary of the financial balances of an individual or organisation, whether it be a sole proprietorship, a business partnership, a corporation, private limited company or other organization such as Government or not-for-profit entity. Assets, liabilities and ownership equity are listed as of a specific date, such as the end of its financial year. A balance sheet is often described as a "snapshot of a company's financial condition". Of the four basic financial statements, the balance sheet is the only statement which applies to a single point in time of a business' calendar year.

A standard company balance sheet has two sides: assets, on the left and financing, which itself has two parts, liabilities and ownership equity, on the right. The main categories of assets are usually listed first, and typically in order of liquidity. Assets are followed by the liabilities. The difference between the assets and the liabilities is known as equity or the net assets or the net worth or capital of the company and according to the accounting equation, net worth must equal assets minus liabilities.

Another way to look at the balance sheet equation is that total assets equals liabilities plus owner's equity. Looking at the equation in this way shows how assets were financed: either by borrowing money (liability) or by using the owner's money (owner's or shareholders' equity). Balance sheets are usually presented with assets in one section and liabilities and net worth in the other section with the two sections "balancing".

A business operating entirely in cash can measure its profits by withdrawing the entire bank balance at the end of the period, plus any cash in hand. However, many businesses are not paid immediately; they build up inventories of goods and they acquire buildings and equipment. In other words: businesses have assets and so they cannot, even if they want to, immediately turn these into cash at the end of each period. Often, these businesses owe money to suppliers and to tax authorities, and the proprietors do not withdraw all their original capital and profits at the end of each period. In other words, businesses also have liabilities.

Types

A balance sheet summarizes an organization or individual's assets, equity and liabilities at a specific point in time. Two forms of balance sheet exist. They are the report form and the account form. Individuals and small businesses tend to have simple balance sheets. Larger businesses tend to have more complex balance sheets, and these are presented in the organization's annual report. Large businesses also may prepare balance sheets for segments of their businesses. A balance sheet is often presented alongside one for a different point in time (typically the previous year) for comparison.

Personal

A personal balance sheet lists current assets such as cash in checking accounts and savings accounts, long-term assets such as common stock and real estate, current liabilities such as loan debt and mortgage debt due, or overdue, long-term liabilities such as mortgage and other loan debt. Securities and real estate values are listed at market value rather than at historical cost or cost basis. Personal net worth is the difference between an individual's total assets and total liabilities.

US Small Business

Sample Small Business Balance Sheet				
Assets (current)		**Liabilities and Owners' Equity**		
Cash	$6,600	**Liabilities**		
Accounts Receivable	$6,200	Notes Payable	$5,000	
Assets (non-current)		Accounts Payable $25,000		
Tools and equipment	$25,000	*Total liabilities*		$30,000
		Owners' equity		
		Capital Stock	$7,000	
		Retained Earnings	$800	
		Total owners' equity		$7,800
Total	$37,800	*Total*		$37,800

A small business balance sheet lists current assets such as cash, accounts receivable, and inventory, fixed assets such as land, buildings, and equipment, intangible assets such as patents, and liabilities such as accounts payable, accrued expenses, and long-term debt. Contingent liabilities such as warranties are noted in the footnotes to the balance sheet. The small business's equity is the difference between total assets and total liabilities.

Public Business Entities Structure

Guidelines for balance sheets of public business entities are given by the International Accounting Standards Board and numerous country-specific organizations/companies. The standard used by companies in the USA adhere to U.S. Generally Accepted Accounting Principles (GAAP). The Federal Accounting Standards Advisory Board (FASAB) is a United States federal advisory committee whose mission is to develop generally accepted accounting principles (GAAP) for federal financial reporting entities.

Balance sheet account names and usage depend on the organization's country and the type of organization. Government organizations do not generally follow standards established for individuals or businesses.

If applicable to the business, summary values for the following items should be included in the balance sheet: Assets are all the things the business owns. This will include property, tools, vehicles, furniture, machinery, and so on.

Assets

Non-current assets (Fixed assets)

1. Property, plant and equipment
2. Investment property, such as real estate held for investment purposes
3. Intangible assets such as (patents, copyrights and goodwill)
4. Financial assets (excluding investments accounted for using the equity method, accounts receivables, and cash and cash equivalents), such as notes receivables
5. Investments accounted for using the equity method
6. Biological assets, which are living plants or animals. Bearer biological assets are plants or animals which bear agricultural produce for harvest, such as apple trees grown to produce apples and sheep raised to produce wool.
7. Loan To (More than one financial period)

Current Assets

1. Prepaid expenses for future services that will be used within a year
2. Accounts receivable
3. Cash and cash equivalents
4. Cash at bank, Petty Cash, Cash On Hand
5. Revenue Earned In Arrears (Accrued Revenue) for services done but not yet received for the year
6. Loan To (Less than one financial period)

Liabilities

1. Accounts payable
2. Provisions for warranties or court decisions (contingent liabilities that are both probable and measurable)
3. Financial liabilities (excluding provisions and accounts payables), such as promissory notes and corporate bonds
4. Liabilities and assets for current tax
5. Deferred tax liabilities and deferred tax assets
6. Unearned revenue for services paid for by customers but not yet provided
7. Interests on loan stock

Equity / capital

The net assets shown by the balance sheet equals the third part of the balance sheet, which is known as the shareholders' equity. It comprises:

1. Issued capital and reserves attributable to equity holders of the parent company (controlling interest)
2. Non-controlling interest in equity

Formally, shareholders' equity is part of the company's liabilities: they are funds "owing" to shareholders (after payment of all other liabilities); usually, however, "liabilities" is used in the more restrictive sense of liabilities excluding shareholders' equity. The balance of assets and liabilities (including shareholders' equity) is not a coincidence. Records of the values of each account in the balance sheet are maintained using a system of accounting known as double-entry bookkeeping. In this sense, shareholders' equity by construction must equal assets minus liabilities, and thus the shareholders' equity is considered to be a residual.

Regarding the items in equity section, the following disclosures are required:

1. Numbers of shares authorized, issued and fully paid, and issued but not fully paid
2. Par value of shares
3. Reconciliation of shares outstanding at the beginning and the end of the period
4. Description of rights, preferences, and restrictions of shares
5. Treasury shares, including shares held by subsidiaries and associates
6. Shares reserved for issuance under options and contracts
7. A description of the nature and purpose of each reserve within owners' equity

Substantiation

Balance sheet substantiation is the accounting process conducted by businesses on a regular basis to confirm that the balances held in the primary accounting system of record (e.g. SAP, Oracle, other ERP system's General Ledger) are reconciled (in balance with) with the balance and transaction records held in the same or supporting sub-systems.

Balance sheet substantiation includes multiple processes including reconciliation (at a transactional or at a balance level) of the account, a process of review of the reconciliation and any pertinent supporting documentation and a formal certification (sign-off) of the account in a predetermined form driven by corporate policy.

Balance sheet substantiation is an important process that is typically carried out on a monthly, quarterly and year-end basis. The results help to drive the regulatory balance sheet reporting obligations of the organization.

Historically, balance sheet substantiation has been a wholly manual process, driven by spreadsheets, email and manual monitoring and reporting. In recent years software solutions have been developed to bring a level of process automation, standardization and enhanced control to the balance sheet substantiation or account certification process. These solutions are suitable for organizations with a high volume of accounts and/or personnel involved in the Balance Sheet Substantiation process and can be used to drive efficiencies, improve transparency and help to reduce risk.

Balance sheet substantiation is a key control process in the SOX 404 top-down risk assessment.

Sample

The following balance sheet is a very brief example prepared in accordance with IFRS. It does not show all possible kinds of assets, liabilities and equity, but it shows the most usual ones. Because it shows goodwill, it could be a consolidated balance sheet. Monetary values are not shown, summary (subtotal) rows are missing as well.

Under IFRS items are always shown based on liquidity from the least liquid assets at the top, usually land and buildings to the most liquid, i.e. cash. Then liabilities and equity continue from the most immediate liability to be paid (usual account payable) to the least i.e. long term debt such a mortgages and owner's equity at the very bottom.

Consolidated Statement of Finance Position of XYZ, Ltd.

As of 31 December 2015

ASSETS

Non-Current Assets (Fixed Assets)

Property, Plant and Equipment **(PPE)**

Less : Accumulated Depreciation

Goodwill

Intangible Assets **(Patent, Copyright, Trademark, etc.)**

Less : Accumulated Amortization

Investments in Financial assets **due after one year**

Investments **in** Associates **and** Joint Ventures

Other Non-Current Assets, e.g. Deferred Tax **Assets,** Lease Receivable **and Receivables due after one year**

Current Assets

Inventories

Prepaid Expenses

Investments in Financial assets due within one year

Non-Current and Current Assets Held for sale

Accounts Receivable (Debtors) due within one year

Less : Allowances for Doubtful debts

Cash and Cash Equivalents

TOTAL ASSETS (this will match/balance the total for Liabilities and Equity below)

LIABILITIES and EQUITY

Current Liabilities (Creditors: amounts falling due within one year)

Accounts Payable

Current Income Tax Payable

Current portion of Loans Payable

Short-term Provisions

Other Current Liabilities, e.g. Deferred income, Security deposits

Non-Current Liabilities (Creditors: amounts falling due after more than one year)

Loans Payable

Issued Debt Securities, e.g. Notes/Bonds Payable

Deferred Tax Liabilities

Provisions, e.g. Pension Obligations

Other Non-Current Liabilities, e.g. Lease Obligations

EQUITY

Paid-in Capital

Share Capital (Ordinary Shares, Preference Shares)

Share Premium

Less: Treasury Shares

Retained Earnings

Revaluation Reserve

Other Accumulated Reserves

Accumulated Other Comprehensive Income

Non-Controlling Interest

TOTAL LIABILITIES and EQUITY (this will match/balance the total for Assets above)

Assets

Fixed Asset

Fixed assets, also known as tangible assets or property, plant, and equipment (PP&E), is a term used in accounting for assets and property that cannot easily be converted into cash. This can be compared with current assets such as cash or bank accounts, which are described as liquid assets. In most cases, only tangible assets are referred to as fixed.

IAS 16 (International Accounting Standard) defines Fixed Assets as assets whose future economic benefit is probable to flow into the entity, whose cost can be measured reliably. Fixed assets belong to one of 2 types: "Freehold Assets" - assets which are purchased with legal right of ownership and used, and "Leasehold Assets" - assets used by owner without legal right for a particular period of time.

Moreover, a fixed/non-current asset can also be defined as an asset not directly sold to a firm's consumers/end-users. As an example, a baking firm's current assets would be its inventory (in this case, flour, yeast, etc.), the value of sales owed to the firm via credit (i.e. debtors or accounts receivable), cash held in the bank, etc. Its non-current assets would be the oven used to bake bread, motor vehicles used to transport deliveries, cash registers used to handle cash payments, etc. While these non-current assets have value, they are not directly sold to consumers and cannot be easily converted to cash.

These are items of value that the organization has bought and will use for an extended period of time; fixed assets normally include items such as land and buildings, motor vehicles, furniture, office equipment, computers, fixtures and fittings, and plant and machinery. These often receive favorable tax treatment (depreciation allowance) over short-term assets.

It is pertinent to note that the cost of a fixed asset is its purchase price, including import duties and other deductible trade discounts and rebates. In addition, cost attributable to bringing and installing the asset in its needed location and the initial estimate of dismantling and removing the item if they are eventually no longer needed on the location.

The primary objective of a business entity is to make profit and increase the wealth of its owners. In the attainment of this objective it is required that the management will exercise due care and diligence in applying the basic accounting concept of "Matching Concept". Matching concept is simply matching the expenses of a period against the revenues of the same period.

The use of assets in the generation of revenue is usually more than a year, i.e. long term. It is therefore obligatory that in order to accurately determine the net income or profit for a period depreciation is charged on the total value of asset that contributed to the revenue for the period in consideration and charge against the same revenue of the same period. This is essential in the prudent reporting of the net revenue for the entity in the period.

Net book value of an asset is basically the difference between the historical cost of that asset and its associated depreciation. From the foregoing, it is apparent that in order to report a true and fair position of the financial jurisprudence of an entity it is relatable to record and report the value of fixed assets at its net book value. Apart from the fact that it is enshrined in Standard Accounting

Statement (SAS) 3 and IAS 16 that value of asset should be carried at the net book value, it is the best way of consciously presenting the value of assets to the owners of the business and potential investor.

Depreciating a Fixed Asset

Depreciation is, simply put, the expense generated by the uses of an asset. It is the wear and tear of an asset or diminution in the historical value owing to usage. Further to this; it is the cost of the asset less any salvage value over its estimated useful life. A fixed asset can be depreciated using the straight line method which is the most common form of depreciation.

Current Asset

In accounting, a current asset is any asset which can reasonably be expected to be sold, consumed, or exhausted through the normal operations of a business within the current fiscal year or operating cycle (whichever period is longer). Typical current assets include cash, cash equivalents, short-term investments (marketable securities), accounts receivable, stock inventory, supplies, and the portion of prepaid liabilities, sometimes referred to as prepaid expenses, which will be paid within a year.

On a balance sheet, assets will typically be classified into current assets and long-term assets.

The current ratio is calculated by dividing total current assets by total current liabilities. It is frequently used as an indicator of a company's liquidity, its ability to meet short-term obligations.

The quick ratio, or acid-test, measures the ability of a company to use its *near cash* or quick assets to extinguish or retire its current liabilities immediately. Quick assets are those that can be quickly turned into cash if necessary.

Investment (Macroeconomics)

In macroeconomics, investment is the amount purchased per unit time of goods which are not consumed at the present time. Types of investment include residential investment in housing that will provide a flow of housing services over an extended time, non-residential fixed investment in things such as new machinery or factories, human capital investment in workforce education, and inventory investment (the accumulation, intentional or unintentional, of goods inventories).

In measures of national income and output, "gross investment" (represented by the variable I) is a component of gross domestic product (GDP), given in the formula GDP = $C + I + G + NX$, where C is consumption, G is government spending, and NX is net exports, given by the difference between the exports and imports, $X - M$. Thus investment is everything that remains of total expenditure after consumption, government spending, and net exports are subtracted (i.e. I = GDP $- C - G - NX$).

"Net investment" deducts depreciation from gross investment. Net fixed investment is the value of the net increase in the capital stock per year.

Fixed investment, as expenditure over a period of time (e.g., "per year"), is not capital but rather leads to changes in the amount of capital. The time dimension of investment makes it a *flow*. By contrast, capital is a *stock*—that is, accumulated net investment up to a point in time.

Investment is often modeled as a function of income and interest rates, given by the relation $I = f(Y, r)$. An increase in income encourages higher investment, whereas a higher interest rate may discourage investment as it becomes more costly to borrow money. Even if a firm chooses to use its own funds in an investment, the interest rate represents an opportunity cost of investing those funds rather than lending out that amount of money for interest.

Liabilities

- A liability is a present obligation of the enterprise arising from past events, the settlement of which is expected to the result in an outflow of a resource embodying economic benefits.
- A liability is an existing obligation based on the evidence available on balance sheet date.
- A liability is recognised when outflow of economic resources in settlement of present obligation can be anticipated and the value of outflow can be reliably measured.

Long-Term Liabilities

- Long-term liabilities are a company's debts or obligations that are to be repaid or performed beyond one year.
  Source of fund
  Examples:
  - Bank Loan.
  - Loan from Financial Institution.
  - Debentures.

Current Liabilities

- Current liabilities are a company's debts or obligations that are to be repaid or performed within one year.
  - Emerge from normal business.
  - Examples:
    - Creditors (Accounts Payable).
    - Outstanding Expenses.
    - Interest accrued but not due on Loan.
    - Provision for Tax.
    - Bank Overdraft.

Provision

Provision means any amount retained by way of providing for any known liability of which amount can not be determined with substantial accuracy.

Provision refers to an amount set aside for meeting claims which are admissible but the amount whereof has not been confirmed.

Examples

- Provision for payment of electricity charges (but bill is not yet received).
- Provision for taxes (till final amount is assessed by authorities.).
- Provision for bonus.
- Amount set aside for writing off bad debts.

Contingent Liability

Contingent liability can be defined as

a. a possible obligation that arises from past events and the existence of which will be confirmed only by occurrence or non-occurrence of one or more uncertain future events not wholly within the control of the enterprise.

b. a present obligation that arises from past events but is not recognised because:

   i. it is not probable that an outflow of resources consisting economic benefits will be required to settle the obligation or

   ii. a reliable estimate of the amount of the obligation cannot be made.

Owners Fund

Owners fund is defined as residual interest of an enterprises after deducting all its liabilities.

Owners fund is the excess of aggregate assets of an enterprises over its aggregate liabilities.

Balance Sheet Equation

Assets = Liabilities + Owners Fund

Therefore,

Owners Fund= Assets – Liabilities

Owners Fund= Capital + Retained Earnings

A = L + O

1. Company borrows from bank

+	+		(+ Bank, + Bank Loan Payable)

1. Issue of shares by company

+		+	(+ Bank, + Equity Shares)

a. Cash purchase of equipment

b. Collection of debtors

a.	+,–			(+ Equipment, – Bank)
b.	+,–			(+ Bank, – Debtors)

a. Company repays bank loan

b. Payment of creditors / suppliers

a.	–	–		(– Loan Payable, – Bank)
b.	–	–		(– Creditors, – Bank)

Company pays dividend to shareholders

–		–	(– Bank, – Reserves)

Company purchases shares from shareholder, pays immediately (buy-back of shares)

–		–	(– Bank, – Equity Capital)

Liability is converted into equity shares e.g., loan is converted into equity shares

–	+	(– Loan Payable, + Equity shares)

Company incurs new liability to pay existing liability, e.g., Creditors are converted into long-term loan

	+,–		(– Creditors, + Loan Payable)

Company distributes stock dividend to stockholders (Bonus Shares)

		+,–	(+ Equity Capital, – Reserves)

Vertical Format of Balance Sheet

Sources of Funds	Rs.	Rs.
Owners Fund		XX
Borrowing Funds		
Secured Loan	XX	

Unsecured Loan	XX	XX
Total Capital Employed		XX

Application of Fund	Rs.	Rs.
Fixed Assets		XX
Investments		XX
Working Capital		
Current Assets	XX	
Current Liabilities	(XX)	
Net Working Capital		XX
Total Assets Employed		XX

Every company has to prepare balance sheet in the form set out in Part I of Schedule VI of Companies Act.

Exercise 1

1. On January 2, owners invest Rs.15,000 in ShriRam Company to begin the business.
2. On January 3, ShriRam Company borrows Rs. 10,000 from DhanLakshmi Bank.
3. On January 5, ShriRam Company purchases Rs. 18,000 of inventory from suppliers. Payment due on Jan 8.
4. On January 9, ShriRam Company sells inventory that cost Rs. 6,000 for Rs. 8,000 in cash.
5. On January 10, ShriRam Company pays for inventory purchased on January 5.
6. On January 12, ShriRam Company sells inventory that cost Rs. 5,000 for Rs. 6,000, on account. Payment will be received on January 31.
7. On January 31, ShriRam Company collects the account receivable and puts in bank.

Prepare Balance sheet of the concern after each transaction.

1. On January 2, owners invest Rs.15,000 in ShriRam Company to begin the business.

ShriRam Company Balance Sheet January 2, Year 1			
Liabilities		Assets	
Capital	15,000	Bank	15,000
Total	15,000	Total	15,000

1. On January 3, ShriRam Company borrows Rs. 10,000 from DhanLakshmi Bank.

ShriRam Company Balance Sheet January 3, Year 1			
Liabilities		Assets	
Paid-up capital	15,000	Bank	25,000
DhanLakshmi Bank Loan	10,000		
Total	25,000	Total	25,000

1. On January 5, ShriRam Company purchases Rs. 18,000 of inventory from suppliers, on account Payment due on January 8

ShriRam Company Balance Sheet January 5, Year 1			
Liabilities		Assets	
Paid-up capital	15,000	Bank	25,000
DhanLakshmi Bank Loan	10,000	Inventory	18,000
Accounts Payable/Creditors	18,000		
Total	43,000	Total	43,000

1. On January 9, ShriRam Company sells inventory that cost Rs. 6,000 for Rs. 8,000 in

ShriRam Company Balance Sheet January 9, Year 1			
Liabilities		Assets	
Paid-up capital	15,000	Bank	33,000
Reserves	2,000	Inventory	12,000
DhanLakshmi Bank Loan	10,000		
Creditors	18,000		
Total	45,000	Total	45,000

1. On January 10, ShriRam Company pays for inventory purchased on January 5.

ShriRam Company Balance Sheet January 10, Year 1			
Liabilities		Assets	
Paid-up capital	15,000	Bank	15,000
Reserves	2,000	Inventory	12,000
DhanLakshmi Bank Loan	10,000		
Creditors	Nil		
Total	27,000	Total	27,00

1. On January 12, ShriRam Company sells inventory that cost Rs. 5,000 for Rs. 6,000, on account. Payment will be received on January 31.

ShriRam Company Balance Sheet January 12, Year 1			
Liabilities		Assets	
Paid-up capital	15,000	Bank	15,000
Reserves	3,000	Inventory	7,000
DhanLakshmi Bank Loan	10,000	Debtors	6,000
Total	28,000	Total	28,000

1. On January 31, ShriRam Company collects the debtors and puts in bank.

ShriRam Company Balance Sheet January 31, Year 1			
Liabilities		Assets	
Paid-up capital	15,000	Bank	21,000
Reserves	3,000	Inventory	7,000
DhanLakshmi Bank Loan	10,000	Debtors	Nil
Total	28,000	Total	28,000

Exercise 2:

Show the effect of each transaction on the balance sheet of M/s. Krishna Book Stores

- Shyam and Murlidhar set up a book stall M/s. Krishna Book Stores in their town. On 1 Jan 2010, Shyam opened new bank account in the name of their partnership by depositing Rs. 1,00,000 cash and Murlidhar brought his own shop worth Rs. 2,00,000 as capital.
- On 2 January 2010, store purchased book of Rs. 75,000 and Stationary of Rs. 10,000 on immediate payment from SK International.
- On 5 January 2010, Stores supplies books of Rs. 90,000 (costing 60,000) to Saraswati Highschool. School paid cheque Rs. 45,000 immediately and reaming amount will be paid on 10 January 2010.
- On 9 January 2010, books costing 47,000 purchased on credit from SSK and Associates.
- On 10 January 2010, Rs. 15,000 received from Saraswati Highschool.
- On 15 January 2010, cheque of Rs. 47,000 paid to creditors.

Balance Sheet as on 1 Jan 2010

Liabilities	Amount	Assets	Amount
Capital			
Shyam	1,00,000	Shop Premises	2,00,000
Murlidhar	2,00,000	Bank	1,00,000
	3,00,000		3,00,000

Balance Sheet as on 2 Jan 2010

Liabilities	Amount	Assets	Amount
Capital			
Shyam	1,00,000	Shop Premises	2,00,000
Murlidhar	2,00,000	Bank	15,000
		Inventory	85,000
	3,00,000		**3,00,000**

Balance Sheet as on 5 Jan 2010

Liabilities	Amount	Assets	Amount
Capital			
Shyam	1,00,000	Shop Premises	2,00,000
Murlidhar	2,00,000	Bank	60,000
Profit and Loss A/c	30,000	Sundry Debtors	45,000
		Inventory	25,000
	3,30,000		3,30,000

Balance Sheet as on 9 Jan 2010

Liabilities	Amount	Assets	Amount
Capital			
Shyam	1,00,000	Shop Premises	2,00,000
Murlidhar	2,00,000	Bank	60,000
Profit and Loss A/c	30,000	Inventory	72,000
Sundry Creditors	47,000	Sundry Debtors	45,000
	3,77,000		3,77,000

Balance Sheet as on 10 Jan 2010

Liabilities	Amount	Assets	Amount
Capital			
Shyam	1,00,000	Shop Premises	2,00,000
Murlidhar	2,00,000	Bank	75,000
Profit and Loss A/c	30,000	Inventory	72,000
Sundry Creditors	47,000	Sundry Debtors	30,000
	3,77,000		**3,77,000**

Balance Sheet as on 15 Jan 2010

Liabilities	Amount	Assets	Amount
Capital			
Shyam	1,00,000	Shop Premises	2,00,000
Murlidhar	2,00,000	Bank	28,000
Profit and Loss A/c	30,000	Inventory	72,000
		Sundry Debtors	30,000
	3,30,000		**3,30,000**

Income Statement

An income statement or profit and loss account (also referred to as a *profit and loss statement* (P&L), *statement of profit or loss, revenue statement, statement of financial performance, earnings statement, operating statement, or statement of operations*) is one of the financial statements of a company and shows the company's revenues and expenses during a particular period. It indicates how the revenues (money received from the sale of products and services before expenses are taken out, also known as the "top line") are transformed into the net income (the result after all revenues and expenses have been accounted for, also known as "net profit" or the "bottom line"). It displays the revenues recognized for a specific period, and the cost and expenses charged against these revenues, including write-offs (e.g., depreciation and amortization of various assets) and taxes. The purpose of the income statement is to show managers and investors whether the company made or lost money during the period being reported.

One important thing to remember about an income statement is that it represents a period of time like the cash flow statement. This contrasts with the balance sheet, which represents a single moment in time.

Charitable organizations that are required to publish financial statements do not produce an income statement. Instead, they produce a similar statement that reflects funding sources compared against program expenses, administrative costs, and other operating commitments. This statement is commonly referred to as the statement of activities. Revenues and expenses are further categorized in the statement of activities by the donor restrictions on the funds received and expended.

The income statement can be prepared in one of two methods. The Single Step income statement takes the simpler approach, totaling revenues and subtracting expenses to find the bottom line. The more complex Multi-Step income statement (as the name implies) takes several steps to find the bottom line, starting with the gross profit. It then calculates operating expenses and, when deducted from the gross profit, yields income from operations. Adding to income from operations is the difference of other revenues and other expenses. When combined with income from operations, this yields income before taxes. The final step is to deduct taxes, which finally produces the net income for the period measured.

Usefulness and Limitations of Income Statement

Income statements should help investors and creditors determine the past financial performance of the enterprise, predict future performance, and assess the capability of generating future cash flows through report of the income and expenses.

However, information of an income statement has several limitations:

- Items that might be relevant but cannot be reliably measured are not reported (*e.g.*, brand recognition and loyalty).
- Some numbers depend on accounting methods used (*e.g.*, using FIFO or LIFO accounting to measure inventory level).
- Some numbers depend on judgments and estimates (*e.g.*, depreciation expense depends on estimated useful life and salvage value).

INCOME STATEMENT GREENHARBOR LLC
For the year ended DECEMBER 31 2010

	€ Debit	€ Credit
Revenues		
GROSS REVENUES (including INTEREST income)		296,397

Expenses:		
ADVERTISING	6,300	
BANK & CREDIT CARD FEES	144	
BOOKKEEPING	2,350	
SUBCONTRACTORS	88,000	
ENTERTAINMENT	5,550	

INSURANCE	750	
LEGAL & PROFESSIONAL SERVICES	1,575	
LICENSES	632	
PRINTING, POSTAGE & STATIONERY	320	
RENT	13,000	
MATERIALS	74,400	
TELEPHONE	1,000	
UTILITIES	1,491	

TOTAL EXPENSES		(195,512)

NET INCOME		100,885

Guidelines for statements of comprehensive income and income statements of business entities are formulated by the International Accounting Standards Board and numerous country-specific organizations, for example the FASB in the U.S..

Names and usage of different accounts in the income statement depend on the type of organization, industry practices and the requirements of different jurisdictions.

If applicable to the business, summary values for the following items should be included in the income statement:

Operating Section

- Revenue - Cash inflows or other enhancements of assets (including accounts receivable) of an entity during a period from delivering or producing goods, rendering services, or other activities that constitute the entity's ongoing major operations. It is usually presented as sales minus sales discounts, returns, and allowances. Every time a business sells a product or performs a service, it obtains revenue. This often is referred to as gross revenue or sales revenue.
- Expenses - Cash outflows or other using-up of assets or incurrence of liabilities (including accounts payable) during a period from delivering or producing goods, rendering services, or carrying out other activities that constitute the entity's ongoing major operations.
    - Cost of Goods Sold (COGS) / Cost of Sales - represents the direct costs attributable to goods produced and sold by a business (manufacturing or merchandizing). It includes *material costs*, *direct labour*, and *overhead costs* (as in absorption costing), and excludes operating costs (period costs) such as selling, administrative, advertising or R&D, etc.
    - Selling, General and Administrative expenses (SG&A or SGA) - consist of the combined payroll costs. SGA is usually understood as a major portion of non-production related costs, in contrast to production costs such as direct labour.

- Selling expenses - represent expenses needed to sell products (e.g., *salaries of sales people, commissions and travel expenses, advertising, freight, shipping, depreciation of sales store buildings and equipment*, etc.).
- General and Administrative (G&A) expenses - represent expenses to manage the business (*salaries of officers / executives, legal and professional fees, utilities, insurance, depreciation of office building and equipment, office rents, office supplies*, etc.).
    - Depreciation / Amortization - the charge with respect to fixed assets / intangible assets that have been capitalised on the balance sheet for a specific (accounting) period. It is a systematic and rational allocation of cost rather than the recognition of market value decrement.
    - Research & Development (R&D) expenses - represent expenses included in research and development.

Expenses recognised in the income statement should be analysed either by nature (raw materials, transport costs, staffing costs, depreciation, employee benefit etc.) or by function (cost of sales, selling, administrative, etc.). (IAS 1.99) If an entity categorises by function, then additional information on the nature of expenses, at least, – depreciation, amortisation and employee benefits expense – must be disclosed. (IAS 1.104) The major exclusive of costs of goods sold, are classified as operating expenses. These represent the resources expended, except for inventory purchases, in generating the revenue for the period. Expenses often are divided into two broad sub classicifications selling expenses and administrative expenses.

Non-operating Section

- Other revenues or gains - revenues and gains from other than primary business activities (e.g., *rent, income from patents*, goodwill). It also includes unusual gains that are either unusual or infrequent, but not both (e.g., *gain from sale of securities* or *gain from disposal of fixed assets*)
- Other expenses or losses - expenses or losses not related to primary business operations, (e.g., *foreign exchange loss*).
- Finance costs - costs of borrowing from various creditors (e.g., interest expenses, bank charges).
- Income tax expense - sum of the amount of tax payable to tax authorities in the current reporting period (current tax liabilities/ tax payable) and the amount of deferred tax liabilities (or assets).

Irregular Items

They are reported separately because this way users can better predict future cash flows - irregular items most likely will not recur. These are reported *net of taxes*.

- Discontinued operations is the most common type of irregular items. Shifting business location(s), stopping production temporarily, or changes due to technological improvement do **not** qualify as discontinued operations. Discontinued operations *must* be shown separately.

Cumulative effect of changes in accounting policies (principles) is the difference between the book value of the affected assets (or liabilities) under the old policy (principle) and what the book value would have been if the new principle had been applied in the prior periods. For example, valuation of inventories using LIFO instead of weighted average method. The changes should be applied retrospectively and shown as adjustments to the *beginning* balance of affected components in Equity. All comparative financial statements should be restated. (IAS 8)

However, changes in estimates (e.g., estimated useful life of a fixed asset) only requires prospective changes. (IAS 8)

No items may be presented in the income statement as extraordinary items under IFRS regulations, but are permissible under US GAAP. (IAS 1.87) *Extraordinary items* are both unusual (abnormal) and infrequent, for example, unexpected natural disaster, expropriation, prohibitions under new regulations. [Note: natural disaster might not qualify depending on location (e.g., frost damage would not qualify in Canada but would in the tropics).]

Additional items may be needed to fairly present the entity's results of operations. (IAS 1.85)

Disclosures

Certain items must be disclosed separately in the notes (or the statement of comprehensive income), if material, including: (IAS 1.98)

- Write-downs of inventories to net realisable value or of property, plant and equipment to recoverable amount, as well as *reversals* of such write-downs
- Restructurings of the activities of an entity and *reversals* of any provisions for the costs of restructuring
- Disposals of items of property, plant and equipment
- Disposals of investments
- Discontinued operations
- Litigation settlements
- Other reversals of provisions

Earnings Per Share

Because of its importance, earnings per share (EPS) are required to be disclosed on the face of the income statement. A company which reports any of the irregular items must also report EPS for these items either in the statement or in the notes.

$$\text{Earnings per share} = \frac{\text{Net income} - \text{Preferred stock dividends}}{\text{Weighted average of common stock shares outstanding}}$$

There are two forms of EPS reported:

- Basic: in this case "weighted average of shares outstanding" includes only actual stocks outstanding.
- Diluted: in this case "weighted average of shares outstanding" is calculated as if all stock options, warrants, convertible bonds, and other securities that could be transformed into shares are transformed. This increases the number of shares and so EPS decreases. Diluted EPS is considered to be a more reliable way to measure EPS.

Sample Income Statement

The following income statement is a very brief example prepared in accordance with IFRS. It does not show all possible kinds of accounts, but it shows the most usual ones. Please note the difference between IFRS and US GAAP when interpreting the following sample income statements.

Fitness Equipment Limited

INCOME STATEMENTS (in millions)

Year Ended March 31,	2009	2008	2007
Revenue	$14,580.2	$11,900.4	$8,290.3
Cost of sales	(6,740.2)	(5,650.1)	(4,524.2)
Gross profit	*7,840.0*	*6,250.3*	*3,766.1*
SGA expenses	(3,624.6)	(3,296.3	(3,034.0)
Operating profit	*$ 4,215.4*	*$ 2,954.0*	*$ 732.1*
Gains from disposal of fixed assets	46.3	-	-
Interest expense	(119.7)	(124.1)	(142.8)
Profit *before* tax	4,142.0	2,829.9	589.3
Income tax expense	(1,656.8)	(1,132.0)	(235.7)
Profit (or loss) for the year1	*$ 2,485.2*	*$ 1,697.9*	*$ 353.6*

DEXTERITY INC. AND SUBSIDIARIES

CONSOLIDATED STATEMENTS OF OPERATIONS (In millions)

Year Ended December 31,	2009	2008	2007
Revenue	$36,525.9	$29,827.6	$21,186.8
Cost of sales	(18,545.8)	(15,858.8)	(11,745.5)
Gross profit	*17,980.1*	*13,968.8*	*9,441.3*

Operating expenses:			
Selling, general and administrative expenses	(4,142.1)	(3,732.3)	(3,498.6)
Depreciation	(602.4)	(584.5)	(562.3)
Amortization	(209.9)	(141.9)	(111.8)
Impairment loss	(17,997.1)	—	—
Total operating expenses	(22,951.5)	(4,458.7)	(4,172.7)
Operating profit (or loss)	*$ (4,971.4)*	*$ 9,510.1*	*$ 5,268.6*
Interest income	25.3	11.7	12.0
Interest expense	(718.9)	(742.9)	(799.1)
Profit (or loss) from continuing operations *before* tax, share of profit (or loss) from associates and non-controlling interest	$ (5,665.0)	$ 8,778.9	$ 4,481.5
Income tax expense	(1,678.6)	(3,510.5)	(1,789.9)
Profit (or loss) from associates, *net of tax*	(20.8)	0.1	(37.3)
Profit (or loss) from non-controlling interest, *net of tax*	(5.1)	(4.7)	(3.3)
Profit (or loss) from continuing operations	*$ (3960.5)*	*$ 5,263.8*	*$ 2,651.0*
Profit (or loss) from discontinued operations,*net of tax*	(1,090.3)	(802.4)	164.6
Profit (or loss) for the year	*$ (2,870.2)*	*$ 4,461.4*	*$ 2,486.4*

Bottom Line

"Bottom line" is the net income that is calculated after subtracting the expenses from revenue. Since this forms the last line of the income statement, it is informally called "bottom line." It is important to investors as it represents the profit for the year attributable to the shareholders.

After revision to IAS 1 in 2003, the Standard is now using profit or loss for the year rather than *net profit or loss* or *net income* as the descriptive term for the bottom line of the income statement.

Requirements of IFRS

On 6 September 2007, the International Accounting Standards Board issued a revised *IAS 1: Presentation of Financial Statements*, which is effective for annual periods beginning on or after 1 January 2009.

A business entity adopting IFRS must include:

- a statement of comprehensive income or
- two separate statements comprising:
    1. an income statement displaying components of profit or loss *and*
    2. a *statement of comprehensive income* that *begins* with profit or loss (bottom line of the income statement) and displays the items of other comprehensive income for the reporting period. (IAS1.81)

All non-owner changes in equity (i.e., *comprehensive income*) shall be presented in either in the statement of comprehensive income (or in a separate income statement and a statement of comprehensive income). Components of comprehensive income may not be presented in the statement of changes in equity.

Comprehensive income for a period includes profit or loss (net income) for that period and other comprehensive income recognised in that period.

All items of income and expense recognised in a period must be included in profit or loss unless a Standard or an Interpretation requires otherwise. (IAS 1.88) Some IFRSs require or permit that some components to be excluded from profit or loss and instead to be included in other comprehensive income. (IAS 1.89)

Items and Disclosures

The statement of comprehensive income should include: (IAS 1.82)

1. Revenue
2. Finance costs (including interest expenses)
3. Share of the profit or loss of associates and joint ventures accounted for using the equity method
4. Tax expense
5. A *single* amount comprising the total of (1) the *post-tax* profit or loss of *discontinued operations* and (2) the *post-tax* gain or loss recognised on the disposal of the assets or disposal group(s) constituting the *discontinued operation*
6. Profit or loss
7. Each component of other comprehensive income classified by nature
8. Share of the other comprehensive income of associates and joint ventures accounted for using the equity method
9. Total comprehensive income

The following items must also be disclosed in the statement of comprehensive income as allocations for the period: (IAS 1.83)

- Profit or loss for the period attributable to non-controlling interests and owners of the parent

- Total comprehensive income attributable to non-controlling interests and owners of the parent

No items may be presented in the statement of comprehensive income (or in the income statement, if separately presented) or in the notes as *extraordinary items*.

Income

Income is the increase in economic benefits during the accounting period in the form of inflows or enhancement of asset or decreases of the liability. The definition of income encompasses revenue and gains.

- Revenue is an income that arises in the ordinary course of activities. e.g. sales.
- Gains are income, which may or may not arises in the ordinary course of activities. e.g. profit on sale of fixed asset.

Expenses

Expense is the decrease in economic benefits during the accounting period in the form of outflows or depletion of asset or incurrence of the liability.

- Expense arises in the ordinary course of activities. e.g. wages.
- Losses may or may not arises in the ordinary course of activities. e.g. loss on sale of fixed asset.

Entity Concept

In accounting, a business or an organization and its owners are treated as two separately identifiable parties. This is called the entity concept. The business stands apart from other organizations as a separate economic unit. It is necessary to record the business's transactions separately, to distinguish them from the owners' personal transactions. This helps to give a correct determination of the true financial condition of the business. This concept can be extended to accounting separately for the various divisions of a business in order to ascertain the financial results for each division.

"The entity view holds the business 'enterprise to be an institution in its own right separate and distinct from the parties who furnish the funds"

Proprietor

An example is a sole trader or one-man business(proprietorship): the sole trader takes money from the business by way of 'drawings': money for his own personal use. Despite it being his business and technically his money, there are still two aspects to the transaction: the business is 'giving' money and the individual is 'receiving' money. Even though there is no other legal distinction between the sole trader and the business, and the sole trader is liable for all of the debts of the business, business transactions will probably still be taxed separately from personal transactions, and the proprietor of the business may also find it useful to see the financial results of the business. For these reasons, the affairs of the individuals behind a business should be kept separate from the affairs of the business itself.

Example

Mr. Honey has three rooms in a house he has rented for $3,000 per month. He has set up a single-member accounting practice and uses one room for the purpose. Under the business entity concept, only 1/3 of the rent or $1,000 should be charged to business, because the other two rooms or $2,000 worth of rent are expended for personal purposes.

The Entity concept of an accounting practice states that the business enterprises is a separate identity apart from its owner.

- Business transaction are recorded in the books of business books of accounts and owners transaction in his personal books of accounts.
- This concept helps in keeping business affairs free from the influence of the personal affairs of the owner.
- Entity concept means that enterprises are liable to owner for capital investment made by the owner.
- Since the owner invested capital, which is also called risk capital he claim on the profit of the enterprise.

Basis of Accounting

A basis of accounting can be defined as the time various financial transactions are recorded. The cash basis (EU VAT vocabulary *Cash accounting*) and the accrual basis are the two primary methods of tracking income and expenses in accounting.

Both can be used in a range of situations, from the accounts of a whole country, a large corporation, a small business or an individual. In many cases, regulatory bodies require individuals, businesses or corporations to use one method or the other. When this is not the case, the choice of which to use is an important decision, as both methods have advantages and disadvantages.

Accrual Basis

The accrual method records income items when they are *earned* and records deductions when expenses are *incurred*. For a business invoicing for an item sold, or work done, the corresponding amount will appear in the books even though no payment has yet been received – and debts owed by the business show as they are incurred, even though they may not be paid until much later.

In the United States tax environment, the accrual basis has been an option since 1916. An "accrual basis taxpayer" looks to the "all-events test" and "earlier-of test" to determine when income is earned. Under the all-events test, an accrual basis taxpayer generally must include income "for the taxable year when all the events have occurred that fix the right to receive income and the amount of the income can be determined with reasonable accuracy." Under the "earlier-of test", an accrual basis taxpayer receives income when (1) the required performance occurs, (2) payment therefore is due, or (3) payment therefore is made, whichever happens earliest. Under the earlier of test outlined in Revenue Ruling 74-607, an accrual basis taxpayer may be treated as a cash basis taxpayer when payment is received before the required performance and before the payment is actually due. An accrual basis taxpayer generally can claim a deduction "in the taxable year in which all the events have occurred that establish the fact of the liability, the amount of the liability can be determined with reasonable accuracy, and economic performance has occurred with respect to the liability."

Similar definition of accrual basis accounting is true for financial accounting purposes, except that revenue can't be recognized until it is earned, even if a cash payment has already been received by the tax authorities.

Modified Accrual Basis

Also referred to as the Modified Cash Basis, combines elements of both accrual and cash basis accounting. The modified method records income when they are earned but deductions when expenses are paid out. The recording of income is then of accrual basis, while the recording of expenses is cash basis. The modified method does not conform to the GAAP.

Accrual Basis of Accounting

- Transaction are recognised as soon as they occur, whether or not cash is actually received or paid.
- Accrual basis ensures better matching between revenue and cost of the enterprise during an accounting period.
- Accrual means recognition of revenue and cost as they are earned or incurred and not as money is received or paid.
- Revenues may not be realised in cash.

Cash may be received simultaneously or before/after revenue is created.

Expense may not be paid in cash.

Cash may be paid simultaneously or before/after expense is made.

Matching Concept

The matching concept is an accounting practice whereby expenses are recognized in the same accounting period when the related revenues are recognized.

The matching concept thus helps avoid misstating earnings for a period. Reporting revenues for a period without reporting the costs of producing those revenues would result in overstated profits.

Prepaid and Outstanding Expenses:

Matching concept is based on the accrual concept as it considers the occurrence of expenses and income and do not concentrate on actual inflow or outflow of cash. This leads to adjustment of items like prepaid and outstanding expenses.

Realisation Concept

Any change in the value of an asset is to be recorded only when the business realise it. When an asset is recorded at its cost of Rs. 15 Lakhs and even if its current cost is Rs. 45 Lakhs such change is not counted unless there is certainty that such change will materialise.

However, we follow a more conservative path. We try to cover all probable losses but do not count any probable gain. That is to say, if we anticipate decrease in value count it, but if there is increase in value ignore it until it is realised.

Profit & Loss A/c (Detailed Format)

Particulars	Amount
Sales	XX
Operating Expenses	(XX)
Operating Profit	XX
Non-Operating Income	XX
Non-Operating Expense	(XX)
Profit before Interest and Tax	XX
Interest	(XX)
Profit before Tax	XX
Tax	(XX)
Profit after Tax	XX

Earnings Before Interest and Taxes

In accounting and finance, earnings before interest and taxes (EBIT), is a measure of a firm's profit that includes all expenses except interest and income tax expenses. It is the difference between operating revenues and operating expenses. When a firm does not have non-operating income, then **operating *income*** is sometimes used as a synonym for **EBIT** and operating profit.

EBIT = revenue – operating expenses (OPEX)

Operating income = revenue – operating expenses

A professional investor contemplating a change to the capital structure of a firm (e.g., through a leveraged buyout) first evaluates a firm's fundamental earnings potential (reflected by earnings before interest, taxes, depreciation and amortization (EBITDA) and EBIT), and then determines the optimal use of debt vs. equity.

To calculate EBIT, expenses (e.g. the cost of goods sold, selling and administrative expenses) are subtracted from revenues. Net income is later obtained by subtracting interest and taxes from the result.

Example statement of income (figures in thousands)	
Revenue	
Sales revenue	$20,438
Operating expenses	
Cost of goods sold	$7,943
Selling, general and administrative expenses	$8,172
Depreciation and amortization	$960
Other expenses	$138
Total operating expenses	$17,213
Operating profit	**$3,225**
Non-operating income	$130
Earnings before Interest and taxes (EBIT)	**$3,355**
Financial income	$45
Income before interest expense (IBIE)	**$3,400**
Financial expense	$190
Earnings before income taxes (EBT)	**$3,210**
Income taxes	$1,027
Net income	**$2,183**

Operating Profit

Operating activities are principal revenue producing activities of the enterprise.

Operating profit is the figure obtained after subtracting personnel, depreciation and other expenses.

Operating profit is the surplus generated by the operations.

Profit Before Interest & Tax

The company irrespective of method of financing, earns this amount. The only other expense to be met at this stage, is the interest expense.

This is the measure of the operational efficiency of the company. This is usually referred as Earnings before Interest and Tax.

Profit Before Tax

Profit before Tax is the surplus after meeting all expenses, including interest.

This is the profit available to company as a result of both its operating as well as financing performance.

Profit After Tax

Profit after Tax is the net amount of surplus earned by the company during the accounting period.

This is the amount available to the company for appropriation. This amount can either distributed to owners or retained in the business as retained earning. Not distributing the profit to owners increases the owners investment in the business.

Exercise 1

In Padmanabham and co. following transaction took place during year 2009-10.

- Goods costing Rs. 1,40,000 purchased for cash.
- Padmanabham paid General expenses of Rs. 4,800.
- Salaries of Rs. 25,500 paid to office staff.
- Padmanabham sales on credit for two month. Total credit sales during year is Rs. 1,40,500 (cost: 90,000) and remaining goods were sold at cash to retail traders for cash at Rs. 69,000.
- Printing and stationary expense were Rs. 5,000 and Telephone expenses were Rs. 18,000.
- Padmanabham paid salary of Apr 2010, Rs. 2,000 in advance to one employee.
- Padmanabham paid Rs. 50,000 towards Bank of Baroda loan, of which Rs. 5,000 was interest component.
- Rs. 3,000 paid as tax.

Prepare profit and loss A/c from the given information of year 2009-10.

Profit and Loss A/c for year ended 31 March 2010	
Particulars	**Amount**
Cash Sales	69,000
Credit Sales	1,40,500
Total Sales	2,09,500
Cost of goods sold	(1,40,000)
Operating Profit	69,500
General Expenses	(4,800)
Salary Expenses	(25,500)
Printing and Stationary Expenses	(5,000)

Telephone Expenses	(18,000)
Profit Before Interest and Tax	16,200
Interest	(5,000)
Profit Before Tax	11,200
Tax	(3,000)
Net profit after Tax	**8,200**

References

- "Balance sheet comparing two year-end balance sheets". Archived from the original on 2007-10-19. Retrieved 2010-05-08
- Williams, Jan R.; Susan F. Haka; Mark S. Bettner; Joseph V. Carcello (2008). Financial & Managerial Accounting. McGraw-Hill Irwin. p. 40. ISBN 978-0-07-299650-0
- "US Small Business Administration sample spreadsheet for a small business". Archived from the original on 2007-07-15. Retrieved 2003-08-10
- Daniels, Mortimer (1980). Corporation Financial Statements. New York: New York : Arno Press. pp. 13–14. ISBN 0-405-13514-9
- Helfert, Erich A. (2001). "The Nature of Financial Statements: The Income Statement". Financial Analysis - Tools and Techniques - A Guide for Managers. McGraw-Hill. p. 40. doi:10.1036/0071395415
- Epstein, Barry J.; Eva K. Jermakowicz (2007). Interpretation and Application of International Financial Reporting Standards. John Wiley & Sons. p. 931. ISBN 978-0-471-79823-1
- Ernst, James. "3 Methods of HOA Accounting and How They Effect Financial Statements". www.echo-ca.org. ECHO. Retrieved 5 August 2014
- Warren, Carl (2008). Survey of Accounting. Cincinnati: South-Western College Pub. pp. 128–132. ISBN 978-0-324-65826-2
- "What are Accruals and the Meaning of Accrued in Accounting?". Simplestudies LLC. 25 February 2010. Retrieved 25 February 2010

4

Financial Statement Analysis and Related Concepts

The recorded transactions are treated as raw data. To retrieve useful information from the data, they are analysed, organized and processed. This process can be divided into horizontal and vertical analysis. The latter part follows preparation of common-size statements. This chapter discusses the methods of managerial accounting in a critical manner providing key analysis to the subject matter.

Financial Statement Analysis

Financial statement analysis (or financial analysis) is the process of reviewing and analyzing a company's financial statements to make better economic decisions. These statements include the income statement, balance sheet, statement of cash flows, and a statement of changes in equity. Financial statement analysis is a method or process involving specific techniques for evaluating risks, performance, financial health, and future prospects of an organization.

It is used by a variety of stakeholders, such as credit and equity investors, the government, the public, and decision-makers within the organization. These stakeholders have different interests and apply a variety of different techniques to meet their needs. For example, equity investors are interested in the long-term earnings power of the organization and perhaps the sustainability and growth of dividend payments. Creditors want to ensure the interest and principal is paid on the organizations debt securities (e.g., bonds) when due.

Common methods of financial statement analysis include fundamental analysis, DuPont analysis, horizontal and vertical analysis and the use of financial ratios. Historical information combined with a series of assumptions and adjustments to the financial information may be used to project future performance. The Chartered Financial Analyst designation is available for professional financial analysts.

History

Benjamin Graham and David Dodd first published their influential book "Security Analysis" in 1934. A central premise of their book is that the market's pricing mechanism for financial securities such as stocks and bonds is based upon faulty and irrational analytical processes performed by many market participants. This results in the market price of a security only occasionally coinciding with the intrinsic value around which the price tends to fluctuate. Investor Warren Buffett is a well-known supporter of Graham and Dodd's philosophy.

The Graham and Dodd approach is referred to as Fundamental analysis and includes: 1) Economic analysis; 2) Industry analysis; and 3) Company analysis. The latter is the primary realm of financial statement analysis. On the basis of these three analyses the intrinsic value of the security is determined.

Horizontal and Vertical Analysis

Horizontal analysis compares financial information over time, typically from past quarters or years. Horizontal analysis is performed by comparing financial data from a past statement, such as the income statement. When comparing this past information one will want to look for variations such as higher or lower earnings.

Vertical analysis is a percentage analysis of financial statements. Each line item listed in the financial statement is listed as the percentage of another line item. For example, on an income statement each line item will be listed as a percentage of gross sales. This technique is also referred to as normalization or common-sizing.

Financial Ratio Analysis

Financial ratios are very powerful tools to perform some quick analysis of financial statements. There are four main categories of ratios: liquidity ratios, profitability ratios, activity ratios and leverage ratios. These are typically analyzed over time and across competitors in an industry.

- *Liquidity ratios* are used to determine how quickly a company can turn its assets into cash if it experiences financial difficulties or bankruptcy. It essentially is a measure of a company's ability to remain in business. A few common liquidity ratios are the current ratio and the liquidity index. The current ratio is current assets/current liabilities and measures how much liquidity is available to pay for liabilities. The liquidity index shows how quickly a company can turn assets into cash and is calculated by: (Trade receivables x Days to liquidate) + (Inventory x Days to liquidate)/Trade Receivables + Inventory.
- *Profitability ratios* are ratios that demonstrate how profitable a company is. A few popular profitability ratios are the breakeven point and gross profit ratio. The breakeven point calculates how much cash a company must generate to break even with their start up costs. The gross profit ratio is equal to (revenue - the cost of goods sold)/revenue. This ratio shows a quick snapshot of expected revenue.
- *Activity ratios* are meant to show how well management is managing the company's resources. Two common activity ratios are accounts payable turnover and accounts receivable turnover. These ratios demonstrate how long it takes for a company to pay off its accounts payable and how long it takes for a company to receive payments, respectively.
- *Leverage ratios* depict how much a company relies upon its debt to fund operations. A very common leverage ratio used for financial statement analysis is the debt-to-equity ratio. This ratio shows the extent to which management is willing to use debt in order to fund operations. This ratio is calculated as: (Long-term debt + Short-term debt + Leases)/ Equity.

DuPont analysis uses several financial ratios that multiplied together equal return on equity, a measure of how much income the firm earns divided by the amount of funds invested (equity).

A Dividend discount model (DDM) may also be used to value a company's stock price based on the theory that its stock is worth the sum of all of its future dividend payments, discounted back to their present value. In other words, it is used to value stocks based on the net present value of the future dividends.

Financial statement analyses are typically performed in spreadsheet software and summarized in a variety of formats.

Recasting Financial Statements

Investors typically are attempting to understand how much cash the company will generate in the future and its rate of profit growth, relative to the amount of capital deployed. Analysts may modify ("recast") the financial statements by adjusting the underlying assumptions to aid in this computation. For example, operating leases (treated like a rental transaction) may be recast as capital leases (indicating ownership), adding assets and liabilities to the balance sheet. This affects the financial statement ratios.

Recasting financial statements requires a solid understanding of accounting theory. Once the cash flow in future years is projected, a discount rate or interest rate will be applied to measure the value of the company and its stock or debt.}

Certifications

Financial analysts typically have finance and accounting education at the undergraduate or graduate level. Persons may earn the Chartered Financial Analyst (CFA) designation through a series of challenging examinations.

Common-size Statements

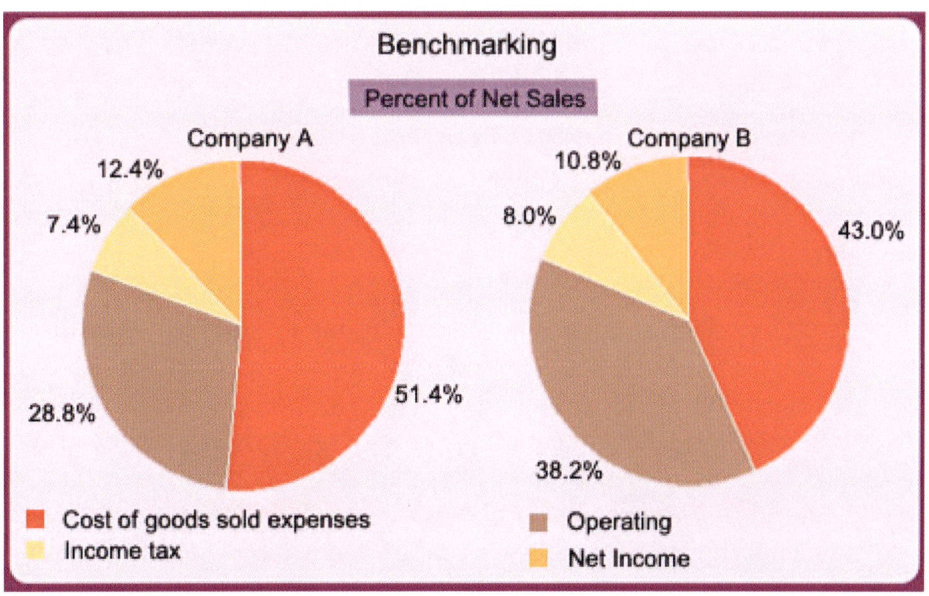

- On the income statement, each item is expressed as a percentage of net sales.
- On the balance sheet, the common size is the total on each side of the accounting equation.
- Common-size statements are used to compare one company to other companies, and to the industry average.
- They are also used to compare financials with earlier years.

Debits and Credits

In double entry bookkeeping, debits and credits (abbreviated Dr and Cr, respectively) are entries made in account ledgers to record changes in value resulting from business transactions. Generally speaking, the source account for the transaction is *credited* (that is, an entry is made on the right side of the account's ledger) and the destination account is *debited* (that is, an entry is made on the left side). Total debits must equal total credits for each transaction; individual transactions may require multiple debit and credit entries to record.

The difference between the total debits and total credits in a single account is the account's *balance*. If debits exceed credits, the account has a debit balance; if credits exceed debits, the account has a credit balance. For the company as a whole, the totals of debit balances and credit balances must be equal as shown in the trial balance report, otherwise an error has occurred.

Accountants use the trial balance to prepare financial statements (such as the balance sheet and income statement) which communicate information about the company's financial activities in a generally accepted standard format.

History

The first known recorded use of the terms is Venetian Luca Pacioli's 1494 work, *Summa de Arithmetica, Geometria, Proportioni et Proportionalita* (translated: *Everything That Is Known About Arithmetic, Geometry, Proportions and Proportionality*). Pacioli devoted one section of his book to documenting and describing the double-entry bookkeeping system in use during the Renaissance by Venetian merchants, traders and bankers. This system is still the fundamental system in use by modern bookkeepers.

One theory is that in its original Latin, Pacioli's *Summa* used the Latin words *debere* (to owe) and *credere* (to entrust) to describe the two sides of a closed accounting transaction. Assets were owed to the owner and the owners' equity was entrusted to the company. At the time negative numbers were not in use. When his work was translated, the Latin words *debere* and *credere* became the English *debit* and *credit*. Under this theory, the abbreviations Dr (for debit) and Cr (for credit) derive from the original Latin. However, Sherman casts doubt on this idea because Pacioli uses *Per* (Latin for "from") for the debtor and *A* (Latin for "to") for the creditor in the Journal entries. Sherman goes on to say that the earliest text he found that actually uses "Dr." as an abbreviation in this context was an English text, the third edition of Ralph Handson's book *Analysis or Resolution of Merchant Accompts* and that Handson uses Dr. as an abbreviation for the English word "debtor." (Sherman could not locate a first edition, but speculates that it too used Dr. for debtor.) The words actually used by Pacioli for the left and right sides of the Ledger are "in dare" and "in havere" (*give* and *receive*). Geijsbeek the translator suggests in the preface: 'if we today would abolish the use of the words debit and credit in the ledger and substitute the ancient terms of "shall give" and "shall have" or "shall receive," the personification of accounts in the proper way would not be difficult and, with it, bookkeeping would become more intelligent to the proprietor, the layman and the student.'

Jackson notes that "debtor" need not be a person, but can be an abstract operator (cf. "divisor" in math) "...it became the practice to extend the meanings of the terms ... beyond their original personal connotation and apply them to inanimate objects and abstract conceptions...".

Aspects of Transactions

To determine whether one must debit or credit a specific account we use either the *accounting equation* approach which consists of five accounting rules or the *traditional approach* based on three rules (for Real accounts, Personal accounts, and Nominal accounts) to determine whether *to debit* or *to credit* an account.

- Real accounts are the assets of a firm, which may be *tangible* (machinery, buildings etc.) or *intangible* (goodwill, patents etc.)
- Personal accounts relate to individuals, companies, creditors, banks etc.
- Nominal accounts relate to expenses, losses, incomes or gains.

Whether a *debit* increases or decreases an account depends on what kind of account it is. An increase to an *asset* account is a debit. An increase to a *liability* or to an *equity* account is a credit.

Kind of account	**Debit**	**Credit**
Asset	Increase	Decrease
Liability	Decrease	Increase
Income/Revenue	Decrease	Increase
Expense	Increase	Decrease
Equity/Capital	Decrease	Increase

Conversely, a decrease to an asset account is a credit. A decrease to a liability or equity account is a debit.

Debits and credits occur simultaneously in every financial transaction in double-entry bookkeeping. In the accounting equation—Assets = Liabilities + Equity—if an asset account increases (a debit), then either another asset account must decrease (a credit), or a liability or equity account must increase (a credit).

For example, when the customer of a bank deposits money into his bank account two things change: the customer's cash-in-hand (asset) decreases and the customer's bank account balance increases. The decrease in the cash-in-hand asset is a credit while the increase in the bank account balance is a debit of equal magnitude.

The bank views the transaction from a different perspective but follows the same rules: the bank's vault cash (asset) increases, which is a debit; the increase in the customer's account balance (liability from the bank's perspective) is a credit. A customer's periodic bank statement generally shows transactions from the bank's perspective, with bank deposits characterized as credits and withdrawals as debits.

Debits are traditionally entered on the left-hand side of a ledger and credits on the right-hand side.

Commercial Understanding

When dealing with one's own business, one must set up various accounts to record all transactions that may take place. When the owner of a business refers to their bank account, they are referring to the business's account, not to their personal account. In addition, all accounts referred to in bookkeeping belong to the business, *not* to other businesses, regardless of their title. For instance, if a business expects to receive money from another person or company and the account is labelled "Receivable A", this does not imply that the account in question belongs to "Receivable A". It is merely a recording of a current asset (a receivable) of one's own business. Therefore, when assessing any transaction, the transaction is from the point of view of one's own business or the business in question.

All accounts must first be classified as one of the five types of accounts (accounting elements). To determine how to classify an account into one of the five elements, the definitions of the five account types must be fully understood i.e. the definition of an asset according to IFRS is as follows, "An asset is a resource controlled by the entity as a result of past events from which future economic benefits are expected to flow to the entity". To understand this definition we can break it down into its constituent parts with an example:

Example: Classify what type of account the business "Bank account" is.

The bank account of a business is "a resource controlled by the entity" as it belongs to the business. "As a result of past events" such as the opening of the business. "From which future economic benefits are expected to flow to the entity" – a business such as a grocers can expect to make money due to the sale of their goods. This basic analogy can be applied to any asset account.

All of the five accounting elements have their own definitions that must be fully understood in order to classify an account correctly.

A business will most often have more than one asset account. An essential asset account in any business is the business's *bank account* The same applies to liability accounts i.e. if I have borrowed money from two sources (called creditors or payables), then I must open two accounts to represent this present liability, called 'Creditor/Payable A' and 'Creditor/Payable B'. In this manner I may have multiple, different accounts. However all these accounts are all classified as one of the five types of accounts, therefore my entire business can be described in terms of its assets, expenses, liabilities, income and equity/capital. This is the extent of "my" business in relation to accounts, regardless of the business' practices (the business may be a retail franchise, furniture shop, restaurant, etc.). With respect to my business, each of the five accounting elements will have a monetary value, and this can be used to assess the financial position of my business at any time (my success, failure, or any other attributes that I might need to know).

Traditionally, transactions are recorded in two separate columns of numbers (known as a ledger or "T-account"): debit transactions in the left hand column and credit transactions in the right hand column. Keeping the debits and credits in separate columns allows each column to be recorded and totaled *independently*. Accounts within the *general ledger* are known colloquially as "T-accounts" due to the "T" shape that the table resembles. Each column of a ledger account lists transactions affecting that account.

Terminology

The words debit and credit are both used differently depending on whether they are used in a bookkeeping (accounting) sense, or non-accounting sense.

In a non-accounting sense, "debit" is:

- a sum of money taken from a bank account.

In a non-accounting sense, "credit" is

- a sum of money placed into a bank account.
- money available to spend.
- money available to borrow.

The reason why individuals see debits and credits in the above manner, is that the bank statement presented by the bank to the customer is the bank's view of the account. The bank views money in a chequing account as money the bank owes to the customer, i.e. a liability, and in the rules of accounting, an increase to a liability account is a credit. Likewise, when a bank lends money to a customer and places the money into the customer's chequing account, the bank has increased its obligation to pay that money, which is a liability, and this increase is a credit and appears in the credit column of a bank statement.

When recording numbers in accounting, a debit value is placed on the left side of a ledger for a debited account and a credit value is placed on the right side of a ledger for a credited account. A debit or a credit either increases or decreases the total balance in each account, depending on what kind of accounts they are.

Each transaction (say, of value £100) is recorded by a debit entry of £100 in one account and a credit entry of £100 in another account. When people say, "debits must equal credits" they do *not* mean that the two columns of any ledger account must be equal. If that were the case, every account would have a zero balance (no difference between the columns) which is often not the case. The rule that *total debits equal the total credits* applies when all accounts are totaled.

More than two accounts may be affected by the same transaction. A transaction for £100 can be recorded as a £100 debit in one account and as multiple credits that total £100 in other accounts.

Example:

I owe creditors A and B £100 each. Thus my liability account for Creditor A has a credit balance of £100 and the same for Creditor B.

Cr: Creditor A (100)

Cr: Creditor B (100)

I pay them off from my bank chequing account, which from my point of view is an asset. I withdraw £200 from my bank account and split it to pay off the two liabilities. In my records, "Creditor A" is one account, "Creditor B" is another account, and "Bank" is a third account. The following transactions affect all three-ledger accounts:

Dr: Creditor A (100)

Dr: Creditor B (100)

Cr: Bank (200)

When I write two £100 cheques for a total of £200, the balance in my bank account is reduced by £200. Based on the law of accounting, a decrease in my cash asset is a credit. The total credit for my asset balance is greater than the total debit. Thus, in my records, my "Bank" ledger account has an asset credit balance, which is reduced by the credit for £200. Amounts in my records for the two creditors are liabilities, which are reduced by the two debits totaling £200.

Therefore, for this transaction, the total amount debited = 200 and the total amount credited = 200. When all three accounts are totaled, the total debits equal the total credits.

At the end of any financial period (say at the end of the quarter or the year), the total debits and the total credits for each account may be different and this difference of the two sides is called the *balance*. If the sum of the debit side is greater than the sum of the credit side, then the account has a "debit balance". If the sum of the credit side is greater, then the account has a "credit balance". If the two sides do equal each other (this would be a coincidence, not as a result of the laws of accounting), then we say we have a "zero balance".

Debit Cards and Credit Cards

Debit cards and credit cards are creative terms used by the banking industry to market and identify each card. From the cardholder's point of view, a credit card account normally contains a credit balance, a debit card account normally contains a debit balance. A debit card is used to make a purchase with one's own money. A credit card is used to make a purchase by borrowing money.

From the bank's point of view, when a debit card is used to pay a merchant, the payment causes a decrease in the amount of money the bank *owes to* the cardholder. From the bank's point of view, your debit card account is the bank's liability. A decrease to the bank's liability account is a debit. From the bank's point of view, when a credit card is used to pay a merchant, the payment causes an increase in the amount of money the bank *is owed by* the cardholder. From the bank's point of view, your credit card account is the bank's asset. An increase to the bank's asset account is a debit. Hence, using a debit card *or* credit card causes a debit to the cardholder's account in either situation when viewed from the bank's perspective.

General Ledgers

General ledger is the term for the comprehensive collection of T-accounts (so called because there was a pre-printed vertical line in the middle of each ledger page and a horizontal line at the top of each ledger page, like a large letter T). Before the advent of computerised accounting, manual accounting procedure used a book (known as a ledger) for each T-account. The collection of all these books was called the general ledger.

"Day Books" or journals are used to list every single transaction that took place during the day, and the list is totalled at the end of the day. These daybooks are not part of the double-entry bookkeeping system. The information recorded in these daybooks is then transferred to the general ledgers. Modern computer software now allows for the instant update of each ledger account – for example, when recording a cash receipt in a cash receipts journal a debit is posted to a cash ledger account with a corresponding credit in the ledger account for which the cash was received. Not every single transaction need be entered into a T-account. Usually only the sum of the book transactions (a batch total) for the day is entered in the general ledger.

The Five Accounting Elements

There are five fundamental elements within accounting. These elements are as follows: Assets, Liabilities, Equity (or Capital), Income (or Revenue) and Expenses. The five accounting elements are all affected in either a positive or negative way. A credit transaction does not always dictate a positive value or increase in a transaction and similarly, a debit does not always indicate a negative value or decrease in a transaction. An asset account is often referred to as a "debit account" due to the account's standard *increasing* attribute on the debit side. When an asset (e.g. an espresso machine) has been acquired in a business, the transaction will affect the debit side of that asset account illustrated below:

Asset	
Debits (Dr)	**Credits (Cr)**
X	

The "X" in the debit column denotes the increasing effect of a transaction on the asset *account balance* (total debits less total credits), because a debit to an asset account is an increase. The asset account above has been *added to* by a debit value X, i.e. the balance has increased by £X or $X. Likewise, in the liability account below, the X in the credit column denotes the increasing effect on the liability account balance (total credits less total debits), because a credit to a liability account is an increase.

All "mini-ledgers" in this section show standard ***increasing*** *attributes for the five elements of accounting.*

Liability	
Debits (Dr)	Credits (Cr)
	X

Income	
Debits (Dr)	Credits (Cr)
	X

Expenses	
Debits (Dr)	Credits (Cr)
X	

Equity	
Debits (Dr)	Credits (Cr)
	X

Summary table of standard increasing and decreasing attributes for the five accounting elements:

ACCOUNT TYPE	DEBIT	CREDIT
Asset	+	–
Liability	–	+
Income	–	+
Expense	+	–
Equity	–	+

Principle

Each transaction that takes place within the business will consist of at least one debit to a specific account and at least one credit to another specific account. A debit to one account can be balanced by more than one credit to other accounts, and vice versa. For all transactions, the total debits must be equal to the total credits and therefore *balance*.

The *general* accounting equation is as follows:

$$Assets = Equity + Liabilities$$

$$A = E + L$$

The equation thus becomes A – L – E = 0 (zero). When the total debits equals the total credits for each account, then the equation balances.

The *extended* accounting equation is as follows:

$$Assets + Expenses = Equity\,/\,Capital + Liabilities + Income$$

$$A + Ex = E + L + I$$

In this form, increases to the amount of accounts on the left-hand side of the equation are recorded as debits, and decreases as credits. Conversely for accounts on the right-hand side, increases to the amount of accounts are recorded as credits to the account, and decreases as debits.

This can also be rewritten in the equivalent form:

$$Assets = Liabilities + Equity / Capital + (Income - Expenses)$$

$$A = L + E + (I - Ex)$$

where the relationship of the Income and Expenses accounts to Equity and profit is a bit clearer. Here Income and Expenses are regarded as temporary or nominal accounts which pertain only to the current accounting period whereas Asset, Liabilities and Equity accounts are permanent or real accounts pertaining to the lifetime of the business. The temporary accounts are closed to the Equity account at the end of the accounting period to record profit/loss for the period. Both sides of these equations must be equal (balance).

Each transaction is recorded in a ledger or "T" account, e.g. a ledger account named "Bank" that can be changed with either a debit or credit transaction.

In accounting it is acceptable to draw-up a ledger account in the following manner for representation purposes:

Bank	
Debits (Dr)	**Credits (Cr)**

Accounts Pertaining to the Five Accounting Elements

Accounts are created/opened when the need arises for whatever purpose or situation the entity may have. For example, if your business is an airline company they will have to purchase airplanes, therefore even if an account is not listed below, a bookkeeper or accountant can create an account for a specific item, such as an asset account for airplanes. In order to understand how to classify an account into one of the five elements, a good understanding of the *definitions* of these accounts is required. Below are examples of some of the more common accounts that pertain to the five accounting elements:

Asset Accounts

Asset accounts are economic resources which benefit the business/entity and will continue to do so. Cash, bank, accounts receivable, inventory, land, buildings/plant, machinery, furniture, equipment, supplies, vehicles, trademarks and patents, goodwill, prepaid expenses, prepaid insurance, debtors (people who owe us money, due within one year), VAT input etc.

Liability Accounts

Liability accounts record debts or future obligations the business/entity owes to others. Accounts payable, salaries and wages payable, income taxes, bank overdrafts, trust accounts, accrued expenses, sales taxes, advance payments (unearned revenue), debt and accrued interest on debt, customer deposits, VAT output etc.

Equity Accounts

Equity accounts record the claims of the owners of the business/entity to the assets of that business/entity. Capital, retained earnings, drawings, common stock, accumulated funds, etc.

Income/Revenue Accounts

Income accounts record all increases in Equity other than that contributed by the owner/s of the business/entity. Services rendered, sales, interest income, membership fees, rent income, interest from investment, recurring receivables,donation etc.

Expense Accounts

Expense accounts record all decreases in the owners' equity which occur from using the assets or increasing liabilities in delivering goods or services to a customer - the costs of doing business. Telephone, water, electricity, repairs, salaries, wages, depreciation, bad debts, stationery, entertainment, honorarium, rent, fuel, utility, interest etc.

Example

Quick Services business purchases a computer for £500, on credit, from ABC Computers. Recognize the following transaction for Quick Services in a ledger account (T-account):

Quick Services has acquired a new computer which is classified as an asset within the business. According to the accrual basis of accounting, even though the computer has been purchased on credit, the computer is already the property of Quick Services and must be recognised as such. Therefore, the equipment account of Quick Services increases and is debited:

Equipment (Asset)	
(Dr)	**(Cr)**
500	

As the transaction for the new computer is made *on credit*, the payable "ABC Computers" has not yet been paid. As a result, a liability is created within the entity's records. Therefore, to balance the accounting equation the corresponding liability account is credited:

Payable ABC Computers (Liability)	
(Dr)	**(Cr)**
	500

The above example can be written in journal form:

	Dr	Cr
Equipment	500	
ABC Computers (Payable)		500

The journal entry "ABC Computers" is indented to indicate that this is the credit transaction. It is accepted accounting practice to indent credit transactions recorded within a journal.

In the accounting equation form:

A = E + L
500 = 0 + 500 (The accounting equation is therefore balanced)

Further examples

1. A business pays rent with cash: You increase rent (expense) by recording a debit transaction, and decrease cash (asset) by recording a credit transaction.
2. A business receives cash for a sale: You increase cash (asset) by recording a debit transaction, and increase sales (income) by recording a credit transaction.
3. A business buys equipment with cash: You increase equipment (asset) by recording a debit transaction, and decrease cash (asset) by recording a credit transaction.
4. A business borrows with a cash loan: You increase cash (asset) by recording a debit transaction, and increase loan (liability) by recording a credit transaction.
5. A business pays salaries with cash: You increase salary (expenses) by recording a debit transaction, and decrease cash (asset) by recording a credit transaction.
6. The totals show the net effect on the accounting equation and the double-entry principle, where the transactions are balanced.

	Account	Debit (Dr)	Credit (Cr)
1.	Rent	100	
	Bank		100
2.	Bank	50	
	Sales		50
3.	Equipment	5200	
	Bank		5200
4.	Bank	11000	
	Loan		11000
5.	Salary	5000	
	Bank		5000
6.	Total (Dr)	$21350	
	Total (Cr)		$21350

T-accounts

The process of using debits and credits creates a ledger format that resembles the letter "T". The term "T-account" is accounting jargon for a "ledger account" and is often used when discussing bookkeeping. The reason that a ledger account is often referred to as a T-account is due to the way the account is physically drawn on paper (representing a "T"). The left side (column) of the "T" for Debit (Dr) transactions and the right side (column) of the "T" for Credit (Cr) transactions.

Debits (Dr)	Credits (Cr)

Contra Account

All accounts have corresponding contra accounts depending on what transaction has taken place e.g., when a vehicle is purchased using cash, the asset account "Vehicles" is *debited* as the vehicle account increases, and simultaneously the asset account "Bank" is *credited* due to the payment for the vehicle using cash. Some balance sheet items have corresponding contra accounts, with negative balances, that offset them. Examples are accumulated depreciation against equipment, and allowance for bad debts (also known as allowance for doubtful accounts) against accounts receivable. United States GAAP utilizes the term *contra* for specific accounts only and doesn't recognize the second half of a transaction as a contra, thus the term is restricted to accounts that are related. For example, sales returns and allowance and sales discounts are contra revenues with respect to sales, as the balance of each contra (a debit) is the opposite of sales (a credit). To understand the actual value of sales, one must net the contras against sales, which gives rise to the term net sales (meaning net of the contras).

A more specific definition in common use is an account with a balance that is the opposite of the normal balance (Dr/Cr) for that section of the general ledger. An example is an office coffee fund: Expense "Coffee" (Dr) may be immediately followed by "Coffee - employee contributions" (Cr). Such an account is used for clarity rather than being a necessary part of GAAP (generally accepted accounting principles).

Real, Personal, and Nominal Accounts

Real accounts are assets. Personal accounts are liabilities and owners' equity and represent people and entities that have invested in the business. Nominal accounts are revenue, expenses, gains, and losses. Accountants close nominal accounts at the end of each accounting period. This method is used in the United Kingdom, where it is simply known as the Traditional approach.

Transactions are recorded by a debit to one account and a credit to another account using these three "golden rules of accounting":

1. Real account: Debit what comes in and credit what goes out
2. Personal account: Debit who receives and Credit who gives.

3. Nominal account: Debit all expenses & losses and Credit all incomes & gains

	Debit	**Credit**
Real (assets)	Increase	Decrease
Personal (liability)	Decrease	Increase
Personal (owner's equity)	Decrease	Increase
Nominal (revenue)	Decrease	Increase
Nominal (expenses)	Increase	Decrease
Nominal (gain)	Decrease	Increase
Nominal (loss)	Increase	Decrease

Balance Sheet Horizontal Format

Financial statements are traditionally prepared for the owners of the organisation. A typical traditional balance sheet is prepared in Horizontal format.

Horizontal Balance Sheet

Liabilities	₹	**Assets**	₹
Capital		Fixed Assets	
Reserves & Surplus		Investments	
Long Terms Loans		Current Assets	
Short Term Loans		Loans & Advances	
Current Liabilities			
Provisions			
Total		**Total**	

Vertical Format

The conventional horizontal form of Balance Sheet is not suitable for financial analysis, precisely because

1. It is designed for the owner.
2. Its presentation and sequence or order of items is relevant only in the event of liquidation; it is unsuitable for financial analysis of a 'going concern'.

Hence financial analysts generally converts horizontal balance sheet, into vertical format which is more suitable for financial analysis, especially in ratio analysis.

Particulars	₹
I. SOURCES OF FUNDS	
1. Owners Fund	
(a) Capital	
(b) Reserves & Surplus	
Less: P & L A/c Dr. Balance	
Misc. Expenditure not w/off	
Own Funds or Net Worth	
2. Loan Funds	
(a) Secured Loan	
(b) Unsecured Loan	
Total Loan Funds	
Total Capital Employed	
II. APPLICATION OF FUNDS	
1. Fixed Assets	
A. Tangible Assets (Gross Block)	
Less: Depreciation	
Net Block	
B. Intangible Assets	
2. Long Term / Trade Investments	
3. Working Capital	
Current Asset	
Less: Current Liabilities	
Net Current Assets	
Total Assets Employed	

Ratio

- Ratio is a relationship between two or more items of the financial statements. E.g. Net Profit Ratio
- Profit A 65 B 45
- Sales A 650 B 300

Ratio Analysis

- A single accounting figure by itself may not communicate any meaningful information but when expressed as a relative to some other figure, it may definitely provide some significant information. Hence ratio analysis proves very beneficial.
- Ratio analysis is not just comparing different numbers from financial statements. It involves comparing the ratio against previous years, against peers, and with the industry average for the purpose of financial analysis.

Ratio Analysis - Advantages

Ratios help stakeholders (like owners, managers, investors, lenders, employees) to draw conclusion about the

- Performance (past, present and future).
- Strengths & weakness.
- And take decision in relation to the firm.

Types of Ratio

The ratios can be classified into following four broad categories:

1. Liquidity Ratios.
2. Capital Structure/Leverage ratios.
3. Activity Ratios.
4. Profitability Ratios.
5. Return Ratios.

Financial Ratio

A financial ratio or accounting ratio is a relative magnitude of two selected numerical values taken from an enterprise's financial statements. Often used in accounting, there are many standard ratios used to try to evaluate the overall financial condition of a corporation or other organization. Financial ratios may be used by managers within a firm, by current and potential shareholders (owners) of a firm, and by a firm's creditors. Financial analysts use financial ratios to compare the strengths and weaknesses in various companies. If shares in a company are traded in a financial market, the market price of the shares is used in certain financial ratios.

Ratios can be expressed as a decimal value, such as 0.10, or given as an equivalent percent value, such as 10%. Some ratios are usually quoted as percentages, especially ratios that are usually or always less than 1, such as earnings yield, while others are usually quoted as decimal numbers, especially ratios that are usually more than 1, such as P/E ratio; these latter are also called multiples.

Given any ratio, one can take its reciprocal; if the ratio was above 1, the reciprocal will be below 1, and conversely. The reciprocal expresses the same information, but may be more understandable: for instance, the earnings yield can be compared with bond yields, while the P/E ratio cannot be: for example, a P/E ratio of 20 corresponds to an earnings yield of 5%.

Sources of Data for Financial Ratios

Values used in calculating financial ratios are taken from the balance sheet, income statement, statement of cash flows or (sometimes) the statement of changes in equity. These comprise the firm's "accounting statements" or financial statements. The statements' data is based on the accounting method and accounting standards used by the organisation.

Purpose and Types of Ratios

Financial ratios quantify many aspects of a business and are an integral part of the financial statement analysis. Financial ratios are categorized according to the financial aspect of the business which the ratio measures. Liquidity ratios measure the availability of cash to pay debt. Activity ratios measure how quickly a firm converts non-cash assets to cash assets. Debt ratios measure the firm's ability to repay long-term debt. Profitability ratios measure the firm's use of its assets and control of its expenses to generate an acceptable rate of return. Market ratios measure investor response to owning a company's stock and also the cost of issuing stock. These are concerned with the return on investment for shareholders, and with the relationship between return and the value of an investment in company's shares.

Financial ratios allow for comparisons

- between companies
- between industries
- between different time periods for one company
- between a single company and its industry average

Ratios generally are not useful unless they are benchmarked against something else, like past performance or another company. Thus, the ratios of firms in different industries, which face different risks, capital requirements, and competition are usually hard to compare.

Accounting Methods and Principles

Financial ratios may not be directly comparable between companies that use different accounting methods or follow various standard accounting practices. Most public companies are required by law to use generally accepted accounting principles for their home countries, but private companies, partnerships and sole proprietorships may not use accrual basis accounting. Large multi-national corporations may use International Financial Reporting Standards to produce their financial statements, or they may use the generally accepted accounting principles of their home country.

There is no international standard for calculating the summary data presented in all financial statements, and the terminology is not always consistent between companies, industries, countries and time periods.

Abbreviations and Terminology

Various abbreviations may be used in financial statements, especially financial statements summarized on the Internet. Sales reported by a firm are usually net sales, which deduct returns, allowances, and early payment discounts from the charge on an invoice. Net income is always the amount *after* taxes, depreciation, amortization, and interest, unless otherwise stated. Otherwise, the amount would be EBIT, or EBITDA.

Companies that are primarily involved in providing services with labour do not generally report "Sales" based on hours. These companies tend to report "revenue" based on the monetary value of income that the services provide.

Note that Shareholders' Equity and Owner's Equity are *not* the same thing, Shareholder's Equity represents the total number of shares in the company multiplied by each share's book value; Owner's Equity represents the total number of shares that an individual shareholder owns (usually the owner with controlling interest), multiplied by each share's book value. It is important to make this distinction when calculating ratios.

Abbreviations

- COGS = Cost of goods sold, or cost of sales.
- EBIT = Earnings before interest and taxes
- EBITDA = Earnings before interest, taxes, depreciation, and amortization
- EPS = Earnings per share

Ratios

Profitability Ratios

Profitability ratios measure the company's use of its assets and control of its expenses to generate an acceptable rate of return

Gross margin, Gross profit margin or Gross Profit Rate

$$\frac{\text{Gross Profit}}{\text{Net Sales}} \text{ :::OR::: } \frac{\text{Net Sales -- COGS}}{\text{Net Sales}}$$

Operating margin, Operating Income Margin, Operating profit margin or Return on sales (ROS)

$$\frac{\text{Operating Income}}{\text{Net Sales}}$$

Note: Operating income is the difference between operating revenues and operating expenses, but it is also sometimes used as a synonym for EBIT and operating profit. This is true if the firm has no non-operating income. (Earnings before interest and taxes / Sales)

Profit margin, net margin or net profit margin

$$\frac{\text{Net Profit}}{\text{Net Sales}}$$

Return on equity (ROE)

$$\frac{\text{Net Income}}{\text{Average Shareholders Equity}}$$

Return on assets (ROA ratio or Du Pont Ratio)

$$\frac{\text{Net Income}}{\text{Average Total Assets}}$$

Return on assets (ROA)

$$\frac{\text{Net Income}}{\text{Total Assets}}$$

Return on assets Du Pont (ROA Du Pont)

$$\left(\frac{\text{Net Income}}{\text{Net Sales}}\right)\left(\frac{\text{Net Sales}}{\text{Total Assets}}\right)$$

Return on Equity Du Pont (ROE Du Pont)

$$\left(\frac{\text{Net Income}}{\text{Net Sales}}\right)\left(\frac{\text{Net Sales}}{\text{Average Assets}}\right)\left(\frac{\text{Average Assets}}{\text{Average Equity}}\right)$$

Return on net assets (RONA)

$$\frac{\text{Net Income}}{\text{Fixed Assets + Working Capital}}$$

Return on capital (ROC)

$$\frac{\text{EBIT}(1 - \text{Tax Rate})}{\text{Invested Capital}}$$

Risk adjusted return on capital (RAROC)

$$\frac{\text{Expected Return}}{\text{Economic Capital}} \text{ :::OR ::: } \frac{\text{Expected Return}}{\text{Value at Risk}}$$

Return on capital employed (ROCE)

$$\frac{\text{EBIT}}{\text{Capital Employed}}$$

Note: this is somewhat similar to (ROI), which calculates Net Income per Owner's Equity

Cash flow return on investment (CFROI)

$$\frac{\text{Cash Flow}}{\text{Market Recapitalisation}}$$

Efficiency ratio

$$\frac{\text{Non-Interest expense}}{\text{Revenue}}$$

Net gearing

$$\frac{\text{Net debt}}{\text{Equity}}$$

Basic Earnings Power Ratio

$$\frac{\text{EBIT}}{\text{Total Assets}}$$

Liquidity Ratios

Liquidity ratios measure the availability of cash to pay debt.

Current ratio (Working Capital Ratio)

$$\frac{\text{Current Assets}}{\text{Current Liabilities}}$$

Acid-test ratio (Quick ratio)

$$\frac{\text{Current Assets -- (Inventories + Prepayments)}}{\text{Current Liabilities}}$$

Cash ratio

$$\frac{\text{Cash and Marketable Securities}}{\text{Current Liabilities}}$$

Operating cash flow ratio

$$\frac{\text{Operating Cash Flow}}{\text{Total Debts}}$$

Activity Ratios (Efficiency Ratios)

Activity ratios measure the effectiveness of the firm's use of resources.

Average collection period

$$\frac{\text{Accounts Receivable}}{\text{Annual Credit Sales} \div 365 \text{ Days}}$$

Degree of Operating Leverage (DOL)

$$\frac{\text{Percent Change in Net Operating Income}}{\text{Percent Change in Sales}}$$

DSO Ratio.

$$\frac{\text{Accounts Receivable}}{\text{Total Annual Sales} \div 365 \text{ Days}}$$

Average payment period

$$\frac{\text{Accounts Payable}}{\text{Annual Credit Purchases} \div 365 \text{ Days}}$$

Asset turnover

$$\frac{\text{Net Sales}}{\text{Total Assets}}$$

Stock turnover ratio

$$\frac{\text{Cost of Goods Sold}}{\text{Average Inventory}}$$

Receivables Turnover Ratio

$$\frac{\text{Net Credit Sales}}{\text{Average Net Receivables}}$$

Inventory conversion ratio

$$\frac{365 \text{ Days}}{\text{Inventory Turnover}}$$

Inventory conversion period (essentially same thing as above)

$$\left(\frac{\text{Inventory}}{\text{Cost of Goods Sold}}\right) 365 \text{ Days}$$

Receivables conversion period

$$\left(\frac{\text{Receivables}}{\text{Net Sales}}\right)365\text{ Days}$$

Payables conversion period

$$\left(\frac{\text{Accounts Payables}}{\text{Purchases}}\right)365\text{ Days}$$

Cash Conversion Cycle

Inventory Conversion Period + Receivables Conversion Period - Payables Conversion Period

Debt Ratios (Leveraging Ratios)

Debt ratios quantify the firm's ability to repay long-term debt. Debt ratios measure financial leverage.

Debt ratio

$$\frac{\text{Total Liabilities}}{\text{Total Assets}}$$

Debt to equity ratio

$$\frac{\text{Long-term Debt + Value of Leases}}{\text{Average Shareholders Equity}}$$

Long-term Debt to equity (LT Debt to Equity)

$$\frac{\text{Long-term Debt}}{\text{Average Shareholders Equity}}$$

Times interest earned ratio (Interest Coverage Ratio)

$$\frac{\text{EBIT}}{\text{Annual Interest Expense}}$$

OR

$$\frac{\text{Net Income}}{\text{Annual Interest Expense}}$$

Debt service coverage ratio

$$\frac{\text{Net Operating Income}}{\text{Total Debt Service}}$$

Market Ratios

Market ratios measure investor response to owning a company's stock and also the cost of issuing stock. These are concerned with the return on investment for shareholders, and with the relationship between return and the value of an investment in company's shares.

Earnings per share (EPS)

$$\frac{\text{Net Earnings}}{\text{Number of Shares}}$$

Payout ratio

$$\frac{\text{Dividends}}{\text{Earnings}}$$

OR

$$\frac{\text{Dividends}}{\text{EPS}}$$

Dividend cover (the inverse of Payout Ratio)

$$\frac{\text{Earnings per Share}}{\text{Dividend per Share}}$$

P/E ratio

$$\frac{\text{Market Price per Share}}{\text{Diluted EPS}}$$

Dividend yield

$$\frac{\text{Dividend}}{\text{Current Market Price}}$$

Cash flow ratio or Price/cash flow ratio

$$\frac{\text{Market Price per Share}}{\text{Present Value of Cash Flow per Share}}$$

Price to book value ratio (P/B or PBV)

$$\frac{\text{Market Price per Share}}{\text{Balance Sheet Price per Share}}$$

Price/sales ratio

$$\frac{\text{Market Price per Share}}{\text{Gross Sales}}$$

PEG ratio

$$\frac{\text{Price per Earnings}}{\text{Annual EPS Growth}}$$

Other Market Ratios

EV/EBITDA

$$\frac{\text{Enterprise Value}}{\text{EBITDA}}$$

EV/Sales

$$\frac{\text{Enterprise Value}}{\text{Net Sales}}$$

Cost/Income ratio

Sector-specific ratios

EV/capacity

EV/output

Capital Budgeting Ratios

In addition to assisting management and owners in diagnosing the financial health of their company, ratios can also help managers make decisions about investments or projects that the company is considering to take, such as acquisitions, or expansion.

Many formal methods are used in capital budgeting, including the techniques such as

- Net present value
- Profitability index
- Internal rate of return
- Modified internal rate of return
- Equivalent annuity

P/B Ratio

The price-to-book ratio, or P/B ratio, is a financial ratio used to compare a company's current market price to its book value. It is also sometimes known as a Market-to-Book ratio. The calculation can be performed in two ways, but the result should be the same each way. In the first way, the company's market capitalization can be divided by the company's total book value from its balance sheet. The second way, using per-share values, is to divide the company's current share price by the book value per share (i.e. its book value divided by the number of outstanding shares).

As with most ratios, it varies a fair amount by industry. Industries that require more infrastructure capital (for each dollar of profit) will usually trade at P/B ratios much lower than, for example, consulting firms. P/B ratios are commonly used to compare banks, because most assets and liabilities of banks are constantly valued at market values. A higher P/B ratio implies that investors *expect* management to create more value from a given set of assets, all else equal (and/or that the market value of the firm's assets is significantly higher than their accounting value). P/B ratios do not, however, directly provide any information on the ability of the firm to generate profits or cash for shareholders.

This ratio also gives some idea of whether an investor is paying too much for what would be left if the company went bankrupt immediately. For companies in distress, the book value is usually calculated without the intangible assets that would have no resale value. In such cases, P/B should also be calculated on a "diluted" basis, because stock options may well vest on sale of the company or change of control or firing of management.

It is also known as the market-to-book ratio and the price-to-equity ratio (which should not be confused with the price-to-earnings ratio), and its inverse is called the book-to-market ratio.

Total Book Value vs Tangible Book Value

Technically, P/B can be calculated either including or excluding intangible assets and goodwill. When intangible assets and goodwill are excluded, the ratio is often specified to be "price to tangible book value" or "price to tangible book".

Value and Limitations

Except in the case of a small minority of companies like property companies and investment trusts that are asset based, book values bear little or no relationship to true values of the companies. The items on the balance sheet are the result of various transactions, recorded using double entry at a particular point in time, to the extent that they do not form part of the profit and loss account to that point in time. The assets and liabilities comprising the book value are mainly stated at historic cost though a few items therein may be stated at valuations.

In many of today's companies, their most valuable assets are not shown on the balances sheet and are therefore not included in the book value. Book values are meaningless in companies such as Apple, Microsoft, Google, Facebook, GlaxoSmithKline, etc. where their intellectual capital, internally generated goodwill, etc. are much more valuable than the assets per their balance sheets but are not included therein.

In Benjamin Graham's days, book values were more relevant as most companies then had significant investments in tangible assets and such assets comprised the bulk of the value of the company. The value of today's companies, other than asset based companies like investment trusts and property companies, is very different from the book values and there is no relationship between their intrinsic values and their book values. That is why Warren Buffett said "In all cases, what is clear is that book value is meaningless as an indicator of value" in his 2000 annual report.

Despite the theoretical limitations of the price-book ratio, academic research has persistently shown that stocks with low price-book ratios persistently outperform stocks with high price-book ratios. Fama and French incorporated a price-book term in their influential three factor model. Penman Richardson and Tuna (2013) show how the ratio can be decomposed into financing and operating components. Foye and Mramor (2016) show that while stocks with low price-book ratios normally outperform, the ratios decomposed elements exhibit a different relationship with returns in different countries, implying that the price-book ratio may have a country-specific interpretation.

Liquidity Ratio

Liquidity Ratio may refer to:

- Reserve requirement, a bank regulation that sets the minimum reserves each bank must hold.
- Quick Ratio (also known as an *Acid Test* or *Liquidity Ratio*), a ratio used to determine the liquidity of a business entity

Liquidity ratio expresses a company's ability to repay short-term creditors out of its total cash. It is the result of dividing the total cash by short-term borrowings. It shows the number of times short-term liabilities are covered by cash. If the value is greater than 1.00, it means fully covered.

The formula is the following:

LR = liquid assets / short-term liabilities.

Reserve Requirement

The reserve requirement (or cash reserve ratio) is a central bank regulation employed by most, but not all, of the world's central banks, that sets the minimum amount of reserves that must be held by a commercial bank. The minimum reserve is generally determined by the central bank to be no less than a specified percentage of the amount of deposit liabilities the commercial bank owes to its customers. The commercial bank's reserves normally consist of cash owned by the bank and stored physically in the bank vault (vault cash), plus the amount of the commercial bank's balance in that bank's account with the central bank.

The required reserve ratio is sometimes used as a tool in monetary policy, influencing the country's borrowing and interest rates by changing the amount of funds available for banks to make loans with. Western central banks rarely increase the reserve requirements because it would cause immediate liquidity problems for banks with low excess reserves; they generally prefer to use open market operations (buying and selling government-issued bonds) to implement their monetary policy. The People's Bank of China uses changes in reserve requirements as an inflation-fighting tool, and raised the reserve requirement ten times in 2007 and eleven times since the beginning of 2010.

An institution that holds reserves in excess of the required amount is said to hold *excess reserves*.

Effects on Money Supply

The Conventional View

The theory that a reserve requirement can be used as a tool of monetary policy is frequently found in economics textbooks. Under the theory, higher the reserve requirement is set, the less funds banks will have to loan out , leading to lower money creation and perhaps to higher purchasing power of the money previously in use. Under this view, the effect is multiplied, because money obtained as loan proceeds can be re-deposited, and a portion of those deposits may again be loaned out, and so on. Under this theory, the effect on the money supply is governed by the following formulas:

$M_1 = MB * m$: definitional relationship between monetary base MB (bank reserves plus currency held by the non-bank public) the narrowly defined money supply, M_1,

$m = \frac{(1+c)}{(c+R)} = \frac{1+\frac{C}{D}}{\frac{C}{D}+R}$: derived formula for the money multiplier m, the factor by which lending and re-ending leads M_1 to be a multiple of the monetary base:

where notationally,

$c =$ the currency ratio: the ratio of the public's holdings of currency (undeposited cash) to the public's holdings of demand deposits; and

$R =$ the total reserve ratio (the ratio of legally required plus non-required reserve holdings of banks to demand deposit liabilities of banks).

However, in the United States (and other countries except Brazil, China, India, Russia), the reserve requirements are generally not frequently altered to implement monetary policy because of the short-term disruptive effect on financial markets.

The Endogenous Money View

Some economists dispute the conventional theory of the reserve requirement. Criticisms of the conventional theory are usually associated with theories of endogenous money.

Jaromir Benes and Michael Kumhof of the IMF Research Department report that the "deposit multiplier" of the undergraduate economics textbook, where monetary aggregates are created at the initiative of the central bank, through an initial injection of high-powered money into the banking system that gets multiplied through bank lending, turns the actual operation of the monetary transmission mechanism on its head. Benes and Kumhof assert that in most cases where banks ask for replenishment of depleted reserves, the central bank obliges. Under this view, reserves therefore impose no constraints, as the deposit multiplier is simply, in the words of Kydland and Prescott (1990), a myth. Under this theory, private banks almost fully control the money creation process.

Required Reserves

United States

In the United States, a reserve requirement (or liquidity ratio) is a minimum value, set by the

Board of Governors of the Federal Reserve System, of the ratio of required reserves to a category of deposit liabilities (called the "Net Transaction Accounts" or "NTAs") owed by depository institutions to their customers (e.g., owed by commercial banks including U.S. branches of a foreign bank, savings and loan association, savings bank, credit union). The deposit liability categories currently subject to reserve requirements are mainly checking accounts. There is no reserve requirement on savings accounts and time deposit accounts owned by individuals. The total amount of all NTAs held by customers with U.S. depository institutions, plus the U.S. paper currency and coin currency held by the nonbank public, is called M1.

A depository institution can satisfy its reserve requirements by holding either vault cash or reserve deposits. An institution that is a member of the Federal Reserve System must hold its reserve deposits at a Federal Reserve Bank. Nonmember institutions can elect to hold their reserve deposits at a member institution on a pass-through basis.

A depository institution's reserve requirements vary by the dollar amount of NTAs held by customers of that institution. Effective November 17, 2015, institutions with net transactions accounts:

- Of less than $15.2 million have no minimum reserve requirement;
- Between $15.2 million and $110.2 million must have a liquidity ratio of 3% of NTAs;
- Exceeding $110.2 million must have a liquidity ratio of 10% of NTAs.

The threshold monetary amounts are recalculated annually according to a statutory formula.

Effective 27 December 1990, a liquidity ratio of zero has applied to CDs and time deposits, owned by entities other than households, and the Eurocurrency liabilities of depository institutions. Deposits owned by foreign corporations or governments are currently not subject to reserve requirements.

When an institution fails to satisfy its reserve requirements, it can make up its deficiency with reserves borrowed from a Federal Reserve Bank or from an institution holding reserves in excess of reserve requirements. Such loans are typically due in 24 hours or less.

An institution's overnight reserves, averaged over some maintenance period, must equal or exceed its average required reserves, calculated over the same maintenance period. If this calculation is satisfied, there is no requirement that reserves be held at any point in time. Hence reserve requirements play only a limited role in money creation in the United States. Since quantitative easing began in 2008, they have been even less important, as an enormous glut of excess reserves now exists (over the whole system, though in theory, individual banks may still run into temporary shortfalls).

The International Banking Act of 1978 requires branches of foreign banks operating in the United States to follow the same required reserve ratio standards.

Countries Without Reserve Requirements

Canada, the UK, New Zealand, Australia, Sweden and Hong Kong have no reserve requirements.

This does not mean that banks can - even in theory - create money without limit. On the contrary, banks are constrained by capital requirements, which are arguably more important than reserve requirements even in countries that have reserve requirements.

It also does not mean that a commercial bank's overnight reserves can become *negative*, in these countries. The central bank will *always* step in to lend the necessary reserves if necessary so that this does not happen; this is sometimes described as "defending the payment system". Historically a central bank might once have run out of reserves to lend and so have had to suspend redemptions, but this can no longer happen to modern central banks because of the end of the gold standard worldwide, which means that all nations use a fiat currency.

A zero reserve requirement cannot be explained by a theory that holds that monetary policy works by varying the quantity of money using the reserve requirement.

Even in the United States, which retains formal (though now mostly irrelevant) reserve requirements, the notion of controlling the money supply by targeting the quantity of base money fell out of favor many years ago, and now the pragmatic explanation of monetary policy refers to targeting the *interest rate* to control the broad money supply.

United Kingdom

In the UK the term clearing banks is sometimes used, meaning banks that have direct access to the clearing system. However, for the purposes of clarity, the term *commercial banks* will be used for the remainder of this section.

The Bank of England, which is the central bank for the entire United Kingdom, previously held to a voluntary reserve ratio system, with no minimum reserve requirement set. In theory this meant that commercial banks could retain zero reserves. The average cash reserve ratio across the entire United Kingdom banking system, though, was higher during that period, at about 0.15% as of 1999.

From 1971 to 1980, the commercial banks all agreed to a reserve ratio of 1.5%. In 1981 this requirement was abolished.

From 1981 to 2009, each commercial bank set out its own monthly voluntary reserve target in a contract with the Bank of England. Both shortfalls and excesses of reserves relative to the commercial bank's own target over an averaging period of one day would result in a charge, incentivising the commercial bank to stay near its target, a system known as *reserves averaging*.

Upon the parallel introduction of quantitative easing and interest on excess reserves in 2009, banks were no longer required to set out a target, and so were no longer penalised for holding excess reserves; indeed, they were proportionally compensated for holding all their reserves at the Bank Rate (the Bank of England now uses the same interest rate for its bank rate, its deposit rate and its interest rate target). In the absence of an agreed target, the concept of excess reserves does not really apply to the Bank of England any longer, so it is technically incorrect to call its new policy "interest on excess reserves".

Canada

Canada abolished its reserve requirement in 1992.

Other Countries

Other countries have *required reserve ratios* (or RRRs) that are statutorily enforced:

Country	Required reserve (in %)	Note
Australia	None	Statutory Reserve Deposits abolished in 1988, replaced with 1% Non-callable Deposits
New Zealand	None	1985
Sweden	None	Effective 1 April 1994
Eurozone	1.00	Effective 18 January 2012. Down from 2% between January 1999 and January 2012.
Czech Republic	2.00	Since 7 October 2009
Hungary	2.00	Since November 2008
South Africa	2.50	
Switzerland	2.50	
Latvia	3.00	Just after the Parex Bank bailout (24.12.2008), Latvian Central Bank decreased the RRR from 7% (?) down to 3%
Poland	3.50	as of 31 December 2010
Romania	8.00	as of 24 May 2015 for lei. And 10% for foreign currency as of 24 October 2016
Russia	4.00	Effective 1 April 2011, up from 2.5% in January 2011.
Chile	4.50	
India	4.00	Jun2 2015, as per RBI.
Bangladesh	6.00	Raised from 5.50. Effective from 15 December 2010
Lithuania	6.00	
Nigeria	20.00	Raised from 15.00. Effective from 25 November 2014
Pakistan	5.00	Since 1 November 2008
Taiwan	7.00	
Turkey	8.50	Since 19 February 2013
Jordan	8.00	
Zambia	8.00	
Burundi	8.50	
Ghana	9.00	
Israel	9.00	the Required Reserve Ratio is called Minimum Capital Ratio
Mexico	10.50	
Sri Lanka	8.00	With effect from 29 April 2011. 8% of total rupee deposit liabilities.
Bulgaria	10.00	Banks shall maintain minimum required reserves to the amount of 10% of the deposit base (effective from 1 December 2008) with two exceptions (effective from 1 January 2009): 1. on funds attracted by banks from abroad: 5%; 2. on funds attracted from state and local government budgets: 0%.
Croatia	14.00	Down from 17%, effective from 2009-01-14

Country	Required reserve (in %)	Note
Costa Rica	15.00	
Malawi	15.00	
Nepal	5.00	From the monetary policy announcement for FY 2011/12 CRR reduced from 5.5% to 5%
Hong Kong	None	
Brazil	45.00	Up from 44%, effective from June, 2014. Term deposits have a (25% + 11%) RRR and savings accounts a (24.5% + 5.5%) ratio.
China	17.00	China cuts bank reserves again to counter slowdown as of 29 February 2016. Chinese Banks
Tajikistan	20.00	
Suriname	25.00	Down from 27%, effective from 2007-01-01
Lebanon	30.00	

Historical Changes in Reserve Ratios

In some countries, the *cash reserve ratios* have decreased over time; in some countries they have increased:

Country	1968	1978	1988	1998
United Kingdom	20.5	15.9	5.0	3.1
Turkey	58.3	62.7	30.8	18.0
Germany	19.0	19.3	17.2	11.9
United States	12.3	10.1	8.5	10.3
India	3	6	10	10-11

(Ratios are expressed in percentage points.)

Quick Ratio

In finance, the Acid-test or quick ratio or liquidity ratio measures the ability of a company to use its *near cash* or quick assets to extinguish or retire its current liabilities immediately. Quick assets include those current assets that presumably can be quickly converted to cash at close to their book values. A company with a quick ratio of less than 1 cannot currently fully pay back its current liabilities.

Formula

$$\text{Quick (Acid Test) Ratio} = \frac{\text{Cash and Cash Equivalent} + \text{Marketable Securities} + \text{Accounts Receivable}}{\text{Current Liabilities}}$$

Note that inventory is excluded from the sum of assets in the quick ratio, but included in the current ratio. Ratios are tests of viability for business entities but do not give a complete picture of the business' health. If a business has large amounts in accounts receivable which are due for payment after a long period (say 120 days), and essential business expenses and accounts payable due for immediate payment, the quick ratio may look healthy when the business is actually about to run out of cash. In contrast, if the business has negotiated fast payment or cash from customers, and long terms from suppliers, it may have a very low quick ratio and yet be very healthy.

Generally, the acid test ratio should be 1:1 or higher, however this varies widely by industry. In general, the higher the ratio, the greater the company's liquidity (i.e., the better able to meet current obligations using liquid assets).

Current Ratio

The current ratio is a liquidity ratio that measures whether or not a firm has enough resources to meet its short-term obligations. It compares a firm's current assets to its current liabilities, and is expressed as follows:

$$\text{Current ratio} = \frac{\text{Current Assets}}{\text{Current Liabilities}}$$

The current ratio is an indication of a firm's liquidity. Acceptable current ratios vary from industry to industry. In many cases a creditor would consider a high current ratio to be better than a low current ratio, because a high current ratio indicates that the company is more likely to pay the creditor back. Large current ratios are not always a good sign for investors. If the company's current ratio is too high it may indicate that the company is not efficiently using its current assets or its short-term financing facilities.

If current liabilities exceed current assets the current ratio will be less than 1. A current ratio of less than 1 indicates that the company may have problems meeting its short-term obligations. Some types of businesses can operate with a current ratio of less than one however. If inventory turns into cash much more rapidly than the accounts payable become due, then the firm's current ratio can comfortably remain less than one. Inventory is valued at the cost of acquiring it and the firm intends to sell the inventory for more than this cost. The sale will therefore generate substantially more cash than the value of inventory on the balance sheet. Low current ratios can also be justified for businesses that can collect cash from customers long before they need to pay their suppliers.

Capital Structure/Leverage Ratios

a. Capital Structure ratios: These ratios provide an insight into the financing techniques used by a business and focus, as a consequence, on the long term solvency position.

   1. Equity ratio: This ratio indicates proportion of owners fund to total fund invested in the business.

$$\text{Equity Ratio} = \frac{\text{Shareholder's Equity}}{\text{Total Capital Employed}}$$

2. Debt ratio:

$$\text{Debt Ratio} = \frac{\text{Total Debt}}{\text{Capital Employed}}$$

Total debt includes short and long term borrowing from financial institution, debentures/ bonds deferred payment arrangements for buying capital equipments, bank borrowings, public deposits and any other interest bearing loan. Capital employed includes total debt and net worth. This ratio is used to analyse long term solvency of the firm.

3. Debt equity ratio:

$$\textit{Debt equity Ratio} = \frac{\textit{Debt + Preference Share Capital}}{\textit{Shareholders Equity}}$$

This ratio indicates the proportion of debt fund in relation to equity. Lenders are very keen to know this ratio since it shows relative weight of debt and equity. A high ratio here means less protection for creditors.A low ratio, on the other hand, indicates a wider safety cushion.

b. Coverage ratios: The coverage ratios measure the firm's ability to service the fixed liabilities. These ratios establish the relationship between fixed claims and what is normally available out of which these claims are to be paid. The fixed claims of:

i. Interest on loans.

ii. Preference Dividends.

iii. Repayment installment of loans.

1. $$\textit{Debt Service Coverage ratios} = \frac{\textit{Earnings available for debt service}}{\textit{Interest + Installments}}$$

Earnings for debt service = Net Profit + Non cash operating expenses like depreciation and other amortisation + non-operating adjustments like loss on sale of fixed assets + Interest on debt funds

Lenders are interested in debt service coverage to judge the firms ability to pay off current interest and instalments.

2. $$\textit{Interest Coverage ratios} = \frac{\textit{EBIT}}{\textit{Interest}}$$

This ratio indicates the extent to which earnings may fall without causing any embarrassment to the company regarding the payment of interest charges. A high ratio means that an enterprise can easily meet its interest obligation even if EBIT suffers a considerable decline. A lower ratio indicates excessive use of debt or inefficient operations.

1. $$\textit{Preference dividend Coverage ratio} = \frac{\textit{EAT}}{\textit{Preference dividend liability}}$$

This ratio measures the ability of a firm to pay dividend on preference shares which carry a stated rate of return.

2. $\text{Capital Gearing ratio} = \dfrac{\text{Preference Share Capital} + \text{Debenture} + \text{Long Term Loan}}{\text{Equity Share Capital} + \text{Reserves \& Surplus} - \text{Losses}}$

Activity Ratios

Activity ratios are also called as Turnover ratios or Performance ratios. These ratios are used to evaluate efficiency with which the company manages and utilises its assets. These ratios are usually calculated with reference to sale/cost of goods sold and are expressed in terms of rate or times. Some of the important activity ratios are as follows:

a. $\text{Capital Turnover Ratio} = \dfrac{\text{Sales}}{\text{Capital Employed}}$

This ratio indicates the firm's ability of generating sales per rupee of long term investments.

b. $\text{Fixed Asset Turnover Ratio} = \dfrac{\text{Sales}}{\text{Capital Asset}}$

This ratio indicates the firm's ability to efficient utilisation of fixed asset in generating sales.

c. $\text{Working Capital Turnover Ratio} = \dfrac{\text{Sales}}{\text{Working Capital}}$

Working Capital Turnover is further segregated into Inventory turnover, Debtors Turnover, Creditors turnover.

i. $\text{Inventory Turnover Ratio} = \dfrac{\text{Cost of Sales or Sales}}{\text{Average or Closing Inventory}}$

$$\text{Average Inventory} = \frac{\text{Opening Stock} + \text{Closing Stock}}{2}$$

Inventory turnover ratio indicates average stock holding period. However it can be directly calculated as

$$\text{Stock holding Period} = \frac{\text{Average Inventory}}{\text{Sales or Cost of sales}}\ X\ 365/12$$

This ratio indicates that how fast inventory is sold. It establishes the relationship between cost of goods sold during the year and average inventory held during the year.

c.

ii. $\text{Debtors Turnover Ratio} = \dfrac{\text{Credit Sales}}{\text{Average Accounts Receivables}}$

This ratio throw light on the collection and credit policies of the firm.

Debtors turnover ratio indicates average collection period. However it can be directly calculated as

$$Debtors\ velocity = \frac{Average\ Debtors}{Credit\ Sales} X\ 365/12$$

iii. $$Creditors\ Turnover\ Ratio = \frac{Credit\ Purchase}{Average\ Accounts\ Payables}$$

This ratio shows the velocity of the debt payment by the firm. This ratios reflect the credit terms granted by creditors.

Average payment period can be calculated as

$$Creditors\ Velocity = \frac{Average\ Creditors}{Credit\ Purchases} X\ 365/12$$

Profitability Ratios:

Profitability ratios measure the profitability as a percentage of sales.

a. $$Net\ Profit\ Ratio = \frac{Net\ Profit\ After\ Tax}{Sales} * 100$$

b. $$Gross\ Profit\ Ratio = \frac{Gross\ Profit}{Sales} * 100$$

c. $$Operating\ Profit\ Ratio = \frac{Operating\ Profit}{Sales} * 100$$

Return Ratios:

Return ratios measure the profitability in relation to capital used. These ratios reflect the final results of the business.

a. $$Return\ on\ Equity\ (ROE) = \frac{Profit\ after\ Taxes}{Net\ worth} * 100$$

Return on equity measures the profitability of equity funds invested in the firm.

b. $$Return\ on\ capital\ employed\ (ROCE)\ /\ Return\ on\ Investment\ (ROI) = \frac{Return}{Capital\ Employed}$$

where,

$$Return = Net\ Profit\ before\ Taxes\ + Interest\ +/-\ Non\ trading\ adjustment$$

$$Capital\ Employed = Equity + Preference + Reserves\ \&\ Surplus + Debentures\ \&\ Other\ Long\ Term\ Loan - Misc.\ Expenditure\ \&\ Losses - Non\ trade\ investments$$

$$Return\ on\ Investment\ (ROI) = Profitability\ Ratio\ X\ Capital\ Turnover\ Ratio$$

ROI can be improved either by improving operating profit ratio or capital turnover or by both.

c. $$Return\ on\ Asset = \frac{Net\ Profit\ After\ Tax}{Average\ Fixed\ Assets}$$

This ratio measures the profitability of the firm in terms of assets employed in the firm.

d. $$Earnings\ per\ Share\ (EPS) = \frac{Net\ Profit\ available\ to\ Equity\ shareholders}{Number\ of\ Equity\ Shares}$$

The profitability per share from the point of view equity share-holders

e. $$Price\ Earning\ Ratio\ (PE) = \frac{Market\ Price\ Per\ share}{Earning\ Per\ Share}$$

The PE ratio indicates the expectation of equity investors about the earnings of the company.

f. $$Dividend\ per\ Share\ (DPS) = \frac{Dividend\ distributed\ to\ Equity\ shareholders}{Number\ of\ Equity\ Shares}$$

Dividend per share ratio indicates the amount of profit distributed per equity share.

Various ratios are good measure of:

- Growth potential of investment.
- Risk characteristics.
- Profitability.
- Degree of liquidity.
- Corporate image.

Fixed-asset Turnover

Fixed-asset turnover is the ratio of sales (on the profit and loss account) to the value of fixed assets (on the balance sheet). It indicates how well the business is using its fixed assets to generate sales.

$$Fixed\ Asset\ Turnover = \frac{Net\ sales}{Average\ net\ fixed\ assets}$$

Generally speaking, the higher the ratio, the better, because a high ratio indicates the business has less money tied up in fixed assets for each unit of currency of sales revenue. A declining ratio may indicate that the business is over-invested in plant, equipment, or other fixed assets.

In A.A.T. assessments this financial measure is calculated in two different ways.

1. Total Asset Turnover Ratio = Revenue / Total Assets

2. Net Asset Turnover Ratio = Revenue / (Total Assets - Current Liabilities)

Inventory Turnover

In accounting, the Inventory turnover is a measure of the number of times inventory is sold or used in a time period such as a year. The equation for inventory turnover equals the cost of goods sold or net sales divided by the average inventory. Inventory turnover is also known as inventory turns, merchandise turnover, stockturn, stock turns, turns, and stock turnover.

Inventory Turnover Formulas

The formula for inventory turnover:

$$\text{Inventory Turnover} = \frac{\text{Net Sales}}{\text{Average Inventory}}$$

or

$$\text{Inventory Turnover} = \frac{\text{Cost of Goods Sold}}{\text{Average Inventory}}$$

or

$$\text{Inventory Turnover} = \frac{\text{Cost of Material Change in inventories (of 1/2 and 1/1 goods)}}{\text{Inventories}}$$

The *most basic* formula for average inventory:

$$\text{Average Inventory} = \frac{\text{Beginning inventory+Ending inventory}}{2}$$

or just

$$\text{Average Inventory} = \text{Ending inventory}$$

Multiple data points, for example the average of the monthly averages, will provide a much more representative turn figure.

The average days to sell the inventory is calculated as follows:

$$\text{Average days to sell the inventory} = \frac{\text{365 days}}{\text{Inventory Turnover Ratio}}$$

Application in Business

A low turnover rate may point to overstocking, obsolescence, or deficiencies in the product line or marketing effort. However, in some instances a low rate may be appropriate, such as where higher inventory levels occur in anticipation of rapidly rising prices or expected market shortages.

Conversely a high turnover rate may indicate inadequate inventory levels, which may lead to a loss in business as the inventory is too low. This often can result in stock shortages.

Some compilers of industry data (e.g., Dun & Bradstreet) use sales as the numerator instead of cost of sales. Cost of sales yields a more realistic turnover ratio, but it is often necessary to use sales for purposes of comparative analysis. Cost of sales is considered to be more realistic because of thc difference in which sales and the cost of sales are recorded. Sales are generally recorded at market value, i.e. the value at which the marketplace paid for the good or service provided by the firm. In the event that the firm had an exceptional year and the market paid a premium for the firm's goods and services then the numerator may be an inaccurate measure. However, cost of sales is recorded by the firm at what the firm actually paid for the materials available for sale. Additionally, firms may reduce prices to generate sales in an effort to cycle inventory. In this article, the terms "cost of sales" and "cost of goods sold" are synonymous.

An item whose inventory is sold (turns over) once a year has higher holding cost than one that turns over twice, or three times, or more in that time. Stock turnover also indicates the briskness of the business. The purpose of increasing inventory turns is to reduce inventory for three reasons.

- Increasing inventory turns reduces holding cost. The organization spends less money on rent, utilities, insurance, theft and other costs of maintaining a stock of good to be sold.
- Reducing holding cost increases net income and profitability as long as the revenue from selling the item remains constant.
- Items that turn over more quickly increase responsiveness to changes in customer requirements while allowing the replacement of obsolete items. This is a major concern in fashion industries.
- When making comparison between firms, it's important to take note of the industry, or the comparison will be distorted. Making comparison between a supermarket and a car dealer, will not be appropriate, as supermarket sells fast-moving goods such as sweets, chocolates, soft drinks so the stock turnover will be higher. However, a car dealer will have a low turnover due to the item being a slow moving item. As such only intra-industry comparison will be appropriate.

Formula:

Some computer programs measure the stock turns of an item using the actual number sold.

$$\text{Turn} = \frac{\text{Number of Units Sold (Over a given period)}}{\text{Average Number of Units (For the period)}}$$

The important issue is that any organization should be consistent in the formula that it uses.

Receivables Turnover Ratio

Receivable Turnover Ratio or Debtor's Turnover Ratio is an accounting measure used to measure how effective a company is in extending credit as well as collecting debts. The receivables turnover ratio is an activity ratio, measuring how efficiently a firm uses its assets.

Formula:

$$\text{Receivable Turnover Ratio} = \frac{\text{Net receivable sales}}{\text{Average net receivables}}$$

A high ratio implies either that a company operates on a cash basis or that its extension of credit and collection of accounts receivable is efficient. While a low ratio implies the company is not making the timely collection of credit.

Relation Ratios

- Days' sales in receivables = 365 / Receivable Turnover Ratio
- Average Collection Period = (Days x AR)/Credit Sales
- Average Debtor collection period: Trade Receivables/Credit Sales x 365 = Average collection period in days,
- Average Creditor payment period: Trade Payables/Credit Purchases x 365 = Average Payment period in days,

Profitability Index

Profitability index (PI), also known as profit investment ratio (PIR) and value investment ratio (VIR), is the ratio of payoff to investment of a proposed project. It is a useful tool for ranking projects because it allows you to quantify the amount of value created per unit of investment.

The ratio is calculated as follows:

$$\text{Profitability index} = \frac{\text{PV of future cash flows}}{\text{Initial investment}}$$

Assuming that the cash flow calculated does not include the investment made in the project, a profitability index of 1 indicates breakeven. Any value lower than one would indicate that the project's present value (PV) is less than the initial investment. As the value of the profitability index increases, so does the financial attractiveness of the proposed project.

Rules for selection or rejection of a project:

- If PI > 1 then accept the project
- If PI < 1 then reject the project

For example:

- Investment = $40,000
- Life of the Machine = 5 Years

CFAT	Year	CFAT
	1	18000
	2	12000
	3	10000
	4	9000
	5	6000

Calculate Net present value at 10% and PI:

Year	CFAT	PV@10%	PV
1	18000	0.909	16362
2	12000	0.827	9924
3	10000	0.752	7520
4	9000	0.683	6147
5	6000	0.621	3726
	Total present value		43679
	(-) Investment		40000
	NPV		3679

PI = 43679/40000 = 1.091 > 1 ⇒ Accept the project

Return Ratio

The return ratio of a dependent source in a linear electrical circuit is the *negative* of the ratio of *the current (voltage) returned to the site of the dependent source* to *the current (voltage) of a replacement independent source*. The terms *loop gain* and *return ratio* are often used interchangeably; however, they are necessarily equivalent only in the case of a single feedback loop system with unilateral blocks.

Calculating the Return Ratio

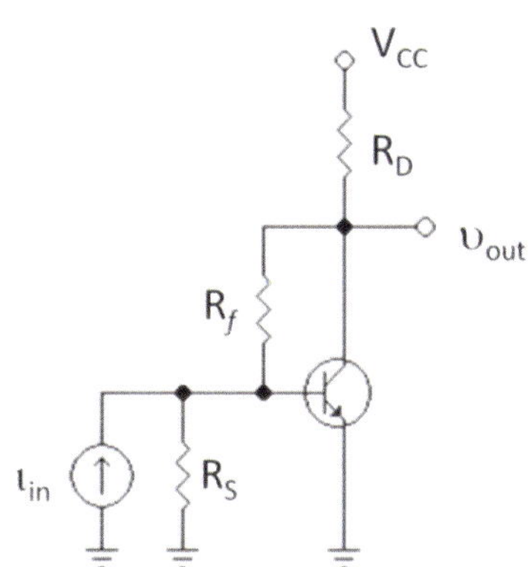

Collector-to-base biased bipolar amplifier

The steps for calculating the return ratio of a source are as follows:

1. Set all independent sources to zero.
2. Select the dependent source for which the return ratio is sought.
3. Place an independent source of the same type (voltage or current) and polarity in parallel with the selected dependent source.
4. Move the dependent source to the side of the inserted source and cut the two leads joining the dependent source to the independent source.
5. For a voltage source the return ratio is minus the ratio of the voltage across the dependent source divided by the voltage of the independent replacement source.
6. For a current source, short-circuit the broken leads of the dependent source. The return ratio is minus the ratio of the resulting short-circuit current to the current of the independent replacement source.

Other Methods

These steps may not be feasible when the dependent sources inside the devices are not directly accessible, for example when using built-in "black box" SPICE models or when measuring the return ratio experimentally. For SPICE simulations, one potential workaround is to manually replace non-linear devices by their small-signal equivalent model, with exposed dependent sources. However this will have to be redone if the bias point changes.

A result by Rosenstark shows that return ratio can be calculated by breaking the loop at any unilateral point in the circuit. The problem is now finding how to break the loop without affecting the bias point and altering the results. Middlebrook and Rosenstark have proposed several methods for experimental evaluation of return ratio (loosely referred to by these authors as simply *loop gain*), and similar methods have been adapted for use in SPICE by Hurst.

Example: Collector-to-base biased Bipolar Amplifier

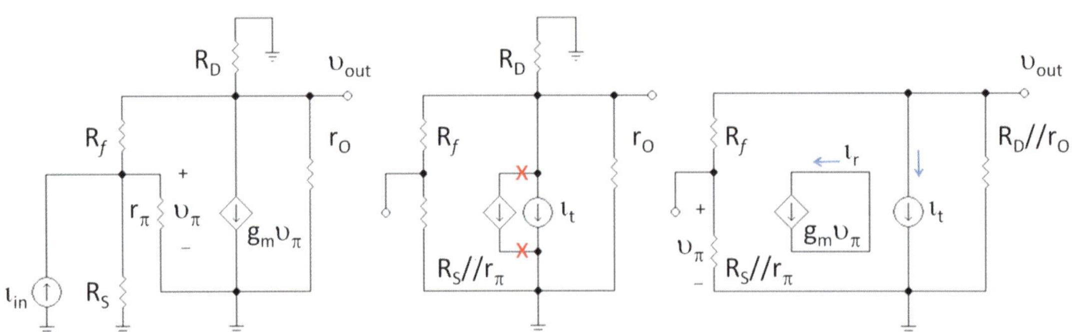

Left - small-signal circuit corresponding to Figure, center - inserting independent source and marking leads to be cut; right - cutting the dependent source free and short-circuiting broken leads

Figure (top right) shows a bipolar amplifier with feedback bias resistor R_f driven by a Norton signal source. Figure (left panel) shows the corresponding small-signal circuit obtained by replacing the transistor with its hybrid-pi model. The objective is to find the return ratio of the dependent current source in this amplifier. To reach the objective, the steps outlined above are followed. Figure (center panel) shows the application of these steps up to Step 4, with the dependent source moved to the left of the inserted source of value i_t, and the leads targeted for cutting marked with an x. Figure (right panel) shows the circuit set up for calculation of the return ratio T, which is

$$T = -\frac{i_r}{i_t}.$$

The return current is

$$i_r - g_m v_\pi .$$

The feedback current in R_f is found by current division to be:

$$i_f = \frac{R_D // r_O}{R_D // r_O + R_F + r_\pi // R_S} i_t .$$

The base-emitter voltage v_π is then, from Ohm's law:

$$v_\pi = -i_f \, (r_\pi // R_S) .$$

Consequently,

$$T = g_m (r_\pi // R_S) \frac{R_D // r_O}{R_D // r_O + R_F + r_\pi // R_S} .$$

Application in Asymptotic Gain Model

The overall transresistance gain of this amplifier can be shown to be:

$$G = \frac{v_{out}}{i_{in}} = \frac{(1 - g_m R_F) R_1 R_2}{R_F + R_1 + R_2 + g_m R_1 R_2} ,$$

with $R_1 = R_S \mid\mid r_\pi$ and $R_2 = R_D \mid\mid r_O$.

This expression can be rewritten in the form used by the asymptotic gain model, which expresses the overall gain of a feedback amplifier in terms of several independent factors that are often more easily derived separately than the overall gain itself, and that often provide insight into the circuit. This form is:

$$G = G_\infty \frac{T}{1+T} + G_0 \frac{1}{1+T} ,$$

where the so-called asymptotic gain G_∞ is the gain at infinite g_m, namely:

$$G_\infty = -R_F ,$$

and the so-called feed forward or direct feedthrough G_0 is the gain for zero g_m, namely:

$$G_0 = \frac{R_1 R_2}{R_F + R_1 + R_2}.$$

Depreciation

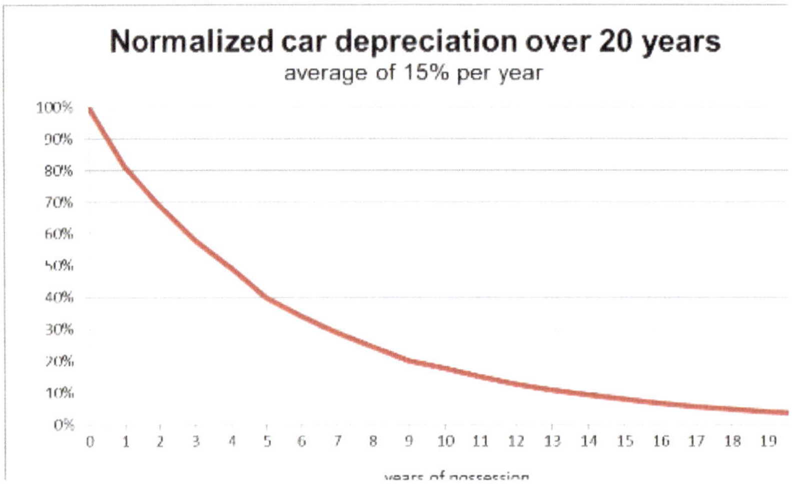

A typical vehicle depreciation over 20 years

In accountancy, depreciation refers to two aspects of the same concept:

- The decrease in value of assets (fair value depreciation)
- The allocation of the cost of assets to periods in which the assets are used (depreciation with the matching principle)

Depreciation is a method of reallocating the cost of a tangible asset over its useful life span of it being in motion. Businesses depreciate long-term assets for both tax and accounting purposes. The former affects the balance sheet of a business or entity, and the latter affects the net income that they report. Generally the cost is allocated, as depreciation expense, among the periods in which the asset is expected to be used. This expense is recognized by businesses for financial reporting and tax purposes. Methods of computing depreciation, and the periods over which assets are depreciated, may vary between asset types within the same business and may vary for tax purposes. These may be specified by law or accounting standards, which may vary by country. There are several standard methods of computing depreciation expense, including fixed percentage, straight line, and declining balance methods. Depreciation expense generally begins when the asset is placed in service. For example, a depreciation expense of 100 per year for five years may be recognized for an asset costing 500.

Accounting Concept

In determining the profits (net income) from an activity, the receipts from the activity must be reduced by appropriate costs. One such cost is the cost of assets used but not immediately consumed in the activity. Such cost so allocated in a given period is equal to the reduction in the value placed on the asset, which is initially equal to the amount paid for the asset and subsequently may or may not be related to the amount expected to be received upon its disposal. Depreciation is any method of allocating such net cost to those periods in which the organization is expected to benefit from use of the asset. The asset is referred to as a depreciable asset. Depreciation is technically a method of allocation, not valuation, even though it determines the value placed on the asset in the balance sheet.

Any business or income producing activity using tangible assets may incur costs related to those assets. If an asset is expected to produce a benefit in future periods, some of these costs must be deferred rather than treated as a current expense. The business then records depreciation expense in its financial reporting as the current period's allocation of such costs. This is usually done in a rational and systematic manner. Generally this involves four criteria:

- cost of the asset,
- expected salvage value, also known as residual value of the assets,
- estimated useful life of the asset, and
- a method of apportioning the cost over such life.

Depreciable Basis

Cost generally is the amount paid for the asset, including all costs related to acquisition. In some countries or for some purposes, salvage value may be ignored. The rules of some countries specify lives and methods to be used for particular types of assets. However, in most countries the life is based on business experience, and the method may be chosen from one of several acceptable methods.

Net Basis

When a depreciable asset is sold, the business recognizes gain or loss based on net basis of the asset. This net basis is cost less depreciation.

Impairment

Accounting rules also require that an impairment charge or expense be recognized if the value of assets declines unexpectedly. Such charges are usually nonrecurring, and may relate to any type of asset. Many companies consider write-offs of some of their long-lived assets because some property, plant, and equipment have suffered partial obsolescence. Accountants reduce the asset's carrying amount by its fair value. For example, if a company continues to incur losses because prices of a particular product or service are higher than the operating costs, companies consider write-offs of the particular asset. These write-offs are referred to as impairments. There are events and changes in circumstances might lead to impairment. Some examples are:

- Large amount of decrease in fair value of an asset.
- A change of manner in which the asset is used.
- Accumulation of costs that are not originally expected to acquire or construct an asset.

- A projection of incurring losses associated with the particular asset.

Events or changes in circumstances indicate that the company may not be able recover the carrying amount of the asset. In which case, companies use the recoverability test to determine whether impairment has occurred. The steps to determine are: 1. Estimate the future cash flow of asset. (from the use of the asset to disposition) 2. If the sum of the expected cash flow is less than the carrying amount of the asset, the asset is considered impaired.

Depletion and Amortization

Depletion and amortization are similar concepts for minerals (including oil) and intangible assets, respectively.

Effect on Cash

Depreciation expense does not require current outlay of cash. However, since depreciation is an expense to the P&L account, provided the enterprise is operating in a manner that covers its expenses (e.g. operating at a profit) depreciation is a source of cash in a statement of cash flows, which generally offsets the cash cost of acquiring new assets required to continue operations when existing assets reach the end of their useful lives.

Accumulated Depreciation

While depreciation expense is recorded on the income statement of a business, its impact is generally recorded in a separate account and disclosed on the balance sheet as accumulated depreciation, under fixed assets, according to most accounting principles. Accumulated depreciation is known as a contra account, because it separately shows a negative amount that is directly associated with another account.

Without an accumulated depreciation account on the balance sheet, depreciation expense is usually charged against the relevant asset directly. The values of the fixed assets stated on the balance sheet will decline, even if the business has not invested in or disposed of any assets. The amounts will roughly approximate fair value. Otherwise, depreciation expense is charged against accumulated depreciation. Showing accumulated depreciation separately on the balance sheet has the effect of preserving the historical cost of assets on the balance sheet. If there have been no investments or dispositions in fixed assets for the year, then the values of the assets will be the same on the balance sheet for the current and prior year (P/Y).

Methods of Depreciation

There are several methods for calculating depreciation, generally based on either the passage of time or the level of activity (or use) of the asset.

Straight-line Depreciation

Straight-line depreciation is the simplest and most often used method. In this method, the company estimates the salvage value (scrap value) of the asset at the end of the period during which it will be used to generate revenues (useful life). (The salvage value is an estimate of the value of the asset at the time it will be sold or disposed of; it may be zero or even negative. Salvage value is also known as scrap value or residual value.) The company will then charge the same amount to depreciation each year over that period, until the value shown for the asset has reduced from the original cost to the salvage value.

Straight-line Method:

$$\text{Annual Depreciation Expense} = \frac{\text{Cost of Fixed Asset} - \text{Residual Value}}{\text{Useful Life of Asset}(\textit{years})}$$

For example, a vehicle that depreciates over 5 years is purchased at a cost of $17,000, and will have a salvage value of $2000. Then this vehicle will depreciate at $3,000 per year, i.e. (17-2)/5 = 3. This table illustrates the straight-line method of depreciation. Book value at the beginning of the first year of depreciation is the original cost of the asset. At any time book value equals original cost minus accumulated depreciation.

book value = original cost − accumulated depreciation Book value at the end of year becomes book value at the beginning of next year. The asset is depreciated until the book value equals scrap value.

Depreciation expense	**Accumulated depreciation at year-end**	**Book value at year-end**
		(original cost) $17,000
$3,000	$3,000	$14,000
3,000	6,000	11,000
3,000	9,000	8,000
3,000	12,000	5,000
3,000	15,000	(scrap value) 2,000

If the vehicle were to be sold and the sales price exceeded the depreciated value (net book value) then the excess would be considered a gain and subject to depreciation recapture. In addition, this gain above the depreciated value would be recognized as ordinary income by the tax office. If the sales price is ever less than the book value, the resulting capital loss is tax deductible. If the sale price were ever more than the original book value, then the gain above the original book value is recognized as a capital gain.

If a company chooses to depreciate an asset at a different rate from that used by the tax office then this generates a timing difference in the income statement due to the difference (at a point in time) between the taxation department's and company's view of the profit.

In the UK used car pricing expert CAP regularly examine their data to find vehicles that devalue at a slower rate than others. They discuss the distinction and differences between percentage depreciate figures and real world cash depreciation to help motorists to reduce their long term costs. When buying a new vehicle it is important to consider if you are likely to change the car in the next three years (when most cars loose between 50% and 60% of their value) and the expected future value (also known as residual value). For example: "If you buy a car for £8,000 which 5 years later is only worth £2,000 you are actually going to have less value than if you have purchased a vehicle for £10,000 that 5 years later is worth £5,000.

Doubling Declining Balance Method

Suppose a business has an asset with $1,000 original cost, $100 salvage value, and 5 years of useful life. First, the straight-line depreciation rate would be 1/5, i.e. 20% per year. Under the double-declining-balance method, double that rate, i.e. 40% depreciation rate would be used. The table below illustrates this:

Depreciation rate	Depreciation expense	Accumulated depreciation	Book value at end of year
			original cost $1,000.00
40%	400.00	400.00	600.00
40%	240.00	640.00	360.00
40%	144.00	784.00	216.00
40%	86.40	870.40	129.60
129.60 - 100.00	29.60	900.00	scrap value 100.00

When using the double-declining-balance method, the salvage value is not considered in determining the annual depreciation, but the book value of the asset being depreciated is never brought below its salvage value, regardless of the method used. Depreciation ceases when either the salvage value or the end of the asset's useful life is reached.

Since double-declining-balance depreciation does not always depreciate an asset fully by its end of life, some methods also compute a straight-line depreciation each year, and apply the greater of the two. This has the effect of converting from declining-balance depreciation to straight-line depreciation at a midpoint in the asset's life.

With the declining balance method, one can find the depreciation rate that would allow exactly for full depreciation by the end of the period, using the formula:

$$\text{rate} = 1 - \sqrt[N]{\frac{\text{residual value}}{\text{cost of fixed asset}}},$$

where N is the estimated life of the asset (for example, in years).

Annuity Depreciation

Annuity depreciation methods are not based on time, but on a level of Annuity. This could be miles driven for a vehicle, or a cycle count for a machine. When the asset is acquired, its life is estimated in terms of this level of activity. Assume the vehicle above is estimated to go 50,000 miles in its lifetime. The per-mile depreciation rate is calculated as: ($17,000 cost - $2,000 salvage) / 50,000 miles = $0.30 per mile. Each year, the depreciation expense is then calculated by multiplying the number of miles driven by the per-mile depreciation rate..

Sum-of-years-digits Method

Sum-of-years-digits is a depreciation method that results in a more accelerated write-off than the straight line method, and typically also more accelerated than the declining balance method. Under this method the annual depreciation is determined by multiplying the depreciable cost by a schedule of fractions.

Sum of the years' digits method of depreciation is one of the accelerated depreciation techniques which are based on the assumption that assets are generally more productive when they are new and their productivity decreases as they become old. The formula to calculate depreciation under SYD method is:

SYD Depreciation = Depreciable Base x (Remaining Useful Life/Sum of the Years' Digits)
Depreciable Base = Cost – Salvage Value

Example: If an asset has original cost of $1000, a useful life of 5 years and a salvage value of $100, compute its depreciation schedule.

First, determine years' digits. Since the asset has useful life of 5 years, the years' digits are: 5, 4, 3, 2, and 1.

Next, calculate the sum of the digits: 5+4+3+2+1=15

The sum of the digits can also be determined by using the formula $(n^2+n)/2$ where n is equal to the useful life of the asset in years. The example would be shown as $(5^2+5)/2=15$

Depreciation rates are as follows:

5/15 for the 1st year, 4/15 for the 2nd year, 3/15 for the 3rd year, 2/15 for the 4th year, and 1/15 for the 5th year.

Depreciable base	Depreciation rate	Depreciation expense	Accumulated depreciation	Book value at end of year
				$1,000 (original cost)
900	5/15	300 =(900 x 5/15)	300	700
900	4/15	240 =(900 x 4/15)	540	460
900	3/15	180 =(900 x 3/15)	720	280
900	2/15	120 =(900 x 2/15)	840	160
900	1/15	60 =(900 x 1/15)	**900**	**100 (scrap value)**

Units-of-production Depreciation Method

Under the units-of-production method, useful life of the asset is expressed in terms of the total number of units expected to be produced:

$$\text{Depreciation Expense} = \frac{\text{Cost of Fixed Asset} - \text{Residual value}}{\text{Estimated Total Production}} \times \text{Actual Production}$$

Suppose, an asset has original cost $70,000, salvage value $10,000, and is expected to produce 6,000 units.

Depreciation per unit = ($70,000–10,000) / 6,000 = $10

10 × actual production will give the depreciation cost of the current year.

The table below illustrates the units-of-production depreciation schedule of the asset.

Units of production	Depreciation cost per unit	Depreciation expense	Accumulated depreciation	Book value at end of year
				$70,000 (original cost)
1,000	10	10,000	10,000	60,000
1,100	10	11,000	21,000	49,000
1,200	10	12,000	33,000	37,000
1,300	10	13,000	46,000	24,000
1,400	10	14,000	**60,000**	**10,000 (scrap value)**

Depreciation stops when book value is equal to the scrap value of the asset. In the end, the sum of accumulated depreciation and scrap value equals the original cost.

Units of Time Depreciation

Units of time depreciation is similar to units of production, and is used for depreciation equipment used in mining or natural resource exploration, or cases where the amount the asset is used is not linear year to year.

A simple example can be given for construction companies, where some equipment is used only for some specific purpose. Depending on the number of projects, the equipment will be used and depreciation charged accordingly.

Group Depreciation Method

Group depreciation method is used for depreciating multiple-asset accounts using straight-line-depreciation method. Assets must be similar in nature and have approximately the same useful lives.‘

Composite Depreciation Method

The composite method is applied to a collection of assets that are not similar, and have different service lives. For example, computers and printers are not similar, but both are part of the office equipment. Depreciation on all assets is determined by using the straight-line-depreciation method.

Asset	Historical cost	Salvage value	Depreciable cost	Life	Depreciation per year
Computers	$5,500	$500	$5,000	5	$1,000
Printers	$1,000	$100	$900	3	$300
Total	$6,500	$600	$5,900	4.5	$1,300

Composite life equals the total depreciable cost divided by the total depreciation per year. $5,900 / $1,300 = 4.5 years.

Composite depreciation rate equals depreciation per year divided by total historical cost. $1,300 / $6,500 = 0.20 = 20%

Depreciation expense equals the composite depreciation rate times the balance in the asset account (historical cost). (0.20 * $6,500) $1,300. Debit depreciation expense and credit accumulated depreciation.

When an asset is sold, debit cash for the amount received and credit the asset account for its original cost. Debit the difference between the two to accumulated depreciation. Under the composite method no gain or loss is recognized on the sale of an asset. Theoretically, this makes sense because the gains and losses from assets sold before and after the composite life will average themselves out.

To calculate composite depreciation rate, divide depreciation per year by total historical cost. To calculate depreciation expense, multiply the result by the same total historical cost. The result, not surprisingly, will equal to the total depreciation per year again.

Common sense requires depreciation expense to be equal to total depreciation per year, without first dividing and then multiplying total depreciation per year by the same number.

Tax Depreciation

Most income tax systems allow a tax deduction for recovery of the cost of assets used in a business or for the production of income. Such deductions are allowed for individuals and companies. Where the assets are consumed currently, the cost may be deducted currently as an expense or treated as part of cost of goods sold. The cost of assets not currently consumed generally must be deferred and recovered over time, such as through depreciation. Some systems permit full deduction of the cost, at least in part, in the year the assets are acquired. Other systems allow depreciation expense over some life using some depreciation method or percentage. Rules vary highly by country, and may vary within a country based on type of asset or type of taxpayer. Many systems that specify depreciation lives and methods for financial reporting require the same lives and methods be used for tax purposes. Most tax systems provide different rules for real property (buildings, etc.) and personal property (equipment, etc.).

Capital Allowances

A common system is to allow a fixed percentage of the cost of depreciable assets to be deducted each year. This is often referred to as a capital allowance, as it is called in the United Kingdom. Deductions are permitted to individuals and businesses based on assets placed in service during or before the assessment year. Canada's Capital Cost Allowance are fixed percentages of assets within a class or type of asset. Fixed percentage rates are specified by type of asset. The fixed percentage is multiplied by the tax basis of assets in service to determine the capital allowance deduction. The tax law or regulations of the country specifies these percentages. Capital allowance calculations may be based on the total set of assets, on sets or pools by year (vintage pools) or pools by classes of assets... Depreciation has got three methods only.

Tax Lives and Methods

Some systems specify lives based on classes of property defined by the tax authority. Canada Revenue Agency specifies numerous classes based on the type of property and how it is used. Under the

United States depreciation system, the Internal Revenue Service publishes a detailed guide which includes a table of asset lives and the applicable conventions. The table also incorporates specified lives for certain commonly used assets (e.g., office furniture, computers, automobiles) which override the business use lives. U.S. tax depreciation is computed under the double declining balance method switching to straight line or the straight line method, at the option of the taxpayer. IRS tables specify percentages to apply to the basis of an asset for each year in which it is in service. Depreciation first becomes deductible when an asset is placed in service.

Additional Depreciation

Many systems allow an additional deduction for a portion of the cost of depreciable assets acquired in the current tax year. The UK system provides a first year capital allowance of £50,000. In the United States, two such deductions are available. A deduction for the full cost of depreciable tangible personal property is allowed up to $500,000 through 2013. This deduction is fully phased out for businesses acquiring over $2,000,000 of such property during the year. In addition, additional first year depreciation of 50% of the cost of most other depreciable tangible personal property is allowed as a deduction. Some other systems have similar first year or accelerated allowances.

Real Property

Many tax systems prescribe longer depreciable lives for buildings and land improvements. Such lives may vary by type of use. Many such systems, including the United States and Canada, permit depreciation for real property using only the straight line method, or a small fixed percentage of cost. Generally, no depreciation tax deduction is allowed for bare land. In the United States, residential rental buildings are depreciable over a 27.5 year or 40 year life, other buildings over a 39 or 40 year life, and land improvements over a 15 or 20 year life, all using the straight line method.

Averaging Conventions

Depreciation calculations require a lot of record-keeping if done for each asset a business owns, especially if assets are added to after they are acquired, or partially disposed of. However, many tax systems permit all assets of a similar type acquired in the same year to be combined in a "pool". Depreciation is then computed for all assets in the pool as a single calculation. These calculations must make assumptions about the date of acquisition. The United States system allows a taxpayer to use a half year convention for personal property or mid-month convention for real property. Under such a convention, all property of a particular type is considered to have been acquired at the midpoint of the acquisition period. One half of a full period's depreciation is allowed in the acquisition period (and also in the final depreciation period if the life of the assets is a whole number of years). United States rules require a mid-quarter convention for per property if more than 40% of the acquisitions for the year are in the final quarter.

Concept of Conservatism

- Conservatism states that the accountant should not anticipate income and should provide for all possible losses.

- As per conservatism concept, it is not prudent to count unrealised gain but it is desirable to guard against all possible losses.
- When there are many alternatives values of an asset an accountant should choose the method which leads to lesser value. For conservatism, there should be three qualitative characteristics, namely
- Prudence, i.e., judgment about possible losses which are to be guarded, as well as gains which are uncertain.
- Neutrality i.e., unbiased outlook is required to identify and record such possible losses and to exclude uncertain gains.
- Faithful representation of alternative values.

Example

1. Closing stock is valued at Cost or market price whichever is lower.
2. Depreciation is charged every year even though cost of the asset has not decreased.

Causes of Depreciation

- Lapse of time.
- natural wear and tear.
- exhaustion of the subject matter.
- Obsolescence of technology.

Objectives of Providing for Depreciation

- To ascertain the true results of operations.
- To present true and fair value of the fixed asset.
- To accumulate funds for the replacement of the asset.

Factors in Measurement

- Estimation of exact amount of depreciation is not easy.
- Generally following factors are considered in calculation of depreciation.
    1. Cost of asset including expenses for installation etc.
    2. Estimated useful life of the asset.
    3. Estimated scrap value (if any) at the time of useful life of the asset.

Reducing Balance Method

Under this method, a fixed percentage of diminishing value of the asset is written off each year.

The annual charges of the depreciation decrease from year to year.

Written Down Value (WDV) = (Acquisition Cost – Depreciation)
Depreciation = WDV * Depr Rate

RBM: The main advantage of this method is that total charge to total revenue is uniform when the depreciation is high, repairs are negligible and as the repairs increases the burden of depreciation gets lesser and lesser.

RBM:

For First Year Depreciation = Acquisition value * Rate
For Second Year on words
Depreciation = Written down value * Rate

Example

Cost of machinery: 50000
Scrap Value of machine: 5000
Useful Life of Asset: 10 Years
Depreciation %: 15% p.a.

Calculate Depreciation as per reducing balance method for first 2 years

RBM:

For First Year
Depreciation = 50000 * 15%
= 7500

For Second Year
Depreciation = 42500 * 15%
= 6375

Machine Hour Method

Where it is possible to keep a record of the actual running hours of each machine, depreciation may be calculated on the basis of hours worked.

The machine hour rate of depreciation is calculated after estimating the total numbers of hours that machine would work during its whole life.

Under machine hour method Depreciation is calculated for each hour the machine works.

Example

Cost of machine: 500000
Estimated working hours: 40000
Scrap Value: 10000
The pattern of distribution of effective working hours:

Year	hours
1-2:	5000 per year
3-5:	7000 per year
6-8:	3000 per year

Compute depreciation p.a.

Solution:

1-2

5000 X (500000 – 10000)

40000

= 61250 p.a.

3-5

7000 X (500000 – 10000)

40000

= 85750 p.a.

6-8

3000 X (500000 – 10000)

40000

= 36750 p.a.

Production Unit Method

Under this method depreciation is determined by comparing annual production with the estimated total production.

The amount of depreciation is computed by the using following formula:

Depreciation for the period =

$$\text{depreciable amount} \quad x \quad \frac{\text{Production during the period}}{\text{Estimated total production}}$$

Example:

Cost of machine: 30000

Estimated total production: 4000

Scrap Value: 2000

Pattern of distribution of production:

Year	Units
1	2000
2	1500
3	500

Solution:

Year 1
2000 X (30000 – 2000)
4000
= 14000

Year 2
1500 X (30000 – 2000)
4000
= 10500

Year 3
500 X (30000 – 2000)
4000
= 3500

Provision

A provision is a liability which can not be measured with a substantial degree of accuracy. A liability is a present obligation of the enterprise arising from past events, the settlement of which is expected to result in an outflow of resources.

Where the liabilities are known but amount s cannot be precisely determined, we estimate for liability and provide for it.

The principle of conservatism supports making of provisions for probable liabilities.

Examples

Product service warranty cost, bad debts, changes in foreign exchange rates in case of international transaction etc.

Goodwill (Accounting)

Goodwill in accounting is an intangible asset that arises when a buyer acquires an existing business. Goodwill represents assets that are not separately identifiable. Goodwill does not include identifiable assets that are capable of being separated or divided from the entity and sold, transferred, licensed, rented, or exchanged, either individually or together with a related contract, identifiable asset, or liability regardless of whether the entity intends to do so. Goodwill also does not include contractual or other legal rights regardless of whether those are transferable or separable from the entity or other rights and obligations. Examples of identifiable assets that are not goodwill include a company's brand name, customer relationships, artistic intangible assets, and any patents or proprietary technology. The goodwill amounts to the excess of the "purchase consideration" (the money paid to purchase the asset or business) over the total value of the assets and liabilities. It is classified as an intangible asset on the balance sheet, since it can neither be seen nor touched. Under US GAAP and IFRS, goodwill is never amortized. Instead, management is responsible for valuing goodwill every year and to determine if an impairment is required. If the fair market value goes below historical cost (what goodwill was purchased for), an impairment must be recorded to bring it down to its fair market value. However, an increase in the fair market value would not be accounted for in the financial statements. Private companies in the United States, however, may elect to amortize goodwill over a period of ten years or less under an accounting alternative from the Private Company Council of the FASB.

Description

The value of goodwill typically arises in an acquisition when one company is purchased by another company. The amount the acquiring company pays for the target company over the target's book value usually accounts for the value of the target's goodwill. If the acquiring company pays less than the target's book value, it gains "negative goodwill," meaning that it purchased the company at a bargain in a distress sale.

Goodwill is difficult to price, but it does make a company more valuable. For example, a company like Coca-Cola (which has been around for decades, makes a widely popular product based on a secret formula, and is generally positively perceived by the public), would have a lot of goodwill. A competitor (a small, regional soda company that has only been in business for five years, has a small customer base, specializes in unusual soda flavors and recently faced a scandal over a contaminated batch of soda), would have far less goodwill, or even negative goodwill.

Because the components that make up goodwill have subjective values, there is a substantial risk that a company could overvalue goodwill in an acquisition. This overvaluation would be bad news for shareholders of the acquiring company, since they would likely see their share values drop when the company later has to write down goodwill. In fact, this happened in the AOL-Time Warner merger of 2001.

Calculating Goodwill

In order to calculate goodwill, the fair market value of identifiable assets and liabilities of the company acquired is deducted from the purchase price. For instance, if company A acquired 100% of company B, but paid more than the net market value of company B, a goodwill occurs. In order to calculate goodwill, it is necessary to have a list of all of company B's assets and liabilities at fair market value.

Fair market value		
Accounts Receivable		$10
Inventory		$5
Accounts payable		$6
Total Net assets	=	$10 + $5 - $6
	=	$9

In order to acquire company B, company A paid $20. Hence, goodwill would be $11 ($20 - $9). The journal entry in the books of company A to record the acquisition of company B would be:

DR Goodwill	$11
DR Accounts Receivable	$10
DR Inventory	$5
CR Accounts Payable	$6
CR Cash	$20

Modern Meaning

Goodwill is a special type of intangible asset that represents that portion of the entire business value that cannot be attributed to other income producing business assets, tangible or intangible.

For example, a privately held software company may have net assets (consisting primarily of miscellaneous equipment and/or property, and assuming no debt) valued at $1 million, but the company's overall value (including customers and intellectual capital) is valued at $10 million. Anybody buying that company would book $10 million in total assets acquired, comprising $1 million physical assets and $9 million in other intangible assets. And any consideration paid in excess of $10 million shall be considered as goodwill. In a private company, goodwill has no predetermined value prior to the acquisition; its magnitude depends on the two other variables *by definition*. A publicly traded company, by contrast, is subject to a constant process of market valuation, so goodwill will always be apparent.

While a business can invest to increase its reputation, by advertising or assuring that its products are of high quality, such expenses cannot be capitalized and added to goodwill, which is technically an intangible asset. Goodwill and intangible assets are usually listed as separate items on a company's balance sheet.

US Practice

History and Purchase vs. Pooling-of-interests

Previously, companies could structure many acquisition transactions to determine the choice between two accounting methods to record a business combination: purchase accounting or pooling-of-interests accounting. Pooling-of-interests method combined the book value of assets and liabilities of the two companies to create the new balance sheet of the combined companies. It therefore did not distinguish between who is buying whom. It also did not record the price the acquiring company had to pay for the acquisition. Since 2001, U.S. Generally Accepted Accounting Principles (FAS 141) no longer allows the pooling-of-interests method.

Amortization and Adjustments to Carrying Value

Goodwill is no longer amortized under U.S. GAAP (FAS 142). FAS 142 was issued in June 2001. Companies objected to the removal of the option to use pooling-of-interests, so amortization was removed by Financial Accounting Standards Board as a concession. As of 2005-01-01, it is also forbidden under International Financial Reporting Standards. Goodwill can now only be impaired under these GAAP standards.

Instead of deducting the value of goodwill annually over a period of maximal 40 years, companies are now required to determine the fair value of the reporting units, using present value of future cash flow, and compare it to their carrying value (book value of assets plus goodwill minus liabilities.) If the fair value is less than carrying value (impaired), the goodwill value needs to be reduced so the carrying value is equal to the fair value. The impairment loss is reported as a separate line item on the income statement, and new adjusted value of goodwill is reported in the balance sheet.

When the business is threatened with insolvency, investors will often deduct the goodwill from any calculation of residual equity because it will likely have no resale value.

Inventory

Electronics inventory.

Inventory or stock means to the goods and materials that a business holds for the ultimate purpose of resale (or repair).

Inventory management is a discipline primarily about specifying the shape and placement of stocked goods. It is required at different locations within a facility or within many locations of a supply network to precede the regular and planned course of production and stock of materials.

The concept of inventory, stock or work-in-process has been extended from manufacturing systems to service businesses and projects, by generalizing the definition to be "all work within the process of production- all work that is or has occurred prior to the completion of production." In the context of a manufacturing production system, inventory refers to all work that has occurred - raw materials, partially finished products, finished products prior to sale and departure from the manufacturing system. In the context of services, inventory refers to all work done prior to sale, including partially process information.

Definition

The scope of inventory management concerns the balance between replenishment lead time, carrying costs of inventory, asset management, inventory forecasting, inventory valuation, inventory visibility, future inventory price forecasting, physical inventory, available physical space, quality management, replenishment, returns and defective goods, and demand forecasting. Balancing these competing requirements leads to optimal inventory levels, which is an ongoing process as the business needs shift and react to the wider environment.

Inventory management involves a retailer seeking to acquire and maintain a proper merchandise assortment while ordering, shipping, handling and related costs are kept in check. It also involves systems and processes that identify inventory requirements, set targets, provide replenishment techniques, report actual and projected inventory status and handle all functions related to the tracking and management of material. This would include the monitoring of material moved into and out of stockroom locations and the reconciling of the inventory balances. It also may include ABC analysis, lot tracking, cycle counting support, etc. Management of the inventories, with the primary objective of determining/controlling stock levels within the physical distribution system, functions to balance the need for product availability against the need for minimizing stock holding and handling costs.

Business Inventory

Reasons for Keeping Stock

There are five basic reasons for keeping an inventory

1. Time - The time lags present in the supply chain, from supplier to user at every stage, requires that you maintain certain amounts of inventory to use in this lead time. However, in practice, inventory is to be maintained for consumption during 'variations in lead time'. Lead time itself can be addressed by ordering that many days in advance.
2. Seasonal Demand: demands varies periodically, but producers capacity is fixed. This can lead to stock accumulation, consider for example how goods consumed only in holidays can lead to accumulation of large stocks on the anticipation of future consumption.
3. Uncertainty - Inventories are maintained as buffers to meet uncertainties in demand, supply and movements of goods.
4. Economies of scale - Ideal condition of "one unit at a time at a place where a user needs it, when he needs it" principle tends to incur lots of costs in terms of logistics. So bulk buying, movement and storing brings in economies of scale, thus inventory.
5. Appreciation in Value - In some situations, some stock gains the required value when it is kept for some time to allow it reach the desired standard for consumption, or for production. For example; beer in the brewing industry

All these stock reasons can apply to any owner or product

Also, some authors mentioned several reasons not to keep high inventory levels:

- *Obsolescence*: due to progress of technology, the bought inventory for future use may become obsolete.

- *Capital Investment*
- *Space Usage*
- *Complicated Inventory Control Systems*:higher number of inventory items complicates the control and monitoring items.

Special terms used in dealing with inventory management

- *Stock Keeping Unit* (SKU) SKUs are clear, internal identification numbers assigned to each of the products and their variants. SKUs can be any combination of letters and numbers chosen, just as long as the system is consistent and used for all the products in the inventory.
- *Stockout* means running out of the inventory of an SKU.
- "New old stock" (sometimes abbreviated NOS) is a term used in business to refer to merchandise being offered for sale that was manufactured long ago but that has never been used. Such merchandise may not be produced anymore, and the new old stock may represent the only market source of a particular item at the present time.

Typology

1. Buffer/safety stock
2. Reorder level
3. Cycle stock (Used in batch processes, it is the available inventory, excluding buffer stock)
4. De-coupling (Buffer stock held between the machines in a single process which serves as a buffer for the next one allowing smooth flow of work instead of waiting the previous or next machine in the same process)
5. Anticipation stock (Building up extra stock for periods of increased demand - e.g. ice cream for summer)
6. Pipeline stock (Goods still in transit or in the process of distribution - have left the factory but not arrived at the customer yet)

Average Daily/Weekly usage quantity X Lead time in days + Safety stock

Inventory Examples

While accountants often discuss inventory in terms of goods for sale, organizations - manufacturers, service-providers and not-for-profits - also have inventories (fixtures, furniture, supplies, etc.) that they do not intend to sell. Manufacturers', distributors', and wholesalers' inventory tends to cluster in warehouses. Retailers' inventory may exist in a warehouse or in a shop or store accessible to customers. Inventories not intended for sale to customers or to clients may be held in any premises an organization uses. Stock ties up cash and, if uncontrolled, it will be impossible to know the actual level of stocks and therefore impossible to control them.

While the reasons for holding stock were covered earlier, most manufacturing organizations usually divide their "goods for sale" inventory into:

- Raw materials - materials and components scheduled for use in making a product.
- Work in process, WIP - materials and components that have begun their transformation to finished goods.
- Finished goods - goods ready for sale to customers.
- Goods for resale - returned goods that are salable.
- Stocks in transit.
- Consignment stocks.
- Maintenance supply.

For example:

Manufacturing

A canned food manufacturer's materials inventory includes the ingredients to form the foods to be canned, empty cans and their lids (or coils of steel or aluminum for constructing those components), labels, and anything else (solder, glue, etc.) that will form part of a finished can. The firm's work in process includes those materials from the time of release to the work floor until they become complete and ready for sale to wholesale or retail customers. This may be vats of prepared food, filled cans not yet labeled or sub-assemblies of food components. It may also include finished cans that are not yet packaged into cartons or pallets. Its finished good inventory consists of all the filled and labeled cans of food in its warehouse that it has manufactured and wishes to sell to food distributors (wholesalers), to grocery stores (retailers), and even perhaps to consumers through arrangements like factory stores and outlet centers.

Capital Projects

The partially completed work (or Work in Process) is a measure of inventory built during the work execution of a capital project, such as encountered in civilian infrastructure construction or oil & gas. Inventory may not only reflect physical items (such as materials, parts, partially-finished sub-assemblies) but also knowledge work-in-process (such as partially completed engineering designs of components and assemblies to be fabricated).

Virtual Inventory

A "virtual inventory" (also known as a "bank inventory") enables a group of users to share common parts, especially where their availability at short notice may be critical but they are unlikely to required by more than a few bank members at any one time.

Costs Associated with Inventory

There are several costs associated with inventory:

- Ordering cost
- Setup cost

- Holding Cost
- Shortage Cost

Principle of Inventory Proportionality

Purpose

Inventory proportionality is the goal of demand-driven inventory management. The primary optimal outcome is to have the same number of days' (or hours', etc.) worth of inventory on hand across all products so that the time of runout of all products would be simultaneous. In such a case, there is no "excess inventory," that is, inventory that would be left over of another product when the first product runs out. Excess inventory is sub-optimal because the money spent to obtain it could have been utilized better elsewhere, i.e. to the product that just ran out.

The secondary goal of inventory proportionality is inventory minimization. By integrating accurate demand forecasting with inventory management, rather than only looking at past averages, a much more accurate and optimal outcome is expected.

Integrating demand forecasting into inventory management in this way also allows for the prediction of the "can fit" point when inventory storage is limited on a per-product basis.

Applications

The technique of inventory proportionality is most appropriate for inventories that remain unseen by the consumer, as opposed to "keep full" systems where a retail consumer would like to see full shelves of the product they are buying so as not to think they are buying something old, unwanted or stale; and differentiated from the "trigger point" systems where product is reordered when it hits a certain level; inventory proportionality is used effectively by just-in-time manufacturing processes and retail applications where the product is hidden from view.

One early example of inventory proportionality used in a retail application in the United States was for motor fuel. Motor fuel (e.g. gasoline) is generally stored in underground storage tanks. The motorists do not know whether they are buying gasoline off the top or bottom of the tank, nor need they care. Additionally, these storage tanks have a maximum capacity and cannot be overfilled. Finally, the product is expensive. Inventory proportionality is used to balance the inventories of the different grades of motor fuel, each stored in dedicated tanks, in proportion to the sales of each grade. Excess inventory is not seen or valued by the consumer, so it is simply cash sunk (literally) into the ground. Inventory proportionality minimizes the amount of excess inventory carried in underground storage tanks. This application for motor fuel was first developed and implemented by Petrolsoft Corporation in 1990 for Chevron Products Company. Most major oil companies use such systems today.

Roots

The use of inventory proportionality in the United States is thought to have been inspired by Japanese just-in-time parts inventory management made famous by Toyota Motors in the 1980s.

High-level Inventory Management

It seems that around 1880 there was a change in manufacturing practice from companies with relatively homogeneous lines of products to horizontally integrated companies with unprecedented diversity in processes and products. Those companies (especially in metalworking) attempted to achieve success through economies of scope - the gains of jointly producing two or more products in one facility. The managers now needed information on the effect of product-mix decisions on overall profits and therefore needed accurate product-cost information. A variety of attempts to achieve this were unsuccessful due to the huge overhead of the information processing of the time. However, the burgeoning need for financial reporting after 1900 created unavoidable pressure for financial accounting of stock and the management need to cost manage products became overshadowed. In particular, it was the need for audited accounts that sealed the fate of managerial cost accounting. The dominance of financial reporting accounting over management accounting remains to this day with few exceptions, and the financial reporting definitions of 'cost' have distorted effective management 'cost' accounting since that time. This is particularly true of inventory.

Hence, high-level financial inventory has these two basic formulas, which relate to the accounting period:

1. Cost of Beginning Inventory at the start of the period + inventory purchases within the period + cost of production within the period = cost of goods available
2. Cost of goods available – cost of ending inventory at the end of the period = cost of goods sold

The benefit of these formulas is that the first absorbs all overheads of production and raw material costs into a value of inventory for reporting. The second formula then creates the new start point for the next period and gives a figure to be subtracted from the sales price to determine some form of sales-margin figure.

Manufacturing management is more interested in *inventory turnover ratio* or *average days to sell inventory* since it tells them something about relative inventory levels.

Inventory turnover ratio (also known as inventory turns) = cost of goods sold / Average Inventory = Cost of Goods Sold / ((Beginning Inventory + Ending Inventory) / 2)

and its inverse

Average Days to Sell Inventory = Number of Days a Year / Inventory Turnover Ratio = 365 days a year / Inventory Turnover Ratio

This ratio estimates how many times the inventory turns over a year. This number tells how much cash/goods are tied up waiting for the process and is a critical measure of process reliability and effectiveness. So a factory with two inventory turns has six months stock on hand, which is generally not a good figure (depending upon the industry), whereas a factory that moves from six turns to twelve turns has probably improved effectiveness by 100%. This improvement will have some negative results in the financial reporting, since the 'value' now stored in the factory as inventory is reduced.

While these accounting measures of inventory are very useful because of their simplicity, they are also fraught with the danger of their own assumptions. There are, in fact, so many things that can vary hidden under this appearance of simplicity that a variety of 'adjusting' assumptions may be used. These include:

- Specific Identification
- Lower of cost or market
- Weighted Average Cost
- Moving-Average Cost
- FIFO and LIFO.

Inventory Turn is a financial accounting tool for evaluating inventory and it is not necessarily a management tool. Inventory management should be forward looking. The methodology applied is based on historical cost of goods sold. The ratio may not be able to reflect the usability of future production demand, as well as customer demand.

Business models, including Just in Time (JIT) Inventory, Vendor Managed Inventory (VMI) and Customer Managed Inventory (CMI), attempt to minimize on-hand inventory and increase inventory turns. VMI and CMI have gained considerable attention due to the success of third-party vendors who offer added expertise and knowledge that organizations may not possess.

Accounting for Inventory

Each country has its own rules about accounting for inventory that fit with their financial-reporting rules.

For example, organizations in the U.S. define inventory to suit their needs within US Generally Accepted Accounting Practices (GAAP), the rules defined by the Financial Accounting Standards Board (FASB) (and others) and enforced by the U.S. Securities and Exchange Commission (SEC) and other federal and state agencies. Other countries often have similar arrangements but with their own accounting standards and national agencies instead.

It is intentional that financial accounting uses standards that allow the public to compare firms' performance, cost accounting functions internally to an organization and potentially with much greater flexibility. A discussion of inventory from standard and Theory of Constraints-based (throughput) cost accounting perspective follows some examples and a discussion of inventory from a financial accounting perspective.

The internal costing/valuation of inventory can be complex. Whereas in the past most enterprises ran simple, one-process factories, such enterprises are quite probably in the minority in the 21st century. Where 'one process' factories exist, there is a market for the goods created, which establishes an independent market value for the good. Today, with multistage-process companies, there is much inventory that would once have been finished goods which is now held as 'work in process' (WIP). This needs to be valued in the accounts, but the valuation is a management decision since there is no market for the partially finished product. This somewhat arbitrary 'valuation' of WIP combined with the allocation of overheads to it has led to some unintended and undesirable results.

Financial Accounting

An organization's inventory can appear a mixed blessing, since it counts as an asset on the balance sheet, but it also ties up money that could serve for other purposes and requires additional expense for its protection. Inventory may also cause significant tax expenses, depending on particular countries' laws regarding depreciation of inventory, as in Thor Power Tool Company v. Commissioner.

Inventory appears as a current asset on an organization's balance sheet because the organization can, in principle, turn it into cash by selling it. Some organizations hold larger inventories than their operations require in order to inflate their apparent asset value and their perceived profitability.

In addition to the money tied up by acquiring inventory, inventory also brings associated costs for warehouse space, for utilities, and for insurance to cover staff to handle and protect it from fire and other disasters, obsolescence, shrinkage (theft and errors), and others. Such holding costs can mount up: between a third and a half of its acquisition value per year.

Businesses that stock too little inventory cannot take advantage of large orders from customers if they cannot deliver. The conflicting objectives of cost control and customer service often pit an organization's financial and operating managers against its sales and marketing departments. Salespeople, in particular, often receive sales-commission payments, so unavailable goods may reduce their potential personal income. This conflict can be minimised by reducing production time to being near or less than customers' expected delivery time. This effort, known as "Lean production" will significantly reduce working capital tied up in inventory and reduce manufacturing costs.

Role of Inventory Accounting

By helping the organization to make better decisions, the accountants can help the public sector to change in a very positive way that delivers increased value for the taxpayer's investment. It can also help to incentive's progress and to ensure that reforms are sustainable and effective in the long term, by ensuring that success is appropriately recognized in both the formal and informal reward systems of the organization.

To say that they have a key role to play is an understatement. Finance is connected to most, if not all, of the key business processes within the organization. It should be steering the stewardship and accountability systems that ensure that the organization is conducting its business in an appropriate, ethical manner. It is critical that these foundations are firmly laid. So often they are the litmus test by which public confidence in the institution is either won or lost.

Finance should also be providing the information, analysis and advice to enable the organizations' service managers to operate effectively. This goes beyond the traditional preoccupation with budgets – how much have we spent so far, how much do we have left to spend? It is about helping the organization to better understand its own performance. That means making the connections and understanding the relationships between given inputs – the resources brought to bear – and the outputs and outcomes that they achieve. It is also about understanding and actively managing risks within the organization and its activities.

FIFO vs. LIFO Accounting

When a merchant buys goods from inventory, the value of the inventory account is reduced by the cost of goods sold (COGS). This is simple where the cost has not varied across those held in stock; but where it has, then an agreed method must be derived to evaluate it. For commodity items that one cannot track individually, accountants must choose a method that fits the nature of the sale. Two popular methods in use are: FIFO (first in - first out) and LIFO (last in - first out).

FIFO treats the first unit that arrived in inventory as the first one sold. LIFO considers the last unit arriving in inventory as the first one sold. Which method an accountant selects can have a significant effect on net income and book value and, in turn, on taxation. Using LIFO accounting for inventory, a company generally reports lower net income and lower book value, due to the effects of inflation. This generally results in lower taxation. Due to LIFO's potential to skew inventory value, UK GAAP and IAS have effectively banned LIFO inventory accounting. LIFO accounting is permitted in the United States subject to section 472 of the Internal Revenue Code.

Standard Cost Accounting

Standard cost accounting uses ratios called efficiencies that compare the labour and materials actually used to produce a good with those that the same goods would have required under "standard" conditions. As long as actual and standard conditions are similar, few problems arise. Unfortunately, standard cost accounting methods developed about 100 years ago, when labor comprised the most important cost in manufactured goods. Standard methods continue to emphasize labor efficiency even though that resource now constitutes a (very) small part of cost in most cases.

Standard cost accounting can hurt managers, workers, and firms in several ways. For example, a policy decision to increase inventory can harm a manufacturing manager's performance evaluation. Increasing inventory requires increased production, which means that processes must operate at higher rates. When (not if) something goes wrong, the process takes longer and uses more than the standard labor time. The manager appears responsible for the excess, even though s/he has no control over the production requirement or the problem.

In adverse economic times, firms use the same efficiencies to downsize, rightsize, or otherwise reduce their labor force. Workers laid off under those circumstances have even less control over excess inventory and cost efficiencies than their managers.

Many financial and cost accountants have agreed for many years on the desirability of replacing standard cost accounting. They have not, however, found a successor.

Theory of Constraints Cost Accounting

Eliyahu M. Goldratt developed the Theory of Constraints in part to address the cost-accounting problems in what he calls the "cost world." He offers a substitute, called throughput accounting, that uses throughput (money for goods sold to customers) in place of output (goods produced that may sell or may boost inventory) and considers labor as a fixed rather than as a variable cost. He defines inventory simply as everything the organization owns that it plans to sell, including buildings, machinery, and many other things in addition to the categories listed here. Throughput accounting recognizes only one class of variable costs: the truly variable costs, like materials and components, which vary directly with the quantity produced

Finished goods inventories remain balance-sheet assets, but labor-efficiency ratios no longer evaluate managers and workers. Instead of an incentive to reduce labor cost, throughput accounting focuses attention on the relationships between throughput (revenue or income) on one hand and controllable operating expenses and changes in inventory on the other.

National Accounts

Inventories also play an important role in national accounts and the analysis of the business cycle. Some short-term macroeconomic fluctuations are attributed to the inventory cycle.

Distressed Inventory

Also known as distressed or expired stock, distressed inventory is inventory whose potential to be sold at a normal cost has passed or will soon pass. In certain industries it could also mean that the stock is or will soon be impossible to sell. Examples of distressed inventory include products which have reached their expiry date, or have reached a date in advance of expiry at which the planned market will no longer purchase them (e.g. 3 months left to expiry), clothing which is out of fashion, music which is no longer popular and old newspapers or magazines. It also includes computer or consumer-electronic equipment which is obsolete or discontinued and whose manufacturer is unable to support it, along with products which use that type of equipment e.g. VHS format equipment and videos.

In 2001, Cisco wrote off inventory worth US $2.25 billion due to duplicate orders. This is considered one of the biggest inventory write-offs in business history.

Stock Rotation

Stock Rotation is the practice of changing the way inventory is displayed on a regular basis. This is most commonly used in hospitality and retail - particularity where food products are sold. For example, in the case of supermarkets that a customer frequents on a regular basis, the customer may know exactly what they want and where it is. This results in many customers going straight to the product they seek and do not look at other items on sale. To discourage this practice, stores will rotate the location of stock to encourage customers to look through the entire store. This is in hopes the customer will pick up items they would not normally see.

Inventory Credit

Inventory credit refers to the use of stock, or inventory, as collateral to raise finance. Where banks may be reluctant to accept traditional collateral, for example in developing countries where land title may be lacking, inventory credit is a potentially important way of overcoming financing constraints. This is not a new concept; archaeological evidence suggests that it was practiced in Ancient Rome. Obtaining finance against stocks of a wide range of products held in a bonded warehouse is common in much of the world. It is, for example, used with Parmesan cheese in Italy. Inventory credit on the basis of stored agricultural produce is widely used in Latin American countries and in some Asian countries. A precondition for such credit is that banks must be confident that the stored product will be available if they need to call on the collateral; this implies the existence of a reliable network of certified warehouses. Banks also face problems in valuing the inventory. The possibility of sudden falls in commodity prices means that they are usually reluctant to lend more than about 60% of the value of the inventory at the time of the loan.

Accounting for Inventory and Goodwill

Inventory Valuation

Inventories should be valued at cost or net realisable value whichever is lower. (AS-2/ IAS 2.9)

This is based on view that no asset should be carried at a value which is in excess of the value realisable by its sale or use.

Net realisable value is the estimated selling price in the ordinary course of business less the estimated cost of completion and estimated cost necessary to make sale.

Example

Cost of semi-finished products at the end of the 2011-12 is Rs. 70000. This products can be finished in the next year by further expenditure of Rs. 10000.

This products can be sold at Rs. 60000 subject to selling commission of 5% on selling price. Determine the value of inventory for the year ended 2011-12.

Solution:

Selling Price	60000
Less: Estimated cost of completion	10000
Less: Commission	3000
Net realisable value	47000

NRV: Rs. 47000

Cost: Rs. 70000

Therefore, value of inventory (lower of cost and NRV): 47000

Techniques of Inventory Valuation

i. Specific identification method.

ii. First in First Out (FIFO).

iii. Last in First Out (LIFO).

iv. Weighted Average Price.

v. Adjusted selling price.

Specific Identification Method

i. Pricing under this method is based on actual physical flow of goods.

ii. It attributes specific cost to identified goods.

iii. This method is generally used to ascertain the cost of inventories of items that are not ordinarily interchangeable or having high value.

iv. Cost of inventory will be determined on the basis of their specific purchase price or production cost.

FIFO

The goods are assumed to be issued from the earliest lot on hand. The stock of goods on hand therefore, consist of the latest purchases.

Example:

Following are the purchases for the month of Jun 2012.

Date	Units	Price p.u.
12	5000	7
17	3000	9
20	6900	9
22	8000	11
27	2000	13

20000 units were issued during the month. Determine the value of closing stock at the end of month.

The closing stock is 4900 units and would consist of:-

2000 units purchased on 27th and 2900 units purchased on 22nd as per FIFO method

2000 X 13 =	26000
2900 X 11 =	31900
Value of Closing Stock	**57900**

LIFO

Under this method good issued are valued at price paid for the latest lot of the goods. In other words stock of goods on hand will be valued at a price paid for earliest lots. LIFO method is based on an irrational assumption that entering last in stores are consumed first.

LIFO method is not permitted for valuing inventories. AS – 2, IAS – 2, Income Tax Act.

Example:

Following are the purchases for the month of Jul 2011.

Date	Units	Price p.u.
11	3000	16
14	6000	20
18	2500	15
25	7000	14
30	9000	19

22000 units were issued during the month. Determine the value of closing stock at the end of month as per LIFO.

The closing stock is 5500 units and would consist of:-
3000 units purchased on 11th and
2500 units purchased on 14th as per LIFO method

3000 X 16 =	48000
2500 X 20 =	50000
Value of Closing Stock	**98000**

Weighted Average Price

Under this method value of inventory is determined by weighted average price per unit. Weighted average price is calculated by using quantity purchased in a lot as weights.

$$\text{Weighted Average price per unit} = \frac{\text{Total cost of goods available for sale during the period}}{\text{Total number of units available for sale during period}}$$

Example:

Compute value of closing stock as per weighted average method

Quantity	Price p.u.	Amount
900	10	9000
400	14	5600
600	18	10800
500	16	8000
800	12	9600
3200	**Total**	**43000**

3000 units were issued during the period.

$$\text{Weighted Average price per unit} = \frac{43000}{3200} = 13.44$$

Hence value of closing stock is
200 X 13.44 = Rs. 2688

Adjusted Selling Price

- This is also known as retail inventory method.
- This method is used where inventory comprises of items, the individual costs of which are not readily ascertainable. The cost of stock is determined by reducing appropriate percentage of gross margin from sales value of the inventory.

Examples:

Compute value of closing stock for month ended 30th Jun 2011.

Particulars	**Amount**
Goods purchased	25000
Transportation cost	5000
Storage cost	2000
Sales during period	50000
Selling price of closing stock	10000

Solution

Particulars	**Amount**
Sales during period	50000
Selling price of closing stock	10000
Total	60000
Less: Goods purchased	25000
Less :Transportation cost	5000
Less: Storage cost	2000
Gross Profit	28000

Gross Profit Margin: 28000/60000 = 46.67%

Particulars	**Amount**
Selling price of closing stock	10000
Less: Gross profit margin	4667
Value of inventory	5333

Window Dressing

- Window Dressing means something done to make a better impression, and implies dishonest or deceptive.
- Window Dressing refers to attempts to mis-represent and present financials in the better light.

- Window dressing is an unethical practice.
- Deliberate deception in the financial statements is fraud.
- Enron - Arthur Anderson.
- Satyam - PWC
- Examples
    - Delay major payment (and not making provision).
    - Include large injection of cash/assets.
    - Hiding sales return.
    - Overstatement of stock /debtors.

References

- Ahorny, Joseph; Saunders, Anthony; Swary, Itzhak (1985). "The Effects of the International Banking Act on Domestic Bank Profitability and Risk". Journal of Money, Credit, and Banking. JSTOR. 17: 493–506. JSTOR 1992444
- White, Gerald I.; Sondhi, Ashwinpaul; Fried, Dov (1998). The Analysis and Use of Financial Statements. John Wiley & Sons, Inc. ISBN 0-471-11186-4
- Accountancy: Higher Secondary First Year (PDF) (First ed.). Tamil Nadu Textbooks Corporation. 2004. pp. 28–34. Retrieved 12 July 2011
- IFRS for SMEs. 1st Floor, 30 Cannon Street, London EC4M 6XH, United Kingdom: IASB (International Accounting Standards Board). 2009. p. 14. ISBN 978-0-409-04813-1
- "Wheres's the "R" in Debit?" by W. Richard Sherman published in The Accounting Historians Journal, Vol. 13, No. 2 (Fall 1986), pp. 137-143
- Pieters, A. Dempsey, H. N. (2009). Introduction to financial accounting (7th ed.). Durban: Lexisnexis. ISBN 978-0-409-10580-3
- Cusimano, David. "Accounting Abbreviations – Helping You Understand Accounting Jargon". Loughborough. Retrieved 18 August 2011
- Tracy, John A. (2004). How to Read a Financial Report: Wringing Vital Signs Out of the Numbers. John Wiley and Sons. p. 173. ISBN 0-471-64693-8
- "Big trends for Inventory Management in 2017 [Infographic] - Magentone Developers Website". Magentone Developers Website. Retrieved 2017-03-16
- Powell, Gary N. (2005). Understanding financial management: a practical guide. Cambridge, MA: Blackwell Pub. p. 59. ISBN 0-631-23100-5

Permissions

All chapters in this book are published with permission under the Creative Commons Attribution Share Alike License or equivalent. Every chapter published in this book has been scrutinized by our experts. Their significance has been extensively debated. The topics covered herein carry significant information for a comprehensive understanding. They may even be implemented as practical applications or may be referred to as a beginning point for further studies.

We would like to thank the editorial team for lending their expertise to make the book truly unique. They have played a crucial role in the development of this book. Without their invaluable contributions this book wouldn't have been possible. They have made vital efforts to compile up to date information on the varied aspects of this subject to make this book a valuable addition to the collection of many professionals and students.

This book was conceptualized with the vision of imparting up-to-date and integrated information in this field. To ensure the same, a matchless editorial board was set up. Every individual on the board went through rigorous rounds of assessment to prove their worth. After which they invested a large part of their time researching and compiling the most relevant data for our readers.

The editorial board has been involved in producing this book since its inception. They have spent rigorous hours researching and exploring the diverse topics which have resulted in the successful publishing of this book. They have passed on their knowledge of decades through this book. To expedite this challenging task, the publisher supported the team at every step. A small team of assistant editors was also appointed to further simplify the editing procedure and attain best results for the readers.

Apart from the editorial board, the designing team has also invested a significant amount of their time in understanding the subject and creating the most relevant covers. They scrutinized every image to scout for the most suitable representation of the subject and create an appropriate cover for the book.

The publishing team has been an ardent support to the editorial, designing and production team. Their endless efforts to recruit the best for this project, has resulted in the accomplishment of this book. They are a veteran in the field of academics and their pool of knowledge is as vast as their experience in printing. Their expertise and guidance has proved useful at every step. Their uncompromising quality standards have made this book an exceptional effort. Their encouragement from time to time has been an inspiration for everyone.

The publisher and the editorial board hope that this book will prove to be a valuable piece of knowledge for students, practitioners and scholars across the globe.

Index

A

Annual Report, 51, 137-139, 142, 196

Auditing Firms, 138

B

Balance Sheet, 93-94, 96, 118, 124, 127-130, 134, 136-137, 140-145, 148-156, 159, 170-171, 173-174, 184-185, 188, 194-195, 203, 207, 214-216, 227-229, 236

Bankrupted Person, 45

Barter Economy, 22

Business Entities, 137, 142, 158, 202

Business Model Development, 6

Business Partners, 3, 28

C

Capital Budgeting Ratios, 195

Capital Markets, 102, 133

Capital Structure Decisions, 1

Capital Surplus, 96-97

Certificate Of Incorporation, 39, 64

Chemical Leasing, 9

Chief Executive Officer, 138

Chief Financial Officer, 138

Co-operative Society, 26, 65-66

Coinage, 18-19

Commercial Bank, 21, 197, 200

Commodity, 12-13, 16-18, 21, 88, 237, 239

Common Law, 32, 34, 48, 61, 85, 138

Common Stock, 96, 98-99, 101-105, 142, 160, 182

Company Accounts, 46, 116, 121

Company Officers, 45

Compensation, 35-36, 68

Contingent Liabilities, 116, 121, 130, 134, 139, 142-143

Contra Account, 184, 216

Cost Of Capital, 1, 103

Counterfeit, 23

Creditors, 45, 57, 63, 67-68, 73, 77-78, 92-93, 97-98, 104, 106, 146, 149, 151, 153-157, 159, 171, 175-176, 178, 187, 197, 204, 206

Credits, 75-76, 112, 174-181, 184

D

Debits, 75-76, 112, 174-181, 184

Decision Support System, 7, 69

Direct Sales Model, 8

Double Entry, 24-25, 70, 72, 78, 174, 196

E

Equity Accounts, 181-182

Expense Accounts, 182

Export Goods, 22, 88

Extensible Business Reporting Language, 140

F

Financial Accounting, 5, 68-69, 135, 139, 141, 166, 228, 234-236, 243

Financial Management, 1, 24, 243

Financial Numbers, 139

Financial Statement, 67-68, 92, 136, 138, 140-141, 171-173, 188

Financial Year, 46, 128, 141

G

Global Standardization, 114

I

Income Tax, 29-30, 49, 51, 57, 59, 68, 141, 146, 159, 161-162, 167, 221, 240

Income/revenue Accounts, 182

Infinite Growth, 83

Insurance Payments, 45

Inventory Turnover, 192, 208, 234

L

Laundering, 23

Legal Capacity, 45

Lenders, 64, 67-68, 113, 187, 204

Liability Accounts, 176, 181

Limited Company, 39, 41, 44-47, 54-56, 63-64, 141

Limited Liability Company, 40-42, 47-56, 58-62, 64

Limited Liability Partnership, 32, 35-39, 41-42, 56, 62

Liquidity Ratio, 191, 197-199, 203

Loans, 23, 26, 28-29, 35, 102, 130, 146, 185, 197, 199, 204

Loyalty Business Models, 9

M

Managerial Talent, 66

Market Liquidity, 16

Market Ratios, 188, 194-195
Marketing Brochure, 139
Mercantilism, 79-90
Middleman Model, 8
Monetary Aggregate, 15
Monetary Policy, 22-23, 69, 197-198, 200, 202
Money Supply, 12, 15, 19, 21-23, 83, 88, 90, 198, 200
Monopolistic Business Model, 9

N
Narrative Coherence, 3
Network Effects Business Model, 9
Nominal Accounts, 175, 181, 184

O
Ownership Equity, 141

P
Partner Compensation, 35
Partnering Firms, 3
Portfolio Management, 1
Preferred Stock, 96, 98-105, 135, 160
Private Company, 44-47, 227-228
Private Investors, 28
Professional Indemnity Insurances, 45
Professional Management, 43
Profitability Index, 210
Profitability Ratios, 172, 188, 206
Public Limited Company, 45, 47
Public Stock Exchange, 45

R
Receivables Turnover Ratio, 210
Redundant Companies, 47
Report Filing, 43
Return Ratios, 206

S
Sales Journals, 72
Security Holders, 63
Share Capital, 38, 43-44, 46-47, 62-63, 93-95, 97, 105, 204
Shareholder Rights, 104
Silent Partner, 32
Small Business Administration, 27-29, 170
Sole Proprietorship, 26-28, 48, 141
Sourcing Business Model, 3
Strategic Outcome, 6
Subscription Business Model, 9
Subsidiaries, 64, 120, 131, 137, 139, 144, 161

T
Tangible Book Value, 196
Tax Burden, 43
Total Book Value, 195-196
Trade Financial Transactions, 63

U
Unlimited Companies, 63-64

W
Wealth Maximization, 43
Working Capital Management, 1